D1172003

A Writer's
Life

A Writer's Life

Scott Young

Doubleday Canada Limited

Canadian Cataloguing in Publication Data
Young, Scott, 1918–
      A writer's life
ISBN 0-385-25469-5

1. Young, Scott, 1918– . 2. Authors, Canadian
(English) – 20th century – Biography.*
3. Novelists. Canadian (English) – 20th century –
Biography.* 4. Sportswriters – Canada – Biography.
I. Title.

PS8547.085Z53 1994   CS18'.5409 C94–931104–9
PR9199.3.Y68Z47 1994

Cover design by Tania Craan
Text design by David Montle
Cover photo by Johnnie Eisen
Printed and bound in the USA
Printed on ∞ acid-free paper

Published in Canada by
Doubleday Canada Limited
105 Bond Street
Toronto, Ontario
M5B 1Y3

To my mother and father, who lived difficult lives mainly in good spirits, and to my brother Bob and sister Dorothy, who helped jog my memory when I needed it, and to the many cousins, uncles and aunts who aren't mentioned in this book at all but would loom large if it were a family history rather than concentrating on the life and times of only one person, me.

CONTENTS

ACKNOWLEDGEMENTS

Most of the photos used in this book are from family albums, with the exception of some taken in Italy and Yugoslavia by Lieutenant Gilbert A. Milne, RCNVR, and others taken at random by various photographers whose credits we have been unable to determine. To all, my thanks.

I

Village Life:
1918 - 1926

≋

"A WONDERFUL-LOOKING COUPLE when they were married," an old woman told me, referring to my parents, Jean Ferguson Paterson and Percy Andrew Young. "Both so good-looking! And with such lovely teeth! When they were walking up the aisle after the ceremony and smiling around the way new-married people do, I heard a woman whisper, 'Isn't it too bad they've both got false teeth, and them so young.' I leaned over and told her, 'them's not false at all, them's their own!'"

That was on September 1, 1917, when my mother was twenty-one and my father twenty-eight, the wedding having taken place in the Presbyterian Church in Glenboro, Manitoba, with the Reverend Robert Paterson, her father, officiating. In the pews were the newly joined Young and Paterson families and their friends and relatives, the farming Youngs of Cypress River being a somewhat more earthy-looking group than the across-the-aisle Patersons of Glenboro and recognizable by the tan lines across their foreheads from the summer's prairie sun, such lines being common among farmers, especially during the annual harvest, which was then well along.

On that day, which you might, if you wished, call pivotal to the life I was soon to begin (sooner than anybody thought at the time), the two heads of family were quite a contrast. One, Reverend Robert Paterson, was a tallish Presbyterian who had helped put himself through theology school by playing semi-pro baseball. He had a shambling walk and hooked nose and huge ears, which he could wiggle at will—and did if he heard whispering in the choir behind him when he was preaching. My mother was the first of three daughters and a son born in Neepawa to him and his wife, the pretty and lissome Agnes Scott, who grew up on a farm near Aurora, Ontario.

The other head of family was John Young, my grandpa Young, short and fierce and white-moustached, a Methodist who bred pedigreed Clydesdales and Percherons, Black Angus cattle, hogs and sheep, and drove a Pierce Arrow touring car. At the time his original 1878 free-land homestead near Cypress River had grown into thousands of acres of prime wheat land and ample pasture, which he ruled. There beside him in the church the day my parents were married was the most serene and lovable person among all the relatives I now remember, my grandma Mary Young (same name, no relation). She had borne thirteen children, nine of whom lived, including my father, Percy. Among the living were seven sons and two daughters.

The couple themselves—a handsome black-haired apprentice druggist and baseball player, Percy Young, and the preacher's lively and talented daughter, by then teaching in country schools, Jean Ferguson Paterson— had known one another for years. There had been many opportunities to meet when Glenboro and Cypress River, ten miles apart, met for curling, baseball, hockey, country fairs and picnics.

By the time he and my mother got serious about one another, Dad had apprenticed as a druggist here and there around Manitoba, including places where mother had been a teenaged teacher in one-room country schools, and where their love began, perhaps hot and heavy, if I may judge from their later lives.

By the time I was born, Dad had completed his apprenticeship (a university course was not required in those days) and purchased his own drugstore in Glenboro. He also played neat and tidy baseball at second base or sometimes shortstop for the town's team.

I was born seven months after their marriage, on April 14, 1918. When my arrival was unmistakably imminent, my mother and dad caught the train to Cypress River, ten miles east, put her in the care of a nurse who specialized in birthing women. A trip by automobile on roads of that time would be too rough for an expectant mother. My father worriedly kissed Mother goodbye and caught a ride back with a friend to look after his drugstore. I was born a few days later. At that time, I suppose it goes without saying, the first flush of their love was unblemished. In the days after my birth he showed up in Cypress at all hours, whenever he could get there by train or automobile, to see "dearie," his pet name for my mother.

She and I returned to Glenboro a week or so later and she must have faced some gossip. There she was, the preacher's a little bit stuck-up eldest daughter, caught out by one of the immutable laws of human reproduction. When I became old enough to understand, or be propagandized, my mother explained the discrepancy to me. Often. "You were two months premature," she assured me and the world. Even her father, she said to clinch the matter, had noticed how much more human I looked two months later, when I *should* have been born.

Coming eventually to know both my mother and father and their aliveness to life and sex, I can only shrug, what does it matter? Whether in the creaking back seat of a horse-drawn buggy, or high in a sun-warmed hayloft, or even in a legitimate honeymoon bed, wherever I began life I'll never know or care and there's no one left to enlighten me. But I got here.

At first, we lived in a tree-shaded two-storey frame house a few minutes' walk from Dad's store. I have a hazy memory of that house, with its big grassy side yard and my father's motorcycle, an Indian, parked in front. He had won the bike in a raffle and often rode it, sometimes with baby Scott aboard, around town and the surrounding country. Mother eventually persuaded him to get rid of it.

I also remember Sunday visits from friends and relatives, mostly Youngs from Cypress River, who fussed over me. And I remember the fresh-cooked doughnuts sizzling in a big pot on a black cookstove when I lined up with other kids on Saturday mornings in the kitchen of our neighbour, Olive Huston. (Her husband, Doc, was the local veterinarian.)

In the 1920s and beyond, several of Dad's brothers—Milt, Hughie, Billy and Herb—still worked parts of what had been the family farm, or got the hell out in protest against Grandpa's tyrannies, and then, broke or badly bent, had to return. Billy was one of those who returned, down from Gilbert Plains with Aunt Ethel and their brood, to find that the old man hadn't changed. When I knew him first, out in the barnyard he always carried a short length of harness, part of a leather trace, the better to snap painfully against the backside of any kid who strayed into his path. I can feel it yet, after being caught with some of my cousins sliding down a strawstack and messing up the rain-resisting shape thereof. Some of those cousins became my lifelong friends as well. We all remembered forever Grandpa Young's iron rule and fierce white moustache.

After my brother Bob was born in March of 1920, we moved from our house to an apartment above the drugstore, a step down in housing. Dad's drugstore was on Glenboro's main street, just across the road from the busy railroad station and the prairie trademark line of grain elevators. I remember vividly a night-time fire in one elevator, with the frightening roar of flames and sparks soaring high before the huge crash as the building collapsed. Around then Dad got me a farm collie, which used to sit on the store's front steps and run barking after passing wagons and buggies. Rather than tie it up, Dad found a farm home for it. Much later, when Mother was recounting things Dad had done that she thought had made me sad, giving the dog away was one of them. "Your Dad should not have given away your dog," she maintained sorrowfully, although I scarcely remembered the dog, let alone grieved over losing him. Children and parents are not always on the same wavelength, and now when I am trying to give a picture of this small boy's life in this small town, the memories refuse to run neatly from one to another in a cohesive whole. The memories are more like leaves falling a few at a time when a wind ruffles a tree.

I think of the cows that many kept in the town for the family's daily milk, cream and butter. Each morning when the cows had been turned out into the lanes in ones or twos from small barns around the town, they were joined by others until a slow-moving parade was heading towards open pasture at the west end of town. Sometimes a flock of us small fry, heading for school, would harry the stragglers, get them to run, just for the fun of it. When the herd filed back in at night, we wouldn't take such liberties. We had all had drummed into us that running a cow and a milk-full udder bouncing around would cause the milk to sour. So we would leave them to be cut out by their owners, taken home and milked.

The raw milk was usually chilled but sometimes was used as is, warm from the udder, or in some households would be poured into the always spotless hand-turned separator (to separate milk from cream). Some cream would be hand-churned into butter, to appear a day or so later when around four each afternoon most Glenboro people stopped work and went home for coffee. At the Magnuses, not far from the drugstore, Mrs. Magnus sometimes let me turn the handle on their coffee grinder just down the basement steps from their kitchen. Their coffee beans, kept on the basement floor in a big burlap bag, were measured out and ground fresh and very strong for each coffee break. Around the kitchen table men and women would chat, usually in Icelandic, sip coffee through a sugar cube held between the teeth, and try to make sure that the kids would not spoil their supper with too many cookies.

In a direct line from the kind of rich food we all ate three or four times a day was the matter of sewage disposal. At the back, abutting the back lane, every house sported a privy, or backhouse, usually a two-holer. Once a week the quiet and non-assertive man who drove Glenboro's "honey wagon" would manoeuvre his team of horses and redolent wagon slowly along the lanes, lift each backhouse's back flap, reach in carefully to retrieve the pail or pails, dump the contents into his wagon, and carefully put the empties back in place. On the way to school some mornings children used to lift these back flaps quietly. If we saw a bare bum we would slam the flap down as hard as we could, then escape down the lane before the owner of that bare bum could get his pants up or her skirts down and charge after us.

A good deal of more or less harmless stealing from gardens was commonplace—carrots, crab apples, tomatoes, whatever we could eat. And not only from gardens. My father's stockroom was in the basement below the store, the door usually open, an invitation to my friends and me to go in and liberate a little candy or some chocolate bars. Once, getting ambitious, I lifted a box of cigars and with three or four of my cronies scampered across the railroad tracks and hid behind a pile of railway ties while we lit one each, puffed, got paler and paler, then hid the remainder in a pumpkin we had hollowed out and craftily replaced in its home field, near a grove of poplars and Manitoba maples called Christie's Bluff. We got away with it for a few days, until the farmer decided that regular visits to his particular pumpkin field by a furtive group of small boys would bear investigation. All he did, apparently, was to hijack the cigars. One day they were there, the next they were gone, and we never heard anything more about it.

My introduction to active sex came when I visited my farm cousins. In those days men in buggies used to tour the back roads leading stallions that could be hired by farmers to breed with their mares. At our home farm my cousins and I used to hide in the barn and crowd in behind a dusty, cobwebby window to watch with extreme interest the mating pro-ceedings: the willing half-squat of the mares, the roaring and squealing of the stallion, the mounting, the dripping—our form of sex education.

Some kids had much nastier pursuits, such as yelling "You killed Jesus!" at offspring of the town's only Jewish family, the Browns, who had a store and whose talented daughter used to catch the train to Winnipeg every week for her music lesson.

Summer was the liveliest time: country fairs, cattle shows, horse races with bookie betting, baseball tournaments for prize money as high as a thousand dollars, winner take all, at which I ran wild with other boys along the sidelines. And then on good Sundays, a day of rest for farm horses and farmers alike, there would be swimming picnics with relatives and friends either on the banks of the Assiniboine River, a little north of our farms and towns, or at the popular Rock Lake, a few miles to the south, towards Baldur. On one Sunday picnic there I noticed that my brother Bob, then four or five years old, although apparently swimming a foot or so below the surface, was not coming up for air. I hauled him out, and it was generally accepted that otherwise he might have drowned. I was a hero. Before picnic days, when we would presumably get clean while swimming, my brother and I would be excused from the Saturday-night bath in a tin tub in the kitchen above the drugstore.

In all this, I realize looking back, there was a strong work ethic, with no excuses. Visiting the family farms, we kids helped with the milking, turned the handle on the cream separator, fed horses and cattle, cleaned out stalls, gathered eggs. When each spring's calves were ready to be weaned, I became an expert. Anybody could do it, but my uncles and cousins appointed me to teach the younger ones—putting my hand in a pail of milk and offering the milky fingers to a tethered calf, which would soon learn to suck on my fingers, get milk that way, and soon do without the fingers and just dig in.

In town there was work to do as well. When I was seven or eight, on Saturday nights I was paid five cents a dozen for crating the loose eggs brought in from nearby farms to trade for other supplies at McKnight and Mott's general store. I also sold *Maclean's* magazine door to door in one summer's national circulation drive, doing well enough to win a gold pocket watch. Those were all mainly summer pursuits, leading in autumn to helping with the harvest. I was not quite strong enough for heavy work but I could drive a team of horses pulling a grain wagon to the elevators at Landseer.

When winter came, we skated and played road hockey, the pucks being frozen horse turds known as road apples. And we also curled, flooding someone's side yard and marking the ends, the scoring areas, by scratching circles in the ice with a nail and marking the circles with wash-day blueing. Each "rock" was a sawn-off round of cordwood with a spike hammered into one side and bent over to form the handle. Along with everyone else in town, I'd be on the CPR platform when the westbound train came in on those great February days when our famous Glenboro curlers, Bert Hames, the McKnight brothers, Reg Doig, Ab Gowanlock, Bung Cartmell and others would arrive home triumphantly from the Manitoba bonspiel—then the world's biggest—laden with trophies.

And then there was the night above the drugstore in 1926 when Gene Tunney beat Jack Dempsey in the famous long-count fight for the heavy-weight championship of the world. My brother and I slept in a room off the parlour at the front of the apartment, and that night I was allowed to stay up and listen to the crackling radio broadcast of the fight. When Dempsey was beaten I went to bed crying and even in bed could not stop sobbing. It was something about defeat, any defeat, that got to me. My father came in and sat on the edge of my bed to comfort me with soothing assurances that Dempsey was all right, and would get Tunney the next time.

At that time our closest relatives were around Glenboro and Cypress River, a smaller circle than before. Somewhere in there Grandpa Paterson moved from Glenboro ("received a call") to a big church in Brandon. After that, each Christmas our family would travel the fifty miles or so to Brandon for, among other things, Grandpa's no-escape mealtime prayers. Breakfast, dinner, supper, it was some variation on the theme of "Lord, have mercy on thy miserable sinners. . ." Knees on the hard floor, elbows on the hard chairs. Nobody dared move until Grandpa at long last would figure that God had our message and would rise, allowing the rest of us to creak to our feet and sit down.

New Year's I liked much better. My parents and brother and I (my sister not yet born) would catch the train in Glenboro to be let off into the snow fifteen miles away at a whistle-stop called Landseer (no town, just a grain elevator). My dad's brothers would be waiting to meet us in open sleighs drawn by snorting, frost-blowing horses, and we'd all be bundled up in buffalo robes for the thrilling race through the snowdrifts, on roads and across fields, to what was always called "the big house" on the home farm, which stood where our homesteading forebears' first cabin had been.

There, my kindly, loving Grandma Young, would feed us thick sugar cookies and fresh bread spread with butter and brown sugar to hold us until the meal was ready. Then we'd all sit down, parents, uncles, aunts and cousins, at the long table, and our trigger-tempered Grandpa Young would stare us into silence and bark out the grace.

It was much later in my life when I heard about the jokes my dad and his brothers would play on one another when they were still at home—such as the time when my staid uncle Herb borrowed Grandpa's favourite buggy one Saturday night to take a girl to a concert in Cypress River. His brothers, knowing that my grandparents would drive that same buggy to church the next morning, waited up for Herb to get home and go sound asleep. Then they tucked a lot of bloomers and petticoats and garters around the floor of the buggy, as if they'd come off—even been ripped off—in frantic haste. When Grandpa and Grandma walked out the next morning in their Sunday finest for the five-mile buggy ride to church, they were stopped by the gleam of pink underwear under the seat. The inquisition took up most of the rest of that Sunday, but for years nobody squealed.

In summer we would sometimes visit the home place in my father's open-sided Star touring car, the replacement for his motorcycle. There'd be Dad, Mother, brother Bob and baby sister Dorothy, who was born in 1925. Through the day we'd have a grand family picnic of lemonade, thick pork or beef sandwiches, Grandma's sugar cookies, the kids taking turns at the handle of the ice-cream freezer, foot races between the house and barn. My brother, then around five, entered family-anecdote Valhalla during one of those races when he was part of a losing photo finish.

"Jim beat!" shouted the cousin acting as finish-line judge.

"I'm Jim!" piped up Bob.

Often on our return trip to Glenboro, our car would stall halfway up Snake Hill a mile west and begin to roll backwards. Dad would reverse into the hillside, turn it around, and drive back down for another try.

If that didn't work, Dad and sometimes I would walk up the hill to the nearest farm, owned by the Sissons family, and get a team of horses to help. Even at my age all such adventures began to assume something of the importance of family folklore.

Then in 1926, when I turned eight, my dad went broke and the warm village life that I had known until then all changed.

2

Upheavals:
1926-1932

~~~

ONE DAY I WAS A quiet happy little eight-year-old, known to everyone, enjoying the small-town life I'd been born into. Without an instant of explanation that I can recall, I was not living in Glenboro any more. Some of the uncles and aunts who years before had fled Grandpa Young's harsh rule had returned to farm near the homestead on properties he made over to them, partly because he was ill and near death. My first stop was in the red-brick farmhouse of my uncle Billy and aunt Ethel and their flock, mainly boys, only half a mile west of the home farm. I started at the same one-room school, Selton, that my cousins attended. I have memories of frequent bad dreams and being slapped once by Uncle Billy to bring me out of one nightmare that sticks in my mind as being caused by some unconscious terror.

Soon, for a reason never specifically explained, I was shuffled back to the homestead to stay with the more placid Uncle Herb and Aunt Beatrice and their children, where I didn't last long either, winding up back at Uncle Billy's. Two other Young family farmers in the area, Uncle Hugh and Aunt Sadie a mile east and Uncle Milt and Aunt Mabel, a couple of miles west, did not get involved in this refugee project. I can assume only that they had made clear to my parents that they preferred a course years later expressed in Sam Goldwyn's immortal "Include me out."

If there was a pattern, it was that the Youngs always were the ones who took me in; the Paterson side of the family seemed to have gone to ground. I became aware of this in a scene that has made me rather partial to strays ever since.

Once I was sent from Uncle Billy's to Glenboro, about fifteen miles, three hours or more, in a team-hauled wagon with my single meagre bag. When the cousin driving the team pulled up in front of the tidy home where my aunt Helen and uncle Frank Ferg lived, and announced that Scott was going to stay with them for a while, Aunt Helen simply said, "No, he's not."

"Well, what should I do?"

"Take him back with you." Back I went, with my bag.

It's a pure speculation, but I believe that my relatives on both sides of the family were fed to the teeth with my parents and felt that the best solution was to refuse to go along.

I was much older before I realized that the disasters of that summer came about because my mother and my father were at their wits end. The blame, if any, went both ways. Before and after their marriage Mother was much admired for her looks, wit and daring, qualities that were attractive to men—an edge she would have for life. But she also admired assertive, successful men, and there she had missed the boat entirely, having acquired an easy-going druggist who was never going to twist anybody's arm or get his own way, or hers.

Before her marriage, she'd been a dashing, lively, slim beauty. In the next few years, during which she bore two more children, Dad sank into debt and her weight soared to two hundred pounds.

My father told me years later that after they left Glenboro in 1926 he never stopped caring for Mother, but the marriage did not improve. She was the pusher and he was too easy to push. The Patersons were town persons and the Youngs strictly country. The two sets of in-laws never meshed.

My dad's easy-going nature meant that he got along with everybody better than with my mother. All I had to do then and for years thereafter, was to mention that my father was Percy Young from Cypress River and my number was made. However, his easy acceptance of hard-luck stories from his drugstore clientele made him a bad businessman. It wasn't in his nature to pressure people who ran up accounts. When the eventual flashpoint came with his bankruptcy, his only solution was to try to remake his life.

At the time, the Hudson's Bay Company was building and staffing a big department store in Winnipeg. Dad applied for a job in the drug department. He went to Winnipeg by train to be interviewed and was accepted. No one explained any of this to me. A sale of our belongings in Glenboro left us with very little that was familiar when we moved to Winnipeg and into a little white frame house he rented on College Street, in the St. James suburb of the sprawling, growing, busy city.

That autumn of 1926 I started at Assiniboine School, across Portage Avenue and many blocks east, a long walk through traffic for a boy accustomed to running down a couple of back lanes to get to class. For my dad, the change must have been even more drastic. Instead of trotting downstairs from our apartment above the store and opening for business, he had the long streetcar ride each morning into downtown Winnipeg. We no longer had a car. Winnipeg then was much the same energetic, multi-immigrant city it is now, but smaller.

We soon moved from the white frame cottage to a slightly larger two-storey house two blocks away on Parkview Street. That house had an entrance hall, parlour to the right of the hall, dining room and kitchen straight ahead. Upstairs were two bedrooms, one for Bob and me, off a sunporch where our parents slept, and a bathroom. When we lived there, money was still tight, but soon Mother had a solution: we would rent out the other bedroom.

Our first boarder, Pete LeSeach, was a handsome and fancy-free bank clerk who was destined to be part of my mother's life and mine for several years. I'm not sure when the relationship between Mother and Pete developed into more than landlady and boarder, but develop it did.

Mother had other male friends too. Some I met, some I didn't. I'd return from school and a man would be with her in the parlour with the door closed. "Oh, that's the insurance man," she would say. She never tried to hide. When Dad worked late, Mother often had the house full of partying bank clerks and others. She played the piano, and everybody drank rye whisky and sang. On hot summer nights the parties spilled into our tiny front yard or the street. When Dad came home late in the evening, he would sometimes join in, but he did not seem to know many of the party-goers.

When I was sent to bed, the noise from below would make sleep impossible. I'd lie there hoping the next song would be the last of the night, and I could go to sleep. But when the house would finally fall quiet, I was sometimes kept awake by arguments between my parents: usually they were about my father's absence. In Mother's view, he should have been around more. Once I came down the stairs to find Mother and Dad standing in the dining room and Mother accusing Dad of playing around with other women.

"Why don't you ever take *me* out?" she said. "What's wrong with *me* to take to your parties? My breasts are low, like the style is. . ." Those were the days of the flappers, flat-chested and slim.

I never spoke of that exchange with my mother, but Dad later told me that in the last years he and Mother were together, he could no longer manage to have any sexual relationship with her.

"I was no good, Scott," he said. "I wanted to, I thought it might solve a lot of things, but when I was thinking that way about her, even in bed, I just couldn't get a hard-on, no matter what I tried. I was pretty sure that it was because we argued all the time. It's hard to get into bed and be loving when you've just had a hell of an argument.

"But I really *didn't believe* I was impotent. I thought it was just with her. So there was a woman at work, I knew she liked me, and I liked her. Anybody would tell you she was one of the best-looking women in the city at the time. We got a hotel room and had a couple of drinks and got into bed—and nothing happened, *nothing!* So I knew then it wasn't just your mother. She thought I was getting sex elsewhere, but I wasn't."

Many years later my brother Bob told me that about that time he once rifled Dad's pockets and found and took a package of condoms, in those days commonly called rubbers, or French safes. One brand came in tins, the lid featuring a female figure, or figures, and the words, *Agnes*, *Mabel* and *Becky*. Bob was awake one night when he overheard the aftermath. Mother and Dad slept in a sunporch just off our bedroom and, he thought, were about to make love when Dad came into our room hunting for the condoms, with Mother calling, "It's all right, Percy, never mind them." What happened next we never knew, but it seemed obvious that Mother was impatient and ready for love, and Dad couldn't find the condoms and obviously didn't want to risk another child.

Fifty years later, when Bob told me of that frantic moment and its aftermath, he said, "I wondered later, many times, if that was the last straw with Mother and Dad, and if I should have had the guts to tell the truth, that I had the condoms and somehow pass them over and maybe get Dad out of the line of fire and avoid the angry battle that followed. But I didn't."

I don't recall having any particular aim in life until I discovered Uncle Jack, Mother's younger brother. Jack, a freelance writer just turned thirty, was handsome and witty. He and his wife, Ruth, would often arrive unannounced from somewhere on the West coast, or the far North. Picture a flapper of the roaring twenties, blonde, trim and, like Jack, game for anything, and you've got Ruth. Jack had lied about his age to enlist in the Canadian Army at fifteen and was only sixteen when he was gassed in the trenches of France, his lungs permanently damaged. In the mid-1920s this led to tuberculosis and years in the sanatorium at Ninette, Manitoba. In that enforced idleness, he had started to write. First he wrote about his war experiences, but branched out when his health recovered enough to leave Ninette. By 1930 the Jack Paterson byline over stories of adventure in the North, had been appearing in various publications of the time, including the broadsheet *Star Weekly*. But it was his freedom of movement that most attracted me.

From his northern travels he knew a lot of bush pilots. One was Roy Brown, whose bush airline was called Wings Limited. When there were big stories in the North, Roy or other bush pilots often flew Jack free of charge — and often were written about, in exchange. Everything exciting in the North was grist to Jack's mill.

The characters in his short stories and articles were often drawn from British Columbia's logging camps in the interior or on Vancouver Island, where he and Ruth lived. He based one memorable character on a daredevil B.C. hunter named Smith whose specialty was cougars. In Jack's articles for magazines, he became Cougar Smith. Jack also wrote many articles about the building of the Hudson Bay Railroad; clouds of insects, locomotives sinking forever out of sight in the muskeg as the rail line was built over several years to connect The Pas to Churchill on Hudson Bay. He and Ruth, and eventually their daughter Helen, nicknamed Bud, moved to where the stories were, from Courtenay, B.C., to Cranberry Portage, Manitoba, where one summer they had to cast off into the nearby lake to escape a forest fire that levelled the town.

To Mother, Jack could do no wrong, then or later, and I think she tended to compare his life unfairly to what she saw as the stodgy life my father led. At parties where Jack and Ruth were always the centre of attention, Dad seemed to be increasingly on the fringe, if there at all. To me also, without loving Dad less, he was much less interesting than Jack.

My admiration grew into friendship for life, with much help from Jack for my fledgling efforts to write. Years later I came to know my father, and to realize that there was more of him in me than I had ever known. Then we became more than father and son, but friends, sharing intimate moments of our lives and problems.

But back in the partying days of Parkview Street, we had no such meeting of our minds. I was more or less adrift when it came to understanding myself, and his marital difficulties left him little time, it seemed, to make real contact with me. Partly I lost myself in reading—but not the book Dad was reading the first time I noticed him reading a book: Darwin's *The Origin of Species*. My reading was mostly boys' adventure stuff. One Christmas at Parkview Dad gave me a thick red *Boy's Own Annual*. I sat in a window seat at the head of the stairs and days later was still reading, until a crashing headache and near-blindness caused a doctor to confine me to a dark room for two days until my headache went away.

I didn't have money to buy other books, and don't even remember a public library where we lived, but I made do, often illegally. Once I was caught by a store detective trying to leave Eaton's department store with my windbreaker packed tight with Tom Swift and Henty books but no sign of money having changed hands. I was marched ignominiously to the store's tiny security office and got off with a tongue-lashing and a phone call to my parents, but no books. Maybe I would have bought the books, given other circumstances, but at that time I rarely had any money except when I was sent to the store for this or that and managed to steal one or more small items. A pound of butter, thirty-five cents, was about the right size, and I'd keep the money.

Our family was chronically broke. Eventually Dad was in trouble at work, as well as at home. I was in Grade Eight, having skipped Grade Seven, when he was fired from The Bay.

This was in 1930 or 1931, the early days of the Great Depression. He tried selling chocolate bars on commission, and kept his boxes of samples in our front vestibule—from whence my brother and I stole them. He found part-time work in a pharmacy, but the streets were full of out-of-work druggists and part-time soon became little or nothing week after week.

I don't remember when he finally gave up. If he said goodbye, it was not to me. What I do remember is that a few days before my thirteenth birthday in 1931 he was no longer around. For a few days I didn't know what was going to happen, except that things were desperate and our family finally had to break up. From then on, things happened fast.

My mother and her Glenboro friend Olive Huston, then living in Winnipeg, took me down one morning to the CPR station off North Main Street. They found a seat for me on the train heading West, and stayed with me a few minutes, everybody reassuring everybody else, and nobody believing a word of it.

Mother gave me a package of sandwiches and a paper bag of clothes, really nothing much, and asked the conductor to keep an eye on me. With the conductor's "All A-board!" they left, and I was on my way to Prince Albert, Saskatchewan.

At the same time my brother, then just turned eleven, was being sent to my grandparents Paterson (back on thy knees, boy, let us thank God for his bounty) at an Indian reserve near Elphinstone in western Manitoba. My sister, Dorothy, her sixth birthday just passed, went with Mother back to Glenboro where she would stay with the Fergs and figure out what to do next.

Dad, we heard later, had landed in Flin Flon, a mining camp about five hundred miles north of Winnipeg. Flin Flon had no road, but a three-times-a-week train from outside. His first job there was driving a team of horses hitched to the town's water wagon, travelling the mining camp's rocky streets selling fresh water to housewives for ten cents a pail. He was, in effect, Flin Flon's water system. A friend told me much later about running into Dad that first spring he was in Flin Flon. His hands were badly chapped and bleeding from carrying water pails from his wagon and house to house in the frigid weather. "I tried to give him some money for gloves, but he wouldn't take it, said a farm boy didn't need gloves. But I bought him some anyway and he wore them."

I enjoyed most of my Prince Albert experience. I was met at the railroad station by Aunt Mary, Dad's older sister, and her well-fixed husband, Frank Culp, an optometrist, Rotarian and seriously henpecked man. That first day Aunt Mary took one look at me, in her view practically in rags, and marched me to a store for outfitting. What I wore on my arrival I never saw again.

That same day, showing me around their comfortably middle-class house, she instructed me on how to pee sitting down, so I wouldn't splash the bathroom floor. Obviously, she felt she had her work cut out. She was kind in her own way, but very firm, and a pillar of the United Church in Prince Albert. A few weeks later, at a golf tournament where I'd gone hoping to get a job as a caddy (I'd done some caddying at the St. Charles Country Club in Winnipeg), I happened to notice Uncle Frank in the beer tent. He stared at me aghast, then hurried after me.

"Don't tell your Aunt Mary about me being, uh, in there," he said, waving at the beer tent. He slipped me a quarter. That worked. I never ratted on him.

My main problem with the Culps was that they expected a lot from me, and I didn't deliver. Their only daughter, my cousin Marie, at age seventeen had fallen and broken a shoulder in a high-school basketball game. She died within two or three days of blood poisoning. Her parents seemed to expect me to live up to their memory of Marie: head of her class, pretty, athletic, a model young person.

Instead, everything I did turned to disaster. I had no skates of my own, but hanging in the basement among Marie's memorabilia were her old skates. Aunt Mary sighed and said I could use them.

Almost instantly, I broke one blade, when my toe caught in a crack in the ice on a rink in the schoolyard while I was playing tag. Next in line were Marie's skis. They'd been stored in a dry basement for a couple of years and were brittle, I guess. The first time I went over a homemade ski jump, just down the hill from the Culps' house, one ski got caught sideways between two saplings. *Crack!*

I was on a roll. The nice pair of pants Aunt Mary had bought me for school—well, I tore the seat out of them. Nothing if not resourceful, mainly out of fear of Aunt Mary, I patched the pants. But the cloth did not match the pants, and my work was not exactly professional. When some Grade Eight kids at school commented on the patch's visibility, I realized that the first time Aunt Mary saw me from behind the game would be up. I spent many meals sidling around the dining room with my back to the wall. Eventually Mary caught on, and it was game over, although I do think she laughed at that time.

Next, in a neighbour's barn I found a barrel full of sexy pulp magazines (*Secrets of the White Slave Trade,* etc.). No doubt intending to save them from harming other young and impressionable schoolmates, I sneaked them all into the house and stored them in my bedroom closet, where Aunt Mary found them. After scolding me, she carried them downstairs and threw them into the furnace.

There were a lot of things she didn't know, at least at first.

That summer I fell in love with a beautiful girl a year older than I was, Suzanne Wood. I set up a tent in the woods behind the house. I told the Culps I wanted to sleep there to escape the summer heat, but I really intended to roam a little in the direction of Suzanne's yard, where she also had a tent.

When darkness fell ("Time for bed, Scott, sleep tight, don't let the bedbugs bite"), I'd yawn mightily, say goodnight to Aunt Mary and Uncle Frank, repair to the tent and turn out the lantern. Later I'd slip through the trees and hurry several blocks to Suzanne's tent, where I never did anything worse than observe her silhouette as she undressed. However, one night when I returned to my tent I found that it was no longer there. In my haste to escape that night I'd neglected to notice that all the bedding was missing, washed and ironed and folded for me to take out when I went to bed. I'd made my goodnights and was probably half a mile away towards Suzanne's tent when Aunt Mary noticed the bedding.

Muttering her version of "Drat that boy, anyway," she went out to my tent, carrying the bedding, took one look, called a couple of times, then took down the tent and went back to the house to wait. She was waiting in the kitchen hours later when I arrived.

Goodbye, tent.

The one really warm memory I have of Prince Albert concerned my grandma Young. I wish I had saved some of her letters to me through all our family's turmoil, letters that were warm, full of heart, and almost illiterate. After Grandpa Young died in the late 1920s she was more or less adrift, and spent the years visiting her offspring. She had come to spend the winter of 1931–32 with the Culps and in her own quiet way seemed to understand what I was up against. On nights when the Culps were out playing bridge or whist or having dinner with friends, we would play checkers on the kitchen table. Once when we were talking about early days on the home farm, she told me about her own arrival there more than fifty years earlier.

There was no Canadian transcontinental railroad at the time, so her trip west with John Young, my grandfather, had to be by train from western Ontario to St. Paul, Minnesota, then north to Winnipeg, where Grandpa bought an axe and a horse and buggy to carry them home, nearly one hundred miles southwest across the prairie.

A day or two later, the young couple arrived in the black of night at the eastern shore of a water-filled slough at the bottom of a hill on which he had built his homesteader cabin.

By the light of a lantern he tethered the horse and took off his clothes. My teenaged grandma hitched up her skirts and there was a certain amount of giggling as she sat on his shoulders, holding his clothes high, to be carried through the slough's chilly water to where they would spend the rest of their lives.

The next morning, snuggled together in the one-room cabin, she was wakened by dogs barking, voices calling and other sounds, and stepped outside to find that a hundred yards away was quite a large Indian encampment. She hadn't been told until then by my laconic grandfather that their cabin was at a traditional crossing of two Indian trails. Tribes were used to camping there and had done so the night before, the sounds of their camp being her always-remembered welcome to where she would spend her life and bear her children.

I can see her now, as we sat and talked in Prince Albert. She had a face not unlike mine as it has become with age, square and not tremendously firm any more. She talked slowly and clearly, smiled a lot, and spoke well of most people. One night she told me that besides the seven sons and two daughters I knew—my father and aunts and uncles—she had borne another four children (two of them twins) who died in infancy. She was my best friend through the fairly steady turmoil of trying to live up to what the Culps had expected of me, a matter soon to come to a head.

❦

When I passed out of Grade Nine with excellent marks in the summer of 1932, my aunt and uncle sat me down in the living room near the DeForest Crosley radio, after "Amos 'n Andy," and told me what their hopes had been when they agreed to take me in.

They then spelled out where I had fallen short (this part took a while) and noted in passing that when I had been sent to them my dad had promised to pay board for me but didn't. The net outcome of the meeting was that these two straitlaced adults admitted they were out of their depth in dealing with a young boy. Their solution was simple: they planned to return me to my mother in Winnipeg. To this end, I was unloaded first for a week or two on another uncle, my father's brother Matt, who ran a grain elevator in Strongfield, Saskatchewan, and I think considered keeping me. But after a week there, I was put on the eastbound train.

In Winnipeg that summer, Mother and my sister had also gathered in my brother from his temporary banishment. I joined them all in a single room in a house on Furby Street.

Mother had no money and was on relief, as welfare was called in those days. The relief allowance for a parent and three children in mid-1932 was $5.62 a week. Somehow we got along, eating and sleeping more or less normally, swimming every day at the Sherbrooke Baths (admission five cents), happy to be back with Mother again, and wishing the clock could be turned back to produce Dad, too.

3

Bicycle Thief:
1932-1934

〰

THAT SINGLE ROOM on Furby Street was sometimes suffocatingly hot. And because our door was the first one to the right of the entrance, it was noisy. Other roomers, coming or going, noisy or quiet, or in whatever state of repair, clumped by a few feet away. The furniture was a card table with one folding chair and a fold-down couch upholstered in a dirty brown cracked leatherette. That was bed for Mother and Dorothy. Bob and I had a mattress on the floor. The electric hotplate rarely was used for much more than boiling coffee or wieners or burning toast. There was no telephone or radio. We had no friends close by—the ones that we'd made in St. James only a year or two before were too far away. To reach them, we'd have had to spend some of the meagre exchequer on streetcar fare.

My brother and sister and I soon got used to our new life, sometimes staying up late in the coolness of the open veranda. And at first there was a heady happiness just in being back together. But for Mother, a lively, good-looking woman of thirty-six, being cooped up with three kids was hard. Bob and Dorothy and I were often alone, especially at night. After all, I was old enough at fourteen to look after my brother and sister. Mother, after making sure we had something to eat, would spend most evenings out. "Just going over to see some friends, kids. I'll be back. Don't stay up too late." On those evenings alone we yarned, sometimes truthfully, about our experiences in Prince Albert (me) and Elphinstone (Bob) and wondered what might happen to us next.

Occasionally we were asked out for dinner by one of Mother's cousins, Lou Black, a tall and angular woman with a silent, forbidding husband named Duncan, who had a good job and I believe gave, or lent, money to Mother. Their daughter, Islay Ruth, was a robust young woman who used to try to get us involved in backyard games that I remember even now with deep ennui. These visits were strained. The Blacks, I think, asked us only because they thought it was the decent, Christian thing to do. Every time our previous family life was mentioned, they handled it by looking stricken. To their way of thinking, marriages did not just break up; someone had to take the blame. It was obvious to us, and I think to Mother, that she was their nominee. The Blacks sometimes brought up the possibility of us getting back together, but each time it was mentioned Mother would grimace. Still, she kept assuring us, something would turn up, things were going to get better.

Eventually her evening absences began to bother me. One night when she went out I followed her to a small and rundown apartment building a few blocks away on Ellice Avenue, and thought I saw Pete LeSeach going into the same building. After that I knew where I might find her if I had to, in some emergency.

I never had to do that, but one day in midsummer she came home with some news. She was excited. She and Pete had worked out a plan, she told us. She would rent a two-bedroom apartment and take in boarders, one being Pete, who thought he could find a couple of other prospects—the stipulation being that the three boarders had to be compatible enough to sleep in one room.

To this end, Pete recruited two other bank clerks, a tall and quiet Maritimer, Mac McLeod, who had a nice woman friend, later his wife, named Nell; and dapper, good-looking Harold Riley. Each of the three would pay Mother what Pete said was the going rate at the time, $35 a month, to cover board, room, laundry and meals. That gave her a total monthly income of $105, from which she would look after rent, groceries and all other expenses for the seven of us.

It was in August, I think, when she took Dorothy, Bob and me over to have a look at our new home. It was a second-storey two-bedroom apartment—or suite, as Winnipeg terminology had it—in the Vansittart block on Stradbrooke Avenue in the Fort Rouge area. We walked through a darkish entranceway, up the single straight staircase, then turned left down the hall. A small elderly man, our new landlord, was waiting at the door of Number Five.

I have to mention here that Mother by 1932 had lost all the weight that had plagued her in her child-bearing years and was just plain good-looking. Also, she knew how to use being a woman. That's the only way I can explain why, in the next few years, our landlord exhibited world-class patience as he waited for the rent. On rent day Mother would dress nicely and take her purse and walk nervously along the hall to the old man's apartment. A couple of hours later she'd come back, and sigh something like, "Well, we're still here."

Of course, we knew nothing of that future the first day we walked into the suite and looked around somewhat goggle-eyed. On our left was a small parlour with a corner fireplace and a window overlooking the street. To our right along the hall was the bathroom and next to it the smaller bedroom, a double bed for Mother and Dorothy and a single for me. The idea was that Bob would sleep either on the bedroom floor or on the chesterfield in the parlour, if that space was available, which it quite often wasn't.

Straight ahead from the front door was a narrow dining room, with table, chairs and sideboard. To the left off the dining room was the bank clerks' bedroom, which had one double bed and one single. In those days it was not the common assumption that any time two people of whatever gender got into one bed, sex of one kind or another, or even several kinds, was preordained. In my youth, boys, girls, men, women, the young and the old slept together as a matter of course, if the available bed space so dictated.

On the other, or non-bank-clerk side of the dining room, was a tiny kitchen in which Mother was to iron, cook and wash dishes. She usually also had on the go a homebrew of potatoes, raisins and so on, known to the hoity-toity as potato champagne but to mother as Draino. Liquor was cheap but Draino was cheaper, and widely popular for that reason.

"It's okay," she said once. "I certainly never have to throw any out."

Living in the apartment directly below us was the perfect new companion for mother, lively and redheaded Flora Britton. They got up to a certain amount of hellery together, which might have startled (in fact, I think, once did startle) Flora's husband, Homer. Mother was clearly the instigator of the hellery. She was more or less on the loose and had more male friends, married and single, than she had need of, and shared the odd leftover with Flora. Flora also made Draino to my mother's recipe, and at least once had to hurry her full and redolent butter crock of liquor up the back stairs and stow it under our stove. That was a time when her wraith-like husband happened to get home earlier than expected. He often complained that our whole block smelled like a distillery, but he never knew, at least at that time, that Flora was one of the distillers.

After we moved into the Vansittart on the first of September, to be ready for school, the reality of the arrangement that had seemed so promising sank in. For their $35 a month the bank clerks got morning and evening meals, plus sandwich lunches to take to work, and laundry. Bank clerks in those days had to wear white shirts to work. Mother ironed twenty white shirts every Saturday. I spent my Saturday mornings in the basement of the block, Saturday being our assigned day to use the washing machine, hand wringer and a heavy contraption called a mangle. This was for ironing what I learned was called flatwork, which I'd iron, pile and carry upstairs—sheets, pillowcases, towels and table linen including napkins (paper ones were unknown, at least to us, at the time).

The boarders also had first go each morning at the single bathroom, next door to our bedroom. The double bed in which Mother and Dorothy slept, was a narrow space away from my single bed, next to a window facing a well into which I dropped apple cores while I was reading in bed. My brother, supposed to sleep on the chesterfield in the living room, sometimes got tired waiting. Often he slept at a riding stable where he made a little money looking after horses after school and happily riding (he was crazy about horses) any that had to be exercised.

None of this was ideal, but it was, finally, a home. My brother adapted better than I did. He'd been bounced around a lot, too, but seemed able to turn his back on the bad patches. I was much less resilient. My time in Prince Albert had had its drawbacks, many of my own making, but I did have my own room, which suddenly I missed. There also I had friends my own age as willing as I was to think up mischief and then get on with it. We could escape into the woods and rivers nearby on both sides of the North Saskatchewan, explore abandoned houses and barns, catch goldeye in the river.

For many months after we moved into the Vansittart, I felt displaced and resentful. One of my problems was Pete LeSeach. He and I never got along, then or later; he tried to rule me and my brother on things that would have been our dad's to do, if he'd been there. My defence against

Pete was usually a hostile silence, or leaving the room, or some other show of rebellion. This, of course, egged him on. Mac and Riley sometimes tried to slow him down when he was playing the heavy too hard, but that is all long ago and far away, and when I grew up I never begrudged Mother what she had to do, or felt she had to do, or even halfheartedly wanted to do.

And she did enjoy Pete's company. He had a zany side that made others laugh. One night when a party was in progress and he was wearing a white suit of which he was proud, he happened to brush against the coal scuttle in front of the fireplace.

When Mother exclaimed, "Oh, Petey! Your suit!" he sat down into the full coal scuttle and kept conversing quite intelligibly while he slowly poured the rest of his beer on his pant legs, from knee to crotch, with the rest of the onlookers rocking with laughter.

Thinking of all this now, I am beset by memories of the years I lived there at the Vansittart, enduring Pete and other things.

I'll whine a little here. No one else made the long walk from the east side of Osborne Street, down Wardlaw and along the great arch of Wellington Crescent to reach Kelvin Technical High School, as I did. And my fellow students seemed all to come from comfortable and stable homes. Some wore suits to school! Some drove or were driven to school in their family cars, whereas I had a long walk.

All kids can be cruel, especially well-off ones. Once my mother bought me some pants at a sale, two dollars a pair. They had to be altered, and it was done badly. Walking to school, followed by classmates, I heard laughter and, "Hey, Young, why is one of your pant legs two inches longer than the other?" I have thought of several defiant responses since, but I didn't have them when I needed them.

I was not the only target of class distinctions. One boy in our room, Lyall Lang, always wore exactly the same garb to school—a sweatshirt and a type of cheap bell bottoms, popular then, called whoopee pants, with a triangular red inset flaring from the narrow knee to the wide cuff. One classmate almost daily dwelled on this evidence that his parents couldn't afford anything better. "Hey, Lang, why do you always wear whoopee pants?"

The riding that Lang and I took daily was still in progress in the spring of 1933 when the annual Winnipeg Inter-High track meet was held among the best young track and fielders from the four Winnipeg high schools of the time—St. John's Tech, Daniel McIntyre, Kelvin and Gordon Bell. This event rated a school holiday and we gathered, competitors and cheering sections, one sunny day at Whittier Park, a racetrack now long gone. Still trying to establish myself somewhere, somehow, I had tried to make the Kelvin team in several track and field events, training and competing in trials with what I convinced myself was real dedication. I fantasized about the cheering and applause that would follow if I won something for the school. I'd show those guys!

Finally I made it onto the junior (or eight-pound) shot-put team, not because I was much good but because each school was allowed two entries in each event and at Kelvin only two of us tried out. When the day of the track meet came, I finished eighth and last in my event, so did not exactly turn my tormentors on their ears.

But—and here is a mighty but—Lang was running the half-mile. He was not thought to be a hot prospect even in our school. The other Kelvin entries and those from other schools mostly wore track shoes and shorts and had been training hard for weeks. Lang had to get home to do a paper route every afternoon, so his daily training had been simply running to and from school and around his paper route.

When the starting gun went off for the half-mile, some of the classy-looking hotshots from other schools sprinted to the front followed by Lang in his sweatshirt, sneakers and whoopee pants. But what's this? After the first two hundred yards Lang was taking the lead! I started to my feet as the distance between Lang and the pack widened. When he came around the racetrack's last turn and into the home stretch, he was still pulling away. At the finish line in front of the grandstand he was a hundred yards ahead of the pack, and I was on my feet yelling and weeping with a joy I've never forgotten.

The next year Lang and I were in different rooms at school, and I found myself with no friends again. Then a corner rink a block away from my home was flooded for hockey and pleasure skating, and I met a few kids my own age who lived in my district. I began to feel more comfortable—in my own neighbourhood, at least. But at school nothing changed. I did, however, try to give myself a personality. Whenever I happened to be in one of the affluent homes near Kelvin, I lied a lot. I told one group in the parlour of a nice home in River Heights that I was part Indian. Soon after I had declared myself one of our original people, I heard a group in the cloakroom arguing for and against my possible Indianness. I came upon them unawares just as someone said thoughtfully, "Well, he does have those high cheekbones. . ."

When there was nothing else immediately available to my tormentors, one would ask, "Hey, Young, don't you have a dad? What does he do?" At that time Dad had just landed a job as a beer waiter in a Flin Flon hotel. I told my tormentors that Dad was a chemist, working on secret scientific formulas at a remote northern mine.

I did have a brief triumph after Christmas one year. As I mentioned, some of my classmates wore suits to school. I didn't have a suit, even a hand-me-down. A day or so before Christmas I answered the door at our suite and a man handed me a long parcel with my name on it. It was a suit from Holt Renfrew in beautiful dark and soft material, and it fitted perfectly.

I later learned that in one of my father's rare letters he'd told Mother that if I didn't have a suit yet he'd like to get me one for Christmas, and would she send my measurements.

On the first day back at school after the holidays I wore the suit along with a white shirt I'd been given at Christmas and a necktie borrowed from one of the bank clerks. The reaction was quick and respectful. "Hey, Young, great suit! Where'd you get it?"

I said it was a Christmas present from my dad, the noted chemist up North.

It was about this time that I began stealing bicycles. I did not do it for the extra money I earned by selling the bikes. Nor can I attribute this part of my life to my parents being separated. I suppose that at that time, going on sixteen, I was feeling pressures that I wasn't even aware of.

I didn't have a bicycle. And every day at school an awful lot of bicycles, mostly padlocked, were lying around. But I couldn't just take one while crowds of rightful owners were nearby. So I would get myself excused from class ahead of the horde, go to where bicycles had been locked, cut a spoke or two with pliers, remove the lock and pedal away.

I don't ever remember a hue and cry—bicycles were stolen throughout the city every day or so. But I do remember in detail certain elements of my short career as a bicycle thief.

One was that I stole a bicycle, told my mother I'd repainted it for a friend, and let it be known around our district that it was for sale. A friend who lived across the street and was panting to own a bicycle alerted his father. I sold it for a few dollars down and four dollars to be paid later.

I stole another one, repainted it, and must have been crazy with self-assurance, because a week or so later, one Saturday afternoon, I rode the bike to a movie theatre on Osborne Street only a block from home and locked it against a post. I enjoyed the movie, then walked out into the afternoon sunshine and approached "my" bike. Then I noticed a car parked nearby with two people in it regarding me with keen interest. Beside the man behind the wheel was a reddish-haired boy I had seen at school. I hesitated, looking at the bike. Then some sixth sense told me to keep walking. The car doors flew open and two converged on me.

"Is this your bike?" the man said harshly.

"No."

"Then why did you stop and look at it?"

When they decided to call the police I decided to get out of there, fast.

They did not attempt to stop me. I walked south past a few store-fronts to a lane that led in the general direction of where I lived.

Turning the corner, I jammed my hand into my pocket, grabbed the key to the bicycle lock and flung it far over the rooftops. A second later the man, boy and a policeman came into the lane yelling for me to stop.

I stopped. The bike owner's father then drove the locked bike, his son, the policeman and the suspect (me) to the Fort Rouge police station a few blocks away.

There I answered a lot of questions, but their case wasn't very good. Okay, the bike had been stolen, but they now had it back. And, as the sergeant pointed out, the bike was locked and whoever had locked it must have the key, but they had searched me and found no key. As he summed it up, there could be suspicion but no proof that I had owned, or purport-ed to own, this or any other bicycle. Finally, reluctantly, they let me go.

I was walking back down the street, my heart rate up considerably, thanking Grandpa Paterson's God for this deliverance, when something nagged at me. I looked down and felt faint. On my right pant leg, the pant leg that bike riders in those days most often caught in a bike's drive-chain or sprocket, I was still wearing my trusty bicycle clip.

It had been there all the time, in plain sight, seen by no one.

I leaned over as if tying a shoelace and slipped the clip into some long grass, then walked on.

A few days later the law did catch up with me, but not on the Case of the Unnoticed Pant Clip. I had been waiting for the four dollars owed me from the sale of the other bike. One evening I went across the street to collect.

The man who had bought the bike for his son was standing on his veranda looking down at me.

He said, not unkindly, "Scott, I'm sorry about this but when I went to register the bike for a licence, they checked the serial number and found the bike had been stolen." He gave me a piece of paper with a man's name and the address of the bicycle licence bureau on it. "You're to go down there and see this man."

I did. He had me cold, of course. I was asked about other stolen bicycles, denied everything, then was charged with theft and given a date in juvenile court. I went home and told my mother. A policeman came around to make sure that I had done so.

A summer morning a week or two later Mother and I left home and walked across the Assiniboine River bridge to the courthouse. I was frightened. Not long before, an out-of-work man, on relief, had been sentenced to jail for stealing a loaf of bread. I feared the worst. I knew nothing about first offences, probation or suspended sentences. The very atmosphere of the small room, I think in the basement of the courthouse, was uncompromising. The charge was read and I pleaded guilty.

My mother then asked to speak. She described our family circumstances, adding that my father, who had been for years in the North just scraping by, was unable to help.

"I blame myself for not being able to provide Scott with what other children have as a matter of course, such as a bicycle, spending money and the kind of parental guidance that most boys his age have, eliminating a lot of temptations," she said.

The judge was not harsh, but he lectured me on the value of honesty in the lives of individuals, families and society as a whole. I listened hard and believed, and do to this day. He found me guilty as charged and suspended the sentence.

Mother and I walked home the way we had come, without any discussion of what had just happened. The events of that day were not mentioned again.

4

Becoming a Writer: 1934-1935

❧

A T KELVIN, GRADE ELEVEN WAS as far as the school went. Grade Twelve, fairly rare in Manitoba at the time, was treated as the equivalent of first-year university. I don't remember even thinking about university. What I needed, and what our family needed, was for me to get a job. I would have taken anything. The one I finally got was definitely a consolation prize, except that in the summer of 1934 there was no such thing as a *bad* job. Later I learned what some men who became my friends and colleagues went through about the same time. Blair Fraser, bound eventually for a distinguished career in journalism, shovelled coal on the Montreal docks to provide for his wife and their child. James H. (Jimmy) Gray also had a wife and child but no job, even though his work had been published in H. L. Mencken's famous *American Mercury.* He spent a lot of the summer of 1934 on his knees on grassy boulevards in affluent parts of Winnipeg, earning his relief payments with a gang of other out-of-luckers by digging up dandelions. The relief, or welfare, creed in those days was simple and virtually foolproof: No work, no relief cheque.

I remember saying once to Jimmy Gray, "Jeez, I'm glad I didn't have a wife and child when I was trying to get a job!"

"Yeah," he said, "but then you were only sixteen."

A few decades later I might have made it to university on scholarships, student loans or part-time jobs, but in 1934, forget it. If there had been a scholarship at Kelvin it would have gone to George Ferguson, who stood first in our class. He had quit school a few years earlier, learned his lesson, then returned, intending to finish high school and go on to Queen's

University in Kingston, which he did. His average, I think, was 82, while mine was 76 with straight 100s all year in math.

I came second to George that year without even going to school very much, preferring to lounge my last school days away on the banks of the Assiniboine River and think. When final exams came, I would rise at four or five in the morning and cram, filling my mind with textbook answers, then I'd go to school and let 'er fly before I forgot.

When the exams were over I applied for work, any work, all over the city. When I did chance across a job opening, some man with a family would get it. Then, finally, the black-jowled owner of a shoeshine parlour on Portage Avenue told me that the next opening he had, he'd hire me. I took the glad tidings home, beaming around. But, beating any possible congratulations to the punch, Pete LeSeach was full of scorn.

"You take a job shining shoes," he declaimed, "you can kiss goodbye to any chance of getting a *decent* job! No bank is going to hire anybody whose experience was shining shoes, for God's sake!"

Against Pete's scorn I made a show of being stubborn, but I never had to fight it out—the shoeshine guy hired somebody else. What I really wanted to be was a bank junior, low man (no juniors were female) on the totem pole in the average branch, and a line of work for which all Canadian banks, without exception, paid $400 a year.

When my final marks were available, I began my tour of the banks. It seemed to me that every boy I knew who had just finished high school was on the same trail. All dressed in our best and neatest, we sat by the hour on hard chairs in wood-panelled waiting rooms while real bankers hurried by. In quiet voices we discussed how great it would be to have a job. I met the same people applying at bank after bank, until I knew by heart what their parents or other relatives advised or tried to fix for them. I came to wish that I knew someone in power, or could think one up and lie about him.

There was a lot of suspense. You'd watch the man in charge running down the recent graduate's report card. If they were good, he might get a brief interview with an assistant manager. Just being asked to fill out an application form, which happened to me a couple of times, would make an applicant feel good all afternoon, like a mountain climber reaching the first plateau. The next level was a more detailed interview, to enable the bank to assess our grasp of who knows what. The next step was real rarefied stuff—to sit among the other late cuts writing a bank's own exams, presumably to check whether one's high school report card was anywhere near the truth.

Tramping around downtown Winnipeg for many days, I went through all the routines except the last one (internal exam) with the old Bank of Toronto, the old Dominion Bank, Bank of Montreal, Royal Bank. Then at the Bank of Nova Scotia the accountant told me I was one of three survivors out of many dozens, and that the winner on the bank's exam would get the job. Each of us that day was put at a desk in the middle of the main office, with a lot of bustle going on around us. Hours later I went home, full of hope. The next day I stayed close to the phone. And the next. And the next.

Eventually I called the bank anonymously to ask about the examinations, and was told the job had been filled. I hitchhiked to my uncle Bob MacInnes's farm near Rathwell, seventy miles or so southwest of the city. Uncle Bob, a kindly, bald man with a great laugh, took me on for the rest of the summer, the terms being room and board. Another summer guest was the beautiful Adelaide Wing, then seventeen, with whom I was soon enamoured. A few days later, working in the summer fallow, I was trudging along beside a team of horses (I had insisted that Adelaide take the seat) when a neighbour who had strung a phone line from town to his barbed-wire fence (an early telephone bootleg) showed up at the house with a message. I was to return right away and report to the accountant at the Bank of Nova Scotia. Adelaide and I ate our noon dinner that day while under the table my left foot was pressed firmly against her right foot, both feet moving a good deal this way and that.

The next day in Winnipeg I called the bank bright and early. The accountant told me (ashamedly) that I had passed the bank exams with the highest marks, but the bank manager's son had not done badly, either, and got the job. However, he hastened to say, one of the bank's accounts nearby was a tobacco wholesaler, John Erzinger Limited. Eddie Gilbert, Erzinger's office manager and a friend of the bank accountant, was looking for a cashier-ledgerkeeper. When he had asked if any of the rejects from the bank's own head-hunting was worth following up, the accountant had recommended me.

"Go across the street to Erzinger's and ask for Eddie Gilbert," the banker said. "Good luck."

I hurried, and found Eddie Gilbert to be a friendly, balding, young man who really never walked—he hurried. He took me in immediately to meet the manager, Stan McClelland, in a tiny office whose glass wall gave him a total view of his domain.

Out there on the firing line, salesmen rushed in and out with their order books, customers stopped by the front counter to pay bills or pick up orders, and the only woman in the place, Stella, took rush orders by phone. Mr. McClelland, who had a toothbrush moustache, apparently had decided even before I got there that he could save a lot of time and effort by giving me the job. He told me something about Erzinger's, long established as a tobacco wholesaler in Winnipeg but now owned by a Saskatoon company, Scales and Roberts, which in turn was owned by the Montreal giant Imperial Tobacco. He needed a bright young guy who could step in right away, because Eddie Gilbert had just been promoted to credit manager and was doing his old job, or jobs, as well as his new one.

"What do you think?" he asked.

"Um. . .?"

"I mean, about taking the job."

So the deal was done. Hallelujah!

The pay was $8 a week. If you are paying attention, as I was, that adds up to $416 a year. ("Too bad about not getting the bank job, Young," I imagined someone saying, and my reply, "Too bad, hell, I'll be making sixteen a year more than those bank guys.") But then, as Eddie Gilbert explained, my hours would be a lot longer than a bank's—from eight to six Monday to Friday, and seven till two Saturday. He showed me around, introduced me to some people, explained a few matters about the company and said, "See you tomorrow!" I went out of there walking on air.

When I got home with the news, Mother and I were alone. She made coffee and we sat and talked. "Now I can pay board!" I said. Hurrying home many blocks on foot from Erzinger's, I'd settled on $5 a week as being what I should give Mother. She said that it was too much, but I insisted. So $5 a week it was, leaving me $3 for high living.

The next morning I reported for work twenty minutes early, which, Eddie Gilbert said at eight o'clock, as he unlocked the door for me and a few others who had showed up, was a good sign. He also told me that he'd forgotten to tell me that the fifty-seven-hour week was augmented once a month by a full evening of stock-taking, which would be that very night.

Then he took me through what I would need to know about the company, the premises and my job as cashier (I was to preside at a front-counter wicket and a cash drawer) and ledgerkeeper (writing orders and payments in ink in big leather-bound ledgers), and checking in our four salesmen with their daily take.

We sold cigars, cigarettes, pipe and cigarette tobacco, pipes, snuff, chocolate bars, pipe cleaners and other smaller items, all wholesale. Our office was on street level, so my cashier's wicket faced the front door to the street. Behind me were a couple of desks, Eddie's and Stella's. Beyond them through a few doors was the warehouse and shipping department, where orders were taken to be filled and piled on the loading platform (opening on a back lane), from which they were delivered to customers by motorcycle (one, for rush orders) and van (one, for everything else). In the basement was equipment to make and repair pipes. And fairly quickly, because nothing was very complicated, I learned the ropes.

On that first day the office closed at six, and we all dispersed along the street to various small cafés for our dinners—twenty-five cents each being provided, in cash, for this purpose. Less than an hour later, we were back at work, counting cigars, cigarettes, chocolate bars, snuff, pipe tobacco, and calling out the numbers for others to enter on forms printed for that purpose.

There were about a dozen employees. One, the order desk's spinster-ish and pleasant Stella, rather fancied the head man in delivery, a former soldier named Albert. Sometimes on real bad-weather nights when Bob, the van driver, might drive some of us home through the Winnipeg cold and dark, Albert and Stella took up a good deal less room than was avail-able to them. Bob lived only about a block from our apartment, with his van garaged nearby, and sometimes I would walk that way and ride to work with him.

One of the perks of the office was free cigarettes and tobacco. I smoked sixty of these free cigarettes one day, felt awful, and gave that up forever to smoke excellent imported pipe tobacco in top-line pipes that I could buy with a 60 percent employee's discount.

For two years, that's the way I lived. I enjoyed the job, but despite pay raises to $12 a week and then to $17 a week (when at eighteen I was promoted to credit manager), I knew that I did not want to do this for life. I wanted to be a writer.

As I've said, one of my heroes was my mother's brother, Jack Paterson, the writer. And my best friend at that time, Jeff Hurley, also wanted to write. Jeff's father, a popular editorial writer for the Winnipeg *Free Press,* had died young and left his widow and son with very little—which Mrs. Hurley wisely decided should be spent taking Jeff and her to England for a year to broaden his horizons. When they returned, broke, George V. Ferguson, the *Free Press* managing editor and a friend of Jeff's father, got Jeff a job as a copy boy, that job being mainly that of a runner. Because I'd often meet Jeff after work, I began hanging around the *Free Press* editorial rooms, making friends with real reporters.

As my ambition grew, I began looking for a typewriter. In a shop window just south of Portage on Main, one lunch-time I saw a new Remington portable, priced at $48, $4 down and $4 a month for eleven months. This was in the summer of 1936. I didn't hesitate. Unbeknownst to anyone at Erzinger's (borrowing from petty cash was a firing offence), I went short to the tune of $4 from Erzinger's petty cash, supposedly guarded by me against all comers, and put a down payment on my first typewriter.

At about that time, Mother had to give up the apartment for a small one in the basement, and eventually had to give that up as well because she'd got so far behind in the rent. We were about to move again, waiting for the axe to fall, when Jeff said, "Why not come and live at our place?"

Jeff's mother also took in boarders on a somewhat higher scale than we'd ever managed, her place being a roomy apartment on River Avenue. I moved in to share his room with him. Each night we sat on our single beds, facing one another, with our typewriters on our knees, and wrote. He sold some of his: a radio play to CBS in New York and some verse to *Poetry Magazine* in Chicago.

Then, not long after I got my typewriter, I sold a short piece to the *Free Press Magazine* for $3, and on the strength of my first byline I applied for a job at the newspaper. Frank Williams, the magazine's editor, recommended me. The executive editor, Dave Rogers, a seasoned veteran of the Toronto *Star* and other newspapers, called me in. There was a job, he said: night copy boy.

"What are you making where you are now?"

I told him $17 a week.

He said he could pay copy boys only $14. Newspapers, he said, didn't offer much of a future. "My advice is to stay where you are."

I demurred.

He said, "Go away and think about it."

I walked out of his office and halfway across the editorial floor, past the semicircular city desk, listening to the typewriters clacking under the fingers of men I admired with the pure, unqualified awe of a neophyte— Pete Whittall, the radio columnist; John Sweeney, who had a neat hand-lettered sign on his desk reading VICE AND CRIME; Jimmy Gray, who later wrote great and durable popular history about the west, beginning with a book called *The Winter Years*, about the depression. Then there was Cy Louth, the police reporter, who was just back from a two-week suspension caused by getting drunk and spending Saturday night throwing newspaper files from the fifth-floor windows and then painting the editorial room's oiled wooden floor in alternating red, white and blue stripes. Burt Gresham, a senior reporter and militiaman who later was taken prisoner and, trying to escape, killed by the Japanese at Hong Kong, always was kind to me and my ambitions to be like him. Ben Malkin. Orton Grain. Eddie Armstrong. J. B. McGeachy, a powerful editorialist, stalked through the room, wearing his trademark white panama suit.

The famous *Free Press* editor John W. Dafoe, arriving from the elevator, must have thought I was on staff because he'd seen me around so much. On his way by me he nodded and said hello.

I turned around and went back into Mr. Rogers's office.

"I've thought it over enough," I said. "Can I have the job?"

"You're crazy," he said, then: "Can you start tomorrow night?"

I said I could. I rushed back to Erzinger's to put my head in at Stan McClelland's door and tell him what I had in mind starting the very next night.

"Sit down," he said.

I did. I liked him. He was no stuffed shirt. Once, I had been told, he had flown an airplane under one of Winnipeg's not especially high river bridges. He also owned one of the first Ford V8s, which he drove fast. A big man, with a reputation with the ladies, he wasn't your average small business manager in those times. He pointed out that I was doing okay where I was, making $17 a week, and that he wouldn't stand in my way but if I stayed he'd pay me $22—which was very good for an eighteen-year-old in the tail end of 1936.

"You have a real good future here, if you want it." he said.

I don't remember what I said but it added up to a respectful, and even fond, no, I'd made up my mind.

"You really want to do it, then?"

"Yes."

He asked me if I knew anybody he could hire to do my job. I said I could, thinking of two close friends of mine who hadn't found work after leaving school—one out of work for a year, the other for six discouraging years. The 1930s were like that.

"Can you get them to come in and see me?"

Feeling like Mr. Benefactor, I said I could. Right away.

"You'll be working nights, you say. How about coming in here days for a couple of weeks, full pay, and whoever we get, show him the ropes?"

That would be $17 a week from Erzinger's and $14 from the *Free Press!* Wow. I walked several feet off the ground back to the *Free Press*, feeling on top of the world.

John Maxfield, the friend who'd been out of work for six years, had the first shot at my job; he didn't make it. The other friend, Jimmy Darricott, got the job and was still there years later.

At the *Free Press*, Jeff and I settled in happily, two copy boys, one day and one night. We wrote some articles with joint bylines—one a personally researched lampoon of the ruses parents used to get rid of their daughters' young men at some arbitrary hour, such as 11 p.m., and how resourceful chaps such as we had ideas on how to thwart such anti-social behaviour.

When the *Free Press Magazine's* Frank Williams felt that with some work it might be worth publishing, he began his note to a higher editor with, "These arrogant young pups. . ."

5

The Sporting Life: 1935

〜〜〜

M Y EARLIEST RECOLLECTION OF SPORT of any kind is of being one in a crowd of young boys, mostly my cousins, at a baseball tournament in Glenboro. We were a wriggling, giggling mass along the first-base line, yelling insults at the opposition and support for our side. These tournaments were most often part of country fairs in small prairie towns, one-day knockout affairs in which the winner normally would have to play three games, usually with the same pitcher, with the size of first prize generally denoting how good the baseball would be—the bigger the prize, the better the teams that would be attracted to compete. Our uncles, aunts and others, dressed not in their Sunday best but not in overalls either, would stand behind us. Sometimes a few elderly onlookers would bring chairs, but mostly not, and the crowd would stretch out to well along the outfield fence, which normally also was part of the racetrack fence for trotters and pacers. My dad was pretty good at his infield position, but the man I remember best from those Glenboro days was a tall pitcher named Whit Meredith, who never seemed to tire no matter how many games he was called upon to play. When I think of those days I am a small eight-year-old in knee breeches and a cap, screaming with the others until darkness fell and the tournament ended.

After my father's bankruptcy and our move to Winnipeg, he played on various Winnipeg teams and I began playing hockey, usually a defenceman because I wasn't as good a rusher as the others, including my younger brother. We weren't in a league, but for games against other neighbourhood teams we'd draw fair crowds, spectators standing on the snow banks surrounding the ice.

All of us normally played the entire game, and when I was finished I would walk home on my skates and take them off in the warm kitchen, rubbing my half-frozen toes to bring the feeling back. My first experience in an organized league came after I'd moved to Prince Albert and tried out on defence for our church league team, boys thirteen and under. After I'd broken Marie's skates I was given a pair of my own and somewhat to my surprise wound up as the captain of our team. That honour had nothing to do with my skill. By my figuring, I was our seventh-best player; ahead of me were the goalie, three defencemen and two forward lines. Our eighth-, ninth- and tenth-best players made up what we called our second line, so small that one onlooker opined that they were the only forward line in hockey that could skate three abreast through a keyhole.

Our best player was Sandy McKenzie. He was a beautiful skater and dazzling stick-handler. I would have loved to play as well, but never did. Sandy scored most of our goals that winter, most of the balance coming from Johnny Chad, who later played for Chicago in the National Hockey League.

Even showing up to play our Saturday morning games was an experience. We played one day when it was 57 below Fahrenheit and another when it was minus 62. In Prince Albert, this was known as a cold snap. When it was 40 below, Uncle Frank would call it Indian summer.

One game that winter lives in my memory as sharply as any heavyweight championship fight or World Series or Olympics of my later times as a sports columnist. We played only on Saturday mornings, in an ancient wooden rink near a railroad track. I'd get up early at Uncle Frank and Aunt Mary's to walk the mile or so to the rink. We'd fire up the coal stove in the dressing room in an attempt to get the temperature high enough that we could take off our mitts and get our skates on. Even with the stove red-hot, the blobs of frost on every nailhead in the wooden walls never melted. Some mornings the rink ice was so brittle from cold that when a train passed, vibrations in the frozen ground would splinter the ice like glass.

I have good reason to remember the final game that season. To become league champions in our age group we needed a win or tie against a remarkably stubborn team of Methodists. (A Presbyterian uncle of mine, hearing this story some years later, asked: "What's so remarkable about Methodists being stubborn?") Our coach had to work that fateful morning and asked me, as captain, to handle the team until he arrived.

Usually he gave our tiny second forward line ice time almost equal to that of the good first line. I would stand on the blueline in those games and marvel at the impassive air with which he would open the gate and unleash those three fifty-pound tigers. I'd feel anything but impassive knowing that the next two minutes would be sheer madness around our goal. One time a fellow defenceman, clearing the puck, also cleared our second-line centreman about twenty feet down the ice, by mistake.

So the day I was handling the team and the game wore on, every time there was a whistle I carefully refrained from even looking at our bench. I knew those three pairs of tiny eyes would be peering mournfully at me, the eyes just barely clearing the boards if their owners stood on tiptoe. So our good line played almost the entire game. We finished in a tie, 2–2, and thus won the championship.

However, when we trooped into the dressing room at the end of the game our cheers were dampened immediately. Our coach had arrived in the last minute of play. When he found that I hadn't played the second line except for one mad shift in the first period when both the Methodist goals had been scored, he came over to where I was unlacing my skates and bawled me out in front of everybody.

"Winning doesn't count as much as you think it does," he said. "It isn't fair to these kids to have them come all this way on a cold morning and leave them on the bench."

It is the only time I have won anything that caused me to go home feeling subdued and sad. I was a bit of a misfit myself because of our family situation, living on the charity of relatives, and it took lessons like that to teach me that others could be vulnerable, too.

That was also my last appearance as a player. It was when school ended that I returned to Winnipeg. That autumn I enrolled in Grade Ten at Kelvin Technical High School, which had a great hockey team. Lacking the ability to play on it, I became Joe Fan, with a vengeance.

When our team was playing, the transit company would send an old trolley car to the school, a special strictly for Kelvin kids. We'd pile on and open the windows and holler the school yell east along Academy Road and north on Sherbrooke, east along Portage and then far north on Main to the old Olympic rink, which is long gone now. People on the streets would stop and smile as we rocked by in the dusk wrestling in the aisles, yelling out the windows, letting everybody know who we were. On those hockey specials, I could forget everything that troubled me.

The bedlam continued unabated in the rink, because our heroes were the best. I can't name any Canadian cabinet ministers of that time without thinking hard, but I remember Burr Keenan at centre and Preston Beattie on defence, Tommy Rathwell, Ken Barker, Al Bertrand, some from my own home room, Mr. Kerr's room.

By the spring of 1935 some of my high-school heroes were with the Winnipeg junior Monarchs when they won the Western championship. Out of school by then, I lined up at five one frigid morning outside the Amphitheatre Rink to pay a dollar for my seat to the Memorial Cup final for the Canadian junior championship. Most of the good seats were sold in pairs, leaving a few choice singles. I got one of those and later I caught a streetcar and hustled off to Erzinger's rejoicing that I'd be seeing, front row centre the Memorial Cup.

I have been grateful many times for knowing what the game was like then. In those days there was no such thing as a deferred penalty, the rule by which a modern team never has to play more than two men short. Any penalty incurred when two of one team are already in the penalty box is deferred until the first of the earlier penalties ends. Not so in 1935. In one game, Monarchs got such a string of penalties at one point that only one player, stocky little Pete Belanger, was left on the ice to protect goalie Paul Gauthier against the full team of Sudbury Wolves. In the great uproar when the Wolves skated in on Pete five abreast, passing the puck back and forth, he recognized the impossibility of the situation by hauling off and slugging the nearest Sudbury player with his stick. Luckily, as he was sent off, some others came on. Monarchs lost that game badly but had won the first one, so all hinged on the third and final contest. I have told many times since, to the glazed eyes of whoever would listen, how Gauthier, before that game, kneeled on the dressing-room bench in his goal pads and prayed—maybe that his teammates would regain their sanity, for all I know. But for whatever reason he got a shutout and Monarchs won the Memorial Cup. Bliss.

Soon after, still at Erzinger's, I began to write. Each night I would sit in my room and peck away at my typewriter. I had more writing heroes besides Uncle Jack by then: Hemingway, Evelyn Waugh, Tiffany Thayer, H. L. Mencken, William Saroyan, James Branch Cabell, Damon Runyon, whoever I was reading that week. I read the *New Yorker, Esquire, American*

Mercury, Harper's, Atlantic, and a good one that didn't last long, *Ringmaster.* At that starting point I never wrote about sports. I saw nothing in the Winnipeg sports scene that might score big with the magazines I was favouring with my output: those above plus the *Saturday Evening Post* and, once in a while, *Black Mask, True Confessions* or *Spicy Western.*

It may be that my best work of that period was an equal partnership with Jeff Hurley in an epic poem entitled "Rape on the Levee." Jeff and I were only hypothetically familiar with rape and had never seen a levee, but had read a lot of Jesse Stuart stories in *Esquire,* and that seemed enough for us to rough out a plot and settle on a plan of action, which was that I would take all the even-numbered verses and he'd take the odd ones. We did it in one night. I read it years later; it wasn't bad. But soon after that I made my first connection with writing sport. One Saturday a leprechaun-like photographer, Harry Steele, must have seen me yearning when he was setting off to cover a Blue Bomber football game because he said, "Hey, kid, why don't you come along and carry my camera bag? That'll get you in."

That was my first experience of Canadian football. From then on I went with Harry to every game. No western team ever had won the Canadian championship at that time, but that November of 1935 Winnipeg won the west with me sitting up to my hips in snow on the timer's bench because that's where Harry was. With no empty seats that day, Harry had told me to stay close to him and I'd be safe.

The same sort of peripheral acceptance got me into the *Free Press* editorial room a week or two later. Winnipeg was playing Hamilton that day in Hamilton for the Canadian championship Grey Cup. Jeff Hurley had told me that the editorial room police radio would carry the game barring interruption from, say, a mass murder, so I quietly eased myself into a chair on the fringe of the real newspapermen who were waiting to put out the Grey Cup extra after the game.

The first great shout from our little group came the instant the broadcast began. It had started two minutes late, for some reason, and Winnipeg already led 6–0! Hamilton had fumbled the Winnipeg kickoff! Herb Peschel had recovered for Winnipeg on the Hamilton eighteen, Russ Rebholz had passed to Joe Perpich in the end zone for the touchdown, and Greg Kabat had converted! (A touchdown was worth only five points in those days.)

O, Lord we sighed, don't toy with us. Apparently the police dispatcher felt the same way. From then on, police calls were made only during stoppages in play, like commercials.

The game wore on. A reporter was sent out to check how downtown Winnipeg was taking it. He hurried back in minutes, so as not to miss anything, and said the streets were deserted and every radio store full to the doors with people who had no radios of their own.

Winnipeg led 12–4 at half-time. But in the third quarter Winnipeg's mightiest lineman, Bert Oja, was penalized for a high tackle. Under the rules of the time, that sent Oja off the field for three minutes, leaving Winnipeg shorthanded. Hamilton scored: 12–10. But then Fritz Hanson, one of the greatest broken-field runners ever in those days when no downfield blocking was allowed, fielded a Hamilton punt and, to our screaming joy, danced his way seventy-eight yards on the icy field through or around the slipping and sliding tacklers and crossed the line standing up. The game ended 18–12.

I went out on the street as the extras were being carried by newsboys from the press room. They ran to the street yelling, "Extra! Extra!" and before they went half a block were sold out and running back for more. The huge front-page headline was "WOWIE! PEGS WIN!" Streetcars were stopped, the streets full of people dancing in the softly falling snow. I watched the first wild public demonstration of my life. I was seventeen.

Reporters today, with degrees in everything from journalism to law, wouldn't recognize the way into journalism that shaped my life and the lives of others. I worked six nights a week from six till two in the morning. If anyone wanted a paste pot cleaned, or a page of a story rushed to the city desk, or a sandwich from across the street at the Spoon Luncheonette, he (it was always a he in those days) simply called, "Boy!" and I ran. I tended the teletype machines, delivering stories to the appropriate departments (news desk, sports, finance, women's) and as a sideline, kept carbon copies of anything on the teletype printers about the Sino–Japanese war then raging. Each night a driver from the On Kee Taxi would sidle into the newsroom for the flimsies I had saved. This was a very unofficial service instituted by a former copy boy, Bert Briggs. The On Kee driver would take the teletype printer flimsies to Kuomintang headquarters in Chinatown, where they were translated to Chinese to be posted on the noticeboard there. In return, one heady night the On Kee

Taxi came again at 2 a.m. and drove Bert Briggs and me to the Nanking restaurant for a grand free meal, with whisky, as thanks for this private public service—which incidentally fuelled a lifelong interest in China, especially its politics and leaders, from Chiang Kai-shek to Mao Tse-tung.

I was still only a copy boy but the tweedy pipe-smoking veteran reporters I revered told me that the only way to get anything published was to go out and find stories, write them and turn them in to the city desk. This I would do on my day off each Saturday. I heard of a man making a snowmobile powered by an airplane engine in his downtown Winnipeg garage. Night city editor Walter Hand spared me embarrassing compliments but printed it.

Meanwhile, the copy boy I had replaced on nights, George Thurston, moved to sports, and had been spending the time unwittingly, I am quite sure, convincing all concerned that he had no future as a sports writer. He was flunked out of sports and later became financial editor of the *Free Press* while, all's well that ends well, I was given the chance at the sports job.

So I began to cover eight hockey games every Saturday and minor sports through the week. I loved it. And that was how, at age eighteen in December of 1936, I became a sports writer: purely by chance. Lucky chance, I've always thought.

The sports editor of the time was W. G. Allen, a gruff small man called Billy by his familiars. His desk was against a wall at the northwest corner of the newsroom, the keystone of a littered rectangle of desks and chairs and typewriters and record books that made up the sports department area. I met W.G. rarely, because I worked nights and he did not live long after I arrived, but I remember him well. At his left sat an upright telephone, and pasted to the adjacent wall were certain useful phone numbers and league schedules. The morning I was told to introduce myself to him as his new staff member I stood respectfully at the corner of his desk, waiting for him to acknowledge me and watching him write a paragraph for his column, in longhand, with a thick black pencil. It was an almost indecipherable scrawl that slanted down from left to right on a copy-paper pad. When he reached the bottom he tore off the page, yelled, "Boy!" and handed the page to day copy boy Hurley, who ran it up the spiral steel stairs that led from the middle of the editorial floor to the composing room and the one particular printer who could read W. G. Allen's handwriting and set it in type. I remember nothing of what Allen said to me that morning, if anything.

Bursting as I was to stun the world with the wit, daring and originality of my prose, I am afraid that at first I tended to look down upon the likes of W. G. Allen as relics of the past. He struck me as being nothing like John Lardner, Joe Williams, Henry McLemore, Grantland Rice, John Kieran, the sports writers I revered at that time. I had yet to learn that there is a time in the lives of some journalists when they use their experience instead of their legs and still can be worth printing. He was old and not well, and in those days before decent pensions, he was kept on because the people who ran the newspaper recognized their responsibility to faithful servants.

He gleaned most of the information for his terse paragraphs from what were called the exchanges. In those days and perhaps even yet in some cases, major newspapers exchanged copies by mail. The *Free Press* received all Canadian newspapers of any consequence, plus the *New York Times* and the old *World-Telegram*. These were cut into sections by a copy boy, who then would deliver the out-of-town editorial pages to the editorial writers, women's pages to the women's department, and so on down to the pile of sports pages from across the country that W. G. Allen would work at, but never get to the bottom of. After a quick scan, maybe leading to a tersely written column item, W. G. threw these pages into a tall wire-mesh wastebasket at his right elbow. He also smoked cigarettes incessantly and flicked the ashes and occasionally live butts into the wastebasket. The resultant conflagrations were famous among day copy boys, who several times a week had to run for water to douse the flames while W. G. stood impassively a few feet away lighting another cigarette as he waited to get back to work. I remember him always in the same outfit: dark suit trousers bagging around his little paunch, his vest unbuttoned and with black pencils sticking from the pockets, tie done up, arm-garters above his elbows to keep his shirtsleeves out of harm's way.

On the three other desks used by the sports department, ancient Underwood typewriters were mounted on wooden platforms that swivelled so that they could be pulled in to work on, or pushed away (sometimes with a crash) when the guy wished to go to the bathroom or, more often at night, when everyone in the sports department except W. G. Allen was on duty, to murmur to me, "If anybody calls I'm in the snakeroom."

It was customary in those days for sports promoters large and small to show their appreciation of our coverage by bringing whisky. They'd often do this in advance, believing from experience that there was a relationship between a forty-ounce bottle of rye and the size of sports-page headlines. They'd stick around for a drink or two and to exchange a few lies, a mutual procedure that in later years became known as public relations. To consume the whisky, some degree of privacy was required, which didn't exist in the big, open editorial floor. Hence, the snakeroom, actually a long, narrow storage room for the Canadian Press news service that occupied part of our floor. Shelves of paper, envelopes, teletype rolls, carbon, flimsies and other supplies reached to the ceiling and left a passage about five feet wide and fifteen feet long. There the amenities could be observed while those present discussed the sports world, usually a lot more interestingly than whatever got into the newspaper.

Our using part of CP's domain as a place to drink was a constant aggravation to the CP bureau chief, Frank Turner, who worked days. Every morning this tall, sombre man in his three-piece suit would moodily inspect his storage room for signs of our passing, such as (once) a sleeping-it-off bowling alley proprietor. One day, pushed beyond endurance, Mr. Turner summoned his night chief, Charlie Edwards.

"You've got to keep those sports department guys out of here, Charlie!" he commanded.

"What have they done now?"

"The usual! When I came in this morning I found the storage place littered with empty mickeys."

Charlie thought for a minute, then said, "Couldn't have been the sports department."

"Why not?"

"They always have forties."

Only rarely at first, but eventually it came to pass that I would be asked to join the men in the snakeroom. One night a visitor noted that rather than fetch some water to mix with my whisky I was taking it straight. Shocked, he said he would show me what straight whisky did to a stomach. He soon returned with a raw steak from the Spoon Luncheonette across the street.

"Had to buy a steak sandwich," he complained. "Didn't even get a discount for them not having to cook it." He laid the steak on a newspaper. "Now, watch this."

He poured a little straight rye whisky onto the steak, which writhed slightly and turned brown. All present, sipping their straight whisky, agreed that it was an interesting demonstration.

When W. G. Allen died, the sports editorship went automatically to Eddie Armstrong, his assistant, an energetic and well-connected younger man who had been running the department anyway in W. G.'s declining years. It was Eddie who had seen what he thought was a spark in me and got me started there. The rest of the department consisted of Cam McKenzie, a handsome, polite, slow-talking dark-haired ladies' man in the early stages of alcoholism, and Clem Shields, of Irish ancestry but with Fleet Street experience. Clem didn't have Cam's vast tolerance for alcohol but he *thought* he did. They were both my friends and helped me a lot.

There was also Scotty Harper, a bow-legged little Scot who worked a regular shift as an International Typographical Union printer, double shifts when he could get them, and wrote about soccer and curling, for which he was paid so much a printed inch. This was called being on space rates. He was a serious, rather beaten-down war veteran, always in a hurry because of the variety of jobs he had, and always broke. He earned more than any of us, but his wife allowed him only twenty-five cents a day spending money. This was for car fare, lunch and other high living, so he tended to be a figure of fun to the free-swinging bachelor McKenzie and stupendously un-henpecked Shields.

Scotty's only breaks came when someone on his soccer or curling beat brought up a bottle for, as they used to say, "the sports boys." Meaning us. Scotty, as conducting officer, thus sometimes had a work-related excuse not to go straight home. After a hang-dog and apologetic phone call to tell his wife of this unforeseen demand on his time, acting it all out on the phone, you'd think practically in tears to look at him, he would hang up and beam happily. Then he would revel in the snakeroom confab, rarely talking himself but chuckling, listening and chiming in with a serious "Aye" when his vote was required.

The one time I remember Scotty really getting into trouble was once when his wife, a large and firmly corseted woman, was spending the summer at a beach cottage. A man from a woman's softball league brought up some whisky. We had been barred from the snakeroom because of a party that was still going on when Frank Turner got in to work one morning, so until things cooled had moved our hospitality headquarters to the *Free Press* Model Kitchen, where by day recipes were tested by a staff of women in impeccable white, like nurses. As the Model Kitchen had running water and ice cubes, and therefore could well have been named the Model Snakeroom, it was locked each night. But we could always find a thirsty janitor to unlock it for us. Once, Scotty's wife being away, he got into his cups a little more than usual and complained bitterly about the tiny allowance he had while his wife lived it up at the beach.

"Even my pension cheque I dinna ever see. . .Well, I see it, aye, it's there now, but I canna spend it, ye ken."

McKenzie, aghast: "You get a wound pension from the war and you can't spend it?"

It turned out that Scotty's wife, knowing the pension cheque would be arriving when she was away, had had a padlock put on the mailbox. She had taken the key with her. All Scotty could do for thrills was stand on tiptoes and look at his pension cheque through the mail slot. McKenzie soon worked Scotty into a state of anger at the iniquity of it all, mainly McKenzie declaiming and Scotty shouting, "Aye! Aye, Cam!" They took a taxi to Scotty's place and broke open the mailbox, and Scotty, for once, spent his pension cheque, explaining to his wife that there had been a city-wide wave of mailbox robberies.

For the above and other reasons my apprenticeship in life as well as journalism went on apace. At first, I was assigned to minor sports, up to and including junior hockey, but when spring arrived I became a baseball expert, covering the Winnipeg Maroons in the class D Northern League. In those early sojourns in the press box fifteen feet above home plate, I was lucky that Johnny Buss, sports editor of our competition, the Winnipeg *Tribune*, was one of the kindest men alive. He taught me how to score baseball, and I've been scoring it ever since, even TV games, so I'll always know what's going on.

The Maroons played in dilapidated Sherbourne Park, now long gone, the infield bald, the uncovered wooden stands unpainted, weathered and rickety. Bruno Haas, the manager, sometimes pitched if a game was gone away. He had spindly legs, a huge torso and very little hair. The league salary limit at the time was $65 a month, but if Bruno really wanted somebody, usually a pitcher, he could go up to $75 by paying the guy an extra $10 to drive the team bus. On the long, instructive (girls in strange towns, drinks I'd never heard of) road trips, Maroons might play a night game, and then, while I was sending the story, Bruno would round up his team and the bus would take off for the next place—Grand Forks, North Dakota; Crookston, Minnesota; Duluth; Superior, Wisconsin; Wausau, Eau Claire, Fargo-Moorhead. . .

As time went on, I tended to take on more than my own work. Sometimes I wrote Clem Shields's weekly column, "The Whirligig." This arrangement with Shields ended one summer when he had put away too much hospitality while covering the Western Canada Hard Courts tennis championships at the Winnipeg Canoe Club. When he phoned on the Friday night before the finals, he asked me to write his column and rambled on drunkenly about this player or that to the effect that they were all a lot of pansies. I was very busy with something else, so went to work on Shields's column in bad grace, leaving in lines about "mincing" out to the court, and such. All in all, it resulted in a remarkable reception for Shields at the finals the next day; he was screamed at for he knew not what, because he hadn't read his own column. He never asked me to write it for him again.

It all seems incredibly telescoped now, that first year or two I spent at the *Free Press*. At first I was new to everything as night copy boy, but the routine was easy—I'd watched Hurley do it. All the same, within days I became a bit player in my first big story, running like hell between the teletype machines and the composing room above with the latest developments in King Edward's abdication, which freed him to marry Wallis Warfield Simpson. Hundreds of thousands of words on that empire-shaking love story poured in on the wires, and I tore them off and ran with them. I would walk home at night excited, exhausted, thinking, "This is the life!"

A few weeks later I was promoted to sports (same pay), but when the R-100 airship tragically crashed late one afternoon with heavy loss of life, at the first newsflash I happened to be in the office with only one other person, city editor Abbie Coo. For the next hour I helped him get an Extra edition edited, set, printed and on the street. My job was to run stories off the teletype machines up the spiral stairs to the composing room where Abbie, old, white-haired, with a swivel front tooth that he could spin like a propeller when he was excited, would scan what I brought and instantly yell out the headline it was to bear. Our Extra beat the opposition to the street. Abbie shuffled past me to pick up the first *Extra* from the pile just in from the press room. "You did well," he said. I was proud, feeling at the centre of things, a real pro. It's a good feeling for a kid to have.

It was about then, in 1937, that, in dire straits, living in one room in a house on Whitehall Avenue, my mother began to think of going north to rejoin my father. My sister had gone to live with Aunt Helen again in Glenboro. My brother had quit school earlier, at age fifteen, and had lied about his age to get a job with a mining company that put him on a train for a remote mine in northwest Ontario. I was with the Hurleys. We were well scattered again.

But Dad, in Flin Flon, was doing better as a grocery clerk and wanted Mother back. She borrowed train fare from a relative and she and my sister went to see him. They both made some commitments, and after a few days she decided to stay; really, no other course I can think of was open to her. Soon my brother joined them and, because of his mining experience and willingness to work underground, he was hired by Hudson Bay Mining and Smelting, the major industry in the area.

So the family was back together again, except for me. I was happy, hoping it would work out, but not very optimistic. I had my own agenda. I liked being a *Free Press* sports writer. Still, I wangled a railroad pass and got to Flin Flon for a week. Mother, Bob and Dorothy seemed okay. In one long talk I had with Dad, the two of us sitting for an hour or two on a huge boulder in the middle of the town, he told me that things between him and Mother had not really changed. I got the idea that she was driving him again to be something he wasn't.

When he said simply, "She beats me, Scott," I wondered how long it would last this time.

Completely on my own then, I worked two years at $14 a week, then was raised to $16. I lived in boarding houses, and got by. The money didn't matter. I felt on top of the world. I'd been started on a weekly column but eventually it was appearing nearly every day. I was getting bylines. I had a free membership to the Winnipeg Canoe Club in return for covering club events. In a smallish sports community, as Winnipeg was then, anyone who writes every day gets a following and I had it, for baseball, basketball, track meets, paddling, hockey, high-school and junior football. I also learned my major lessons, as usual, one at a time.

One came this way. The Manitoba junior football championship had been won by the Young Men's Hebrew Association. I was assigned to Regina for the western junior final. I had the flu at the time and nagging pains around the area of my appendix but I couldn't bear to miss my first genuine out-of-province assignment and was afraid to go to a doctor in case he ordered me to bed. But because I felt so miserable I decided not to travel with the team and its supporters, who'd be partying all night. I took a different train.

A few days later G. Sydney Halter, a Jewish lawyer, approached me. We were good friends, having met through sports. (Later he became president of the Canadian Amateur Athletic Union and then commissioner of the Canadian Football League.) Being a friend he came right out with it: I was thought by some people to be anti-Jewish because I had not travelled with the YMHA team and their families and fans on the trip to Regina.

It was a lesson in how easily a person can be branded. One thing for sure: from then on, Rube Ludwig, Rosy Adelman, Lou Mogul, Benny Hatskin, Mitch Pechet and all the rest of the Jewish athletes who enlivened the Winnipeg sports scene then and later found in me a faithful Boswell. I even switched my custom, such as it was, to a Jewish bootlegger, Fanny Templin, sister of one of the Winnipeg Blue Bombers' linemen, Lou Mogul. Covering all the angles.

Even at that time, I had a strong sense that for much of my life I would be involved for much of the time with sports, and would have fun at it. Which has been the case.

6

Wedding Bells:
1936-1940

THE FIRST TIME I WAS aware of Rassy Ragland, I was on the lawn at the Winnipeg Canoe Club, facing a wide stretch of the Red River where it meanders through the city to empty into Lake Winnipeg a few dozen miles to the north. Kneeling paddlers in racing shells, singles, doubles and fours, were digging deep, warming up for the club's first regatta of the 1938 season and showing off for the girlfriends or would-be girlfriends lounging on blankets on the lawn, all in all a pretty sight that I never would have been part of except that a few weeks earlier, as a member of the sports press, I'd been given a free membership to the Canoe Club and its golf course, tennis courts, canteen, rambling clubhouse with a big ballroom for dances by night and table tennis by day.

Into this idyllic setting sounded a piercing cry, "Dee-yar!" At the same time I overheard a voice from a group of girls on a lawn blanket, muttering, "That woman!"

I turned to see a vividly dark-haired young female heading down the ramp from the clubhouse, waving at the dee-yar in question, a handsome and muscular paddler who missed a stroke to return her wave.

The friend I was with, a male fellow member of the much downscale Winnipeg Swimming Club, whose gathering place was a broken-down house about a mile down river, said, "That's Rassy Ragland. She goes with Jack McDowell, the guy who waved back. If things go the way they have been lately, he'll be on our Olympic team."

"What as?" I asked.

"Paddling. Doubles and fours."

As the regatta went on, I was fairly busy, watching, making notes for the sports-page story I'd be writing later. Many of the results involving Rassy's dee-yar seemed to be foregone conclusions. McDowell and a short, immensely muscled and wide-shouldered paddler named Doug Groff were one-two in the singles, won the doubles and were on the winning fours.

Over the next year or so, I saw a lot of Rassy at regattas, club dances, on the tennis courts. . . She didn't work, drove her father's car whenever she wanted it, had never known joblessness in the family (her father, born in Virginia, was in charge of western Canada operations for Barrett Roofing) and she knew little or nothing of the kind of life I had led. She also had a habit that bothered me: when she wanted something from someone else she might say, "I'll *make* Banwell do it," "I'll *make* Busby drive me there," and seemed surprised if I said, as I did occasionally, "Don't you mean you'll *ask* him?"

She was also dismissive of girls whom I sometimes took to club dances, particularly one, Merle Davies, who I was going around with on a non-exclusive basis, although necking in a canoe up river we did have very good balance together, and never spilled a drop.

I'd met Merle through her stepfather, Lou Davies, a power in thorough-bred racing throughout western Canada. Besides writing a racing column for the *Free Press* under the nom de plume Yorkshire Lad, he was the track handicapper at the two local racing strips, Polo Park and Whittier Park, chart-caller and, most important for the future, proprietor of a past-perfor-mances program that had a lock on sales of that kind of material at all western Canadian tracks. I'd met Merle first at the Davies apartment at Sunday afternoon parties that Lou and Merle's mother, Carrie, held for the Winnipeg sports crowd. She was visiting for the summer before returning to Montreal, where she lived with an aunt. Both Lou and Carrie encouraged me to get Merle out and around where she'd meet people and enjoy herself. Enjoying herself was never difficult for Merle. She was pretty, lively and friendly, and she soon had her own entourage of young males at the canoe club, who quickly overtook my original finders' rights, such as they were.

As the next few months went by, I saw a lot of Rassy one way or another, often at her initiative. When the Canadian Canoe championships were held at Lachine, Quebec, in 1939, part of the exercise being to choose Canada's paddling team for the 1940 Olympics, Jack McDowell, Doug Groff and other strong members of the Winnipeg Canoe Club paddling elite were competing. Most of the finals, as I recall, were on a Saturday and probably wouldn't make the late papers. Radio sports news was fairly sketchy then. Rassy asked me if she could come to the *Free Press* wire room with me so she could get the CCA results firsthand. She hung over the machines as the results came in. Her dee-yar was doing himself proud. Winnipeg paddlers swept most events, meaning that they would be the backbone of our paddling team in Finland at the 1940 Olympics (which, as it turned out, were cancelled because of World War Two).

In the following months, Rassy and I went out together a good deal. Then one night she told me she had broken off her engagement to McDowell. His friends tried hard to get her to reverse that decision, telling her that McDowell was a far better prospect than I was—no doubt true. The whole situation was pretty ridiculous: dark-haired, headstrong beauty turns down athletic hero in favour of ink-stained wretch, who'll do her dirt. Author, author.

A year or so earlier my friend Jeff Hurley had worked his way to Toronto on a cattle train and had caught on as a copy boy and junior reporter at the *Globe and Mail.* He and his mother (the *Free Press* had got her a railroad pass) were living in a downtown attic. When I visited, also on a pass, he wanted me to join them, but I have to admit in retrospect that I had grown apart, as warm as our friendship and Mrs. Hurley's help once had been. To get back west I sat up all night in the day coach. I had one dozen oranges to eat on that trip.

I don't recall exactly how Paris Eakins, Mark McClung and I got together, except that we were all working at the *Free Press* and in the summer of 1939 all looking for a place to live. I found a furnished bachelor apartment on Furby Street near Portage, renting at $37.50 a month, which I couldn't handle by myself on $25 a week, but would be fine if split three ways.

Mark was just back from several years at Oxford. He was witty, somewhat older and much more sophisticated than Paris and I, full of racy stories about the life of an Oxford man. More important, his was the kind of educated background that the *Free Press* didn't have much of. He wrote mainly agricultural stories under the aegis of a noted farm writer of the time, E. Cora Hind, a friend of his mother, the writer and feminist Nellie McClung. In his reporting Mark showed a nice touch in talking to farmers and writing about their problems with drought, rust, grasshoppers and the shortage of good farm help.

Paris was equally bright, and for various reasons connected—as I was—with being born and raised among the curling and hockey and base-ball and farming people of rural Manitoba, with their own brand of wit. He was more my style. He had done well in school, was from a well-known western Manitoba family and had got his *Free Press* job because of good work for the weekly Minnedosa *Tribune*. He was a stocky, freckled, sandy-haired, bustling and witty young man with an engagingly explosive laugh, and he wanted to be a sports writer. Both he and Mark had quickly become dependable reporters, well liked on the *Free Press*, and the three of us got along well together. Given the available space, Paris and I shared the Murphy bed, which folded into the wall when not in use. The chesterfield could have been used as a bed, but for $4, McClung bought an ancient secondhand single cot, which he called the Buggery, because when he got it home and shook it out he had to stamp on a few cockroaches.

In other ways, we were compatible on a grand scale. Often when our shifts ended at night we would repair to our favourite bootlegger in the downtown area and drink beer until our funds ran out, or morning came, when we would make our way homeward through the crowds of decent people heading downtown to their jobs. Our bootlegger was north of the city's main east–west thoroughfare, Portage Avenue, meaning we had to cross that wide and busy street to get to our apartment. On mornings when we felt fit and strong, we would take long runs down a side street, yelling for the decent people to get out of the way, and at Portage would try to broadjump across the very wide sidewalk, which none of us ever did.

Mark McClung's mother lived on Lantern Lane in Victoria, B.C. She was a member of various boards and committees that often brought her east on visits that Mark dreaded, feeling (correctly) that he never quite lived up to his mother's expectations.

One morning I awoke to hear hammering on the door. When none of us stirred to answer it, a woman's voice called, "Mark! It's Mummy!" I opened my eyes to see McClung hurrying silently from the Buggery to our tiny vestibule, where he opened the closet door and pushed through the coats until he was out of sight except for one hand reaching back to close the closet door. Paris was watching, too. He winked at me but neither of us moved, or spoke.

Meanwhile, from the hall the knocking and calling continued. "It's Mummy, Mark! I'm just here between trains, on my way to Ottawa."

Knock, knock. "I brought you some of our own lovely flowers from Lantern Lane!"

After her voice died away down the hall, a few more minutes passed. By that time Paris and I were wide awake. Finally, McClung, his sandy red hair awry, opened the closet door and peered out watchfully. He said nothing. It was too early to get up. We all went back to sleep.

As a sports writer, I worked usually at night. In the afternoons when McClung and Eakins were at work, Rassy might drop in to the apartment. That meant we were together a lot, alone, our sexual urges very strong, but we always stopped short of the ultimate. I had been sexually active, as today's terminology has it, but not with her. Fear of pregnancy controlled many such situations, and marriage had never been mentioned between us. Meanwhile, I had learned something about her temper. She flung a tobacco tin at me once when I was defending my serious attachment to my first real lover, Amy Conway, a lovely woman—she still is, more than fifty years later—which was not going well because of my dalliance with Rassy.

I have to digress here for a patch of rather painful self-analysis. I didn't realize it at the time, but perhaps stemming from years of being bounced around from one home to another, in dealing with women I tended to escalate far too many passing fancies into marriage proposals.

Luckily, most of the girls I asked had more sense than I did, but this uncontrollable tic, or whatever it was, did become somewhat folkloristic. Years later I happened to overhear two women discussing me, one stating that I had once asked her to marry me. The other, Birdeen Allen, Ralph Allen's widow, a longtime dear friend, retorted, "So what? He asks everybody to marry him." After considering the matter I had to admit that Birdeen's opinion was well founded, although I never asked her to marry me. At one time in Winnipeg, Ralph with the *Tribune* and me with the *Free Press*, Ralph and I had been considered in competition for Birdeen. (This was before I got serious with Rassy.) For a few months we had all lived in the same boarding house. Someone often played the piano at night after dinner and we danced. Birdeen flirted with a lot of men, one of them me. I heard (others being eager to bring me the news) that once in a beer parlour session Ralph was ribbed about this apparent competition, the well-known columnist versus the cub sports writer. Ralph eventually asked her to choose, and she wrote me a note, in effect giving me a vote in her decision. I wrote her a frank note in reply, saying that while I had no idea what was going to happen to me, Ralph was a sure thing.

The morning after I had written that note, I found an envelope under my door. In it was another note from Birdeen, saying that she had received mine, and that I was "noble." We both had long lives after that, hers much too short. In our married states for many years we spent a lot of time together, Ralph, Birdeen, Rassy and me, playing bridge through long weekends, fishing, watching Grey Cups at their house or ours, Allen and I often golfing together, major boosters of each other's work. I was always happy to be where Birdeen was.

However, her comment that I asked every passing female to marry me had some truth to it. Before I married, too often I translated simple sexual attraction into daydreams of having a home of my own. As I said, these random proposals usually died natural deaths. Amy, my first real lover, a legal secretary about my age, was one who turned me down. She had missed a period, which had happened before, but this time she was nearly a month late and the situation was looking serious. One evening when she was ironing some clothes in the kitchen of her parents' apartment, I suggested that we should get married.

"No!"

"Why not?"

"Because you ask me only when I'm pregnant," she said.

A few days later she phoned me from the law office where she worked and said, "We can stop worrying." Her period had begun.

Once shortly after that, one of my proposals was accepted by the sister of a good friend, but then was broken by mutual consent. I now know that I was simply not ready, but she too has remained a friend. The fact was that being engaged hadn't stopped me from being strongly attracted to other women. One of those women was Rassy.

Anyway, to end my digression, one night when Rassy and I were spending a rather hot and heavy time on the apartment's chesterfield, as young people tend to do, even yet, I was moved to remark, "Maybe we should get married."

"When?" she said, sitting up abruptly. As a result, a few months later, on June 18, 1940, with McClung and Eakins as ushers and also hunting for a new place to live, we married. The church, Wardlaw United, was filled with a mixture of the sports mob, Paterson and Young relatives, and

Rassy's upscale connections. The reception was held in her parents' large apartment a few blocks away. One minor dilemma stemmed from the fact that one of those present was Granny Paterson, attending for the first time in her life a gathering at which liquor was being served. On the flip side, most of my sports crowd friends had rarely, if ever, attended a function where liquor was *not* being served.

When I saw Granny Paterson, short and well corseted and looking somewhat like Queen Mary, beaming benignly around the crowded apartment, I hastened to the kitchen bar.

"Take a tray of nothing but apple juice straight to that lady over there," I directed. "Be sure she tastes it."

I figured that then Granny would believe that everybody else was drinking apple juice, too.

It might have worked, but as soon as that apple juice tray appeared in the doorway, it looked to many of the seriously thirsty a lot like straight whisky. They closed in with a rush, hands reaching and grabbing.

Granny Paterson got the last glass.

Seconds later, every end table, fireplace mantel, coffee table, windowsill and other open space in the living room contained a glass of apple juice with only one sip missing.

And then there were the other essential matters. Rassy changed to her travelling clothes. When she came out ready to leave with me for the train, she was the most beautiful woman I had ever seen, slim, her hair so dark it was nearly black, contrasting with her pale and perfect complexion. We caught the train and sat holding hands tightly on the plush seats as the night rushed by outside.

Our married life had begun.

Of course, we thought it would last forever.

That night in a hotel in Kenora we had sex a little clumsily for the first time. This, with declining clumsiness, continued night and day for the following week of our honeymoon in a Lake of the Woods cottage. In both of us, both twenty-two, all the pent-up urges of previous months came to fruition. With a few words one would signal to the other and bed was the result. We emerged only for meals.

When we returned to Winnipeg we found that Rassy's parents and sister had had my grungy apartment cleaned, papered and painted. It all looked so beautiful. We were very happy together. It was the first real home I'd had since childhood.

~

By that time I was earning $25 a week, which had been comfortable enough with two roomies to share the $37.50 a month rent but was no longer enough. With a wife to support I felt that I should get a raise. Abbie Coo, the city editor, had promised me one but then changed his mind, or higher management changed it for him.

I campaigned hard to get someone to see the light. For the first weeks home from our honeymoon I was working a split shift—from 8 a.m. until noon, remaking the provincial (early) edition's sports pages to include the overnight news and the popular columnists from news services; then going home to Rassy; to be back on duty at 8 p.m. or earlier to cover whatever was going on in sports that night. As the climax to my campaign for more money, I went to George V. Ferguson, the managing editor, and put my case.

I expected that he would agree that I was doing a sterling job, then would discuss how big a raise he could give me without breaking the bank.

Instead, he said, "You're doing a good job. Working hard. But I have to tell you that I could fill your job tomorrow for less than you're making. There are dozens of guys like Paris Eakins out there, just itching. I've got the applications right here on my desk. The truth is, Scott, and I hate to say this, but you will never be worth more than $25 a week to the Winnipeg *Free Press*."

I should have thanked him for that—I've used the line myself often enough since. I suppose the worst thing was that, for the time in which the words were spoken, they were true. Shed a tear for poor S. Young.

So that was that, but $25 a week forever looked like too bleak a future.

In the two previous years I had applied for jobs as far away as Australia. The Sydney *Morning Herald* politely replied that a rumour I'd heard that ice hockey was about to land on their shores had not caused them to look for a hockey writer. The winter before Rassy and I were married, I had spent vacation time travelling on railroad passes (the railroads routinely provided passes to reporters in those days) to show my clippings and apply to the Montreal *Star* and the Toronto *Telegram*, to no avail. But after my conversation with George V. Ferguson, I tried the Canadian Press,

Canada's main news agency, with bureaus all across the country and also in New York and London.

I knew the people in CP's Winnipeg bureau and had met some higher-ups during the 1939 Canadian tour by Queen Elizabeth and King George VI. The day the tour was in Winnipeg everybody in our sports department was converted to tour coverage. My assignment was to listen to live radio reports and write running copy, which was snatched from me page by page by my successors among the copy boys, to be rushed to the composing room and set in type for the overall lead story in the front page of the tour Extra.

That had been a year earlier. The legendary Gillis Purcell, CP's general superintendent, told me later that he had noticed my work, and in many ways he was the human embodiment of the saying that an elephant never forgets. When I applied to CP the answer was swift. CP would move Rassy and me and our meagre few boxes, which did include four pieces of Limoges, a wedding present from a big-wheel friend of her father at Barrett Roofing, to Toronto, where I would start on the CP rewrite desk—at the same $25 a week I'd been getting. But at CP I'd have prospects. I jumped at the chance.

But before we left Winnipeg we had to face another huge and daunting truth. Not surprisingly, considering everything, Rassy was pregnant. She told me adamantly that she did not want me involved in what she decided should happen next. I think she partly blamed herself and partly she wanted to protect me. Whatever the case, she tried various home remedies (hot baths, obscure drugs, jumping off a toilet seat) that did not work. Then she talked to friends and acquaintances who knew someone, or knew someone who knew someone. One referred her to a backstreet abortionist, a horrid alternative in those days when there was no way to terminate a pregnancy legally with proper medical assistance.

Rassy told me nothing of those details beforehand, and planned it so that I would be away on a baseball road trip. When I did get home, I found her deathly ill, only slowly recovering. Afterwards, she would cry when she tried to tell me about what had happened—a terrifyingly painful and crude procedure that cost $15 and was performed on some woman's kitchen table. We both regretted it forever. We could have survived with a baby born then, but neither of us, both twenty-two and inexperienced, wanted to face having a baby before we had even got used to one another.

I remember the rest of that summer now in short scenes. We both were very emotional. One night we went to a movie that ended with an unhappy renunciation scene. We walked home through the Winnipeg streets weeping uncontrollably, trying to comfort each other, knowing that it was not about the movie. Loving each other to the utmost did not change, but we had learned a terrible lesson.

Then something did happen that focused us on other matters. During the summer of 1940 the war had been going badly and was getting worse. The previous September I had tried to join the navy. When I applied, I had been told to leave my name. "Don't call us, we'll call you." If I had been a member of a yacht club or had some other sailing experience to offer beyond the fact that I'd owned a kayak and sometimes paddled canoes on the Red River, I might have been accepted, as others with some semblance of seagoing experience were. Of course, I could have joined the army. When I was still in high school I had been in a militia unit, one member of a Vickers machine-gun crew, training once or twice a week at lugging heavy tripods, Vickers gun and belt ammunition around vacant lots or the Winnipeg Armouries while being yelled at to move faster. But after the navy turn-down, I thought for now at least I'd done my duty. Besides, if I was going to die in action I didn't fancy doing so in the mud and gore of some far-off infantry battle in Europe.

Like a lot of others I decided to wait and see. Some, such as my *Free Press* friend Ben Malkin, who had a hunched way of walking that made him the least likely soldier I could imagine, joined the army right away. The first week.

I asked Ben why.

"Because I'm Jewish."

His contention was that as the Jews had been Hitler's main and most publicized victims before war began, they should be the first to join. He wanted to demonstrate in the only way open to him individually that this Jew was not shirking his duty. In fact, he virtually led a movement. I went one night to watch his unit drill in north Winnipeg. In the roll call five out of every six names called out were identifiably Jewish. But Benny is the one I remember. In later life when he was first a war correspondent and then an editorial page writer in Ottawa, every time we met my first thought was of Ben, joining the army in 1939 when he didn't have to, except in response to his deeply held conviction that he *had* to.

7

The Big Time:
1940-1942

≈≈≈

W HEN RASSY AND I ARRIVED at Toronto's Union Station on a cut-
tingly damp November morning in 1940, thirty-six hours after we
boarded the train in Winnipeg, we were met by my uncle Jack Paterson.
Over the years he had sold articles and fiction to *Maclean's* magazine and
had recently moved to Toronto as its assistant editor. He loaded our lug-
gage into his car and took off through a Toronto that bore little resem-
blance to the city of today—streetcars running on Bay and Yonge, busi-
nesses long since gone, no subway, no parking meters. Jack told us that
good apartments were getting scarce because of the influx of war workers,
but there was one near where he and Ruth lived. It was no Taj Mahal, he
said, but might do for starters. He drove us there to look at it and we took
it. It was one room, a kitchen and bathroom, furnished with a card table,
three folding chairs, a bed that folded into the wall and not much else.

He and I left Rassy with Ruth and drove back downtown to the CP
newsroom, which at the time occupied the eleventh floor of the
Metropolitan building at the southwest corner of Victoria and Adelaide. I
was introduced to men at various levels of boss-dom and was told that,
after a couple of days to get settled, I would work on the day rewrite desk,
learning the ropes, and then probably would be moved to night rewrite.
That was my introduction to the kind of newsroom bedlam that I'd live in
for the next couple of years.

I learned from the beginning that it was a dirty place to work. Fresh
copy from a dozen or more teletype machines tended to smear when handled. So did the carbons on each "book" of multiple flimsies on which we

typed. We were all fast, even though the typing styles varied all the way from expert to my own technique, two forefingers and one thumb. At the end of each of my "books" of rewrites, I'd pull the carbons (as many as ten) in one big yank. This would free the flimsies, which were then delivered by copy boys to the several wire editors, who either threw them away or added them to the pile waiting to be sent by teletype on the west wire, Ontario wire, Canadian wire or New York wire (this only if a story had a U.S. angle that our allies at Associated Press might wish to use). With all the machines going, spewing out news from around Canada and the world, the noise was considerable. Bedlam was not too strong a description. On top of all this—the hammering of teletype machines, editors yelling advice or insults or comments on the incoming news—there was one extra: sometimes many or all of the men around the newsroom would break into song, never missing a beat in punching out news being relayed across the country. The songs might be from musicals, but most popular, words and music best known, were hymns.

Thus anyone walking into the newsroom might hear as part of the din a full-voiced treatment of "The Old Rugged Cross," "What a Friend We Have in Jesus," "Eternal Father Strong to Save Whose Hand Doth Guide the Restless Wave."

I can recall news editor Ab Fulford (father of writer Robert Fulford, who was a child at the time) leaning in his office doorway to listen with a smile, as did Charles Bruce, the fine writer, novelist and poet who was CP's general superintendent when I arrived. Bruce had replaced Gillis Purcell, who had been sent to England as press officer for the senior Canadian military man of the time, Gen. Andrew G. L. McNaughton.

My eight-hour shift on night rewrite started each day at 6 p.m. and ended each morning about 2, allowing me to catch a northbound streetcar up Yonge Street, then a westbound one on St. Clair. I got off at Oakwood and after a few minutes' walk would be with Rassy, telling her the day's happenings. Besides the card table, which we ate on, and the folding chairs, soon we had a chesterfield that Rassy had found in the hall, about to be thrown out. It had been painted orange with ordinary house paint by its previous owner. Rassy asked the janitor if we could have it, and he helped her carry it in; a surprise for me when I got home that night.

As I mentioned before, our bed folded out of the wall. When it was in place, getting to the bathroom or the kitchen involved walking across the bed. In the morning, if we'd left the window open, pigeons were often to be found drowsing on the drainboard, but from 6 a.m. on old trolleys looped every few minutes, usually moving the pigeons, if not us. We got used to it.

We were happy there. For our first Christmas, we waited until the afternoon of Christmas Eve when the tree price at a lot on a nearby corner had been dropped to fifty cents, and then lugged home a nice fat little tree. We had no decorations, and I left Rassy making some out of coloured paper. When I got in that night a little early (Christmas being a slow news shift), Rassy had decorated the tree with bits of paper fashioned into the shape of flowers. When we were in bed it looked fine, the little tree and its decorations glowing in the light from a nearby streetlight. After a few minutes Rassy said, "There's a note on the tree for you. I want you to open it now."

I got up and found it, and read, "This is our first Christmas and we don't have much except each other, but I have cut up little bits of my heart for you, to put on our first tree."

For many years, as our trees got bigger and fancier, those first decorations, bits of Rassy's heart, were always the first to go on.

❧

In my first few months at CP, meeting people, some of whom were friends forever, attending our first CP office parties, I loved my job. What I wrote, perhaps only short items, might have seemed trivial to others, but it was a nice change to write about things that were worth sending across the country.

My job was to go through the final afternoon papers, then the early *Globe and Mail*, looking for anything that might be of widerinterest. I would rewrite each such story, expanding or contracting, and put my flimsies in the rewrite basket to be picked up and distributed among the wire editors.

The only blip in this routine would come on Fridays, when early in the evening someone would go around and take beer orders, collect the money, go to the nearest beer store (I think near Church) and bring the orders back in time for the usual low-stakes Friday-night poker game that began when the first people came off shift and ended before dawn.

Only rarely was I sent out to cover a live story. One of these occasions was a meeting of the Ontario Hockey Association at the Royal York Hotel, where free liquor flowed. When the time came to walk back to the office and write my story, I hesitated. No doubt emboldened by the drinks I'd already had, I poured a full glass of whisky and carried it several blocks from the Royal York to CP without anyone looking at me twice. I took the full glass to our affable white-haired night editor, Russ Wheatley.

"What's this?" he asked.

"Whisky," I said, and helped him drink it, sharing sipping rights with others. For this I became a minor short-term legend among my colleagues.

In 1941 suddenly all that changed. On the night of April 18 there was a major escape of captured German airmen from a camp near Antler in northern Ontario. When I arrived on day rewrite the next morning I was told to go home and grab my typewriter and warm clothes and catch the next train north.

On the same train with me were several locally or nationally famous reporters. They, however, had sleeping berths and whisky, and talked of other big stories they had scooped everybody on. These veterans included Percy Cole from the *Evening Telegram*, but the main contingent was from the Toronto *Star* – Greg Clark and Fred Griffin the most prominent, but also Robinson McLean, who had covered the war in Ethiopia for the *Telegram* before moving to the *Star*, photographer Strathy Smith, and a young reporter named J. D. (Douglas) MacFarlane, later in the war to be famous as the officer in charge of the Canadian forces newspaper, the *Maple Leaf.*

I liked being the only CP man in that august company. I had a feeling that here was my chance to make my mark.

We soon learned that no passenger trains stopped at Antler. The closest we could get to the action would be Heron Bay, a few miles to the east. A telegram had reached me en route that a telegrapher with his Morse key had been sent to handle my stories. When we reached Heron Bay, he met me and set up his equipment in the railway station waiting room. Through him, I sent out all the news that was available at that early stage, mainly that some escapees hiding in a hunt cabin on which a search party was converging had tried to rush the searchers, mainly soldiers from a lakehead regiment, and in the shooting that followed two escapees had been killed, others wounded.

It seemed to me then more important than ever that I get not only to Antler, but also to the camp itself and get the story firsthand. An army major had been sent in hastily from Ottawa to issue statements on what progress was being made, if any, but he didn't know much either.

Mainly, all we knew for sure was that thirty prisoners had dug a tunnel, probably over a period of weeks, and that the escape was undetected until two shivering escapees were found outside the camp's barbed wire. The other twenty-eight had scattered in many directions. The searchers trying to track down the Germans included an army unit from the Algonquin Regiment at the lakehead, all the Ontario Provincial Police in the area, some others from the Royal Canadian Mounted Police under an inspector Allan Thomas Belcher, and local guides.

Rumours ran rampant. Since the escape had taken place on Hitler's birthday, it was suspected that some of the German airmen might be met along the Lake Superior shore by Nazi sympathizers from the German–American Bund in the United States. Another rumour was that some of the escapees had caught a westbound freight train and now could be approaching the prairies. Many freight trains had passed through the area after the escape and some of the escapees might have got aboard somehow, although searches of all such trains had found nothing.

In an attempt to get closer to the action, I spoke to the crew of one freight train heading west. They said they couldn't stop at the camp itself, but agreed to let me off at Antler. From the station there was still a walk of a few miles to the camp. The temperature was far below zero. I realized there might be another way to reach the camp, by using a railway handcar, known as a jigger. I persuaded one railway section man at Antler to let me and another reporter, Percy Cole, use one that was sitting on a siding.

So Percy Cole and I set out, pumping this vehicle by hand, to cover the last few miles between Antler and the camp.

When we neared the camp area, however, we found that our handcar had been spotted. Rows of soldiers lined the track, their rifles aimed at us. We told them that we wanted to speak to the camp commandant, Maj. Charles Lindsey. Impossible, we were told; he'd had a long night and was resting. But when an officer did agree to take a message to him, Maj. Lindsey granted us an interview. Percy Cole and I were conducted in to see him, and then to see and speak to some of the wounded in the camp hospital. Even while we were taking notes there I was trying to figure out the next move. There's no use being first to a story unless you have a way to get it out. We had no phones and no access to any other method of communication. However. . .

We learned that a funeral service would be held that morning for the two Germans who had been killed by the soldiers. Those of us who had made it to the camp (more had followed me and Cole) were allowed to watch. We stood in frigid wind on a slope near the prisoners who were attending the service. I was making notes about the scene when from the west I heard a train whistle, getting closer by the minute. Unobtrusively, I slipped away from the funeral and headed downhill towards the railway tracks, where I figured the train might stop. It did, for a few minutes, while I hurried to the caboose and asked the trainman, "Can I ride with you to Heron Bay?" He shrugged and made me tea and asked questions about the escape as we wound our way east.

In Heron Bay I wrote my story in longhand and handed it page by page to the telegrapher. Soon it was being dot-dashed in Morse to CP Toronto, the first report from the scene that now was a major story in both Canada and the States. That afternoon's early editions of the *Star* and *Telegram*, both with men on the scene, had to use CP for the first eyewitness report from the camp. I heard later of hot messages that flowed north to the other reporters, stating, "CP carries first eyewitness reports. Where were you?" From then on they knew I was there. Percy Cole said to me, "Goddamn you, Young, you look as if you're not even paying attention half the time, and then you do this to us!?"

But lest anyone think I was overcome with modesty at my good luck and quick thinking, I received a message from Charlie Bruce: "Good work. Do you want us to send someone to help, another reporter or two?"

I replied oratorically that although reporters from the *Star*, the *Tely*, and the *Free Press* in Winnipeg had just arrived, I did not feel "outnumbered."

Charlie, of course, got it. He must have laughed: a rookie reporter, just turned twenty-three, blowing his own horn so loudly. Later, when I knew him better, I could imagine the relish with which he wrote his reply to my boastful words: "Struggle manfully on."

In the next few days, I had another bit of good luck. The *Star* had found a railroader's house to rent in Antler as a base for their staffers. Greg Clark told me there was room for me if I wanted it. But to me Antler had become somewhat of a backwater. I now had obtained a full freight train schedule. I could always get back if I had to.

So I consulted my freight schedule, caught the next eastbound, and in less than an hour or so was in Heron Bay again. By then the *Star* seemed to be keeping track of me. Wherever I went, there was a *Star* man with me. Whether this suspicion was well-founded or not, when I arrived in Heron Bay I was met on the station platform by Doug MacFarlane, a persuasive man and first-rate journalist, so I listened politely as he told me that Heron Bay was the wrong place to be and that we should both get back to Antler and the comfortable *Star* quarters there.

"Besides," he added conclusively, "there's no room at the hotel. I tried. There's a westbound coming through in a few minutes. What you should do, kid, is catch it with me and we'll go back to Antler."

"Ah, I don't know," I said. All my life I've resisted doing what other people suggest I should. Then, just checking, I wandered a hundred yards or so from the station to the hotel, a two-storey building, and found the manager.

"Got a room?" I asked.

"Sure do. In fact, I've got two empty right now."

"I'll take them both," I said.

With the choice of two rooms, I got lucky again and picked one that was immediately above a lounge where searchers and reporters tended to sit and have a drink or two if they could find someone who had a bottle. Perhaps at one time there'd been a stove in that downstairs room, with a stove pipe leading through a hole in the ceiling to heat the room above, the hole now covered by a metal grille.

I immediately found that conversations in the lounge could be heard perfectly if one lay on the floor with one ear on the grille. I heard some interesting facts that way, enhancing my growing reputation for getting news that other people didn't have. A day or two later the army officer in charge of the search angrily summoned me to his room and demanded to know my source. I didn't tell him what I perhaps should have—namely, that when he was talking about matters he didn't want published or widely known, he should stay away from old stovepipe holes.

I developed one other technique during that assignment that I used from time to time over the years. There was no liquor store for many miles around, so when searchers staggered in off the trail exhausted from slogging through the woods and snowbanks, any person who could offer a drink or two had just made a loyal friend.

I arranged for CP to send me several bottles of good Canadian whisky from the nearest liquor store. The night it arrived I happened to see an Ontario Provincial Police officer coming out through the snowbanks on snowshoes and looking exhausted. I asked him a few questions and finally got the right one: "Would you like a drink?" We got some glasses and went to my room. Over the next few days we made this a regular evening happening.

Eventually, as other reporters came in from both Canadian and U.S. newspapers, the hotel became jammed and I had another reporter sleeping on the floor of my bedroom.

After about a week, almost all the escapees had been captured. One or two had made it to western Canada before being nabbed. Others, in twos or threes, had taken shelter in hunt cabins and were captured by a variety of means – tracks that could be followed, a wisp of smoke where someone had lit a fire to get warm, and so on. Finally, only four were left at large. For days there'd been nothing new to report, and editors were calling back their troops.

One night when the main Toronto contingent had just left by train, I was wakened by a hand that reached across my sleeping roommate and touched my shoulder. When I looked up, I saw my Ontario Provincial Police drinking partner beckoning me. Downstairs I caught up to him. "We got the last four," he said quietly. "They're being held in the station waiting room. Your telegrapher is over there, too."

I found the four weary Germans, who had been discovered in a boxcar during one of the routine freight train searches. They showed all the signs of the days they'd spent on the run: their hands and faces were frostbitten; they hungrily ate sandwiches and drank steaming coffee, and they huddled as close as they could to the stove in the middle of the room. My OPP benefactor lifted the lid and dropped in more wood.

Two Germans then stretched out on the benches, eyes closed. I asked one of the others how he'd been captured originally. He'd been a fighter pilot, he said, shot down over the English Channel. I asked his name. "Ackenhausen," he said. Among others in the waiting room were soldiers, my telegrapher and a few OPP and RCMP officers.

My typewriter was on the table beside the telegrapher. I wrote a quick bulletin for CP:

"HERON BAY, Ont. The last four German prisoners among those who escaped from a prison-of-war camp near here a week ago were captured tonight in a boxcar that was part of a freight train about to pull out for western Canada. MORE."

I handed that sheet to the telegrapher, and the bulletin clicked out into CP Toronto for transmission to newspapers across Canada and the U.S. As editors in far-off cities made room on front pages for the apparent end to this major story, I continued talking to Ackenhausen.

He told me how he and his companions had spent the week, narrow escapes from searchers who had passed a few yards from where they were hiding, the food they'd packed for their escape running low. . .

Suddenly, the senior RCMP man, Inspector Belcher, stepped swiftly to my side, grabbed my notes and threw them into the fire.

I jumped up. "What the hell are you doing?"

"You are breaking the law," he snapped. "Under the Geneva Convention on treatment of prisoners of war, they may not be interviewed for publication. You are under arrest."

I argued that this railway station was my office, my place of business, and he had no right to do what he had just done with no warning or explanation. It was a tense scene. Here I was with a clean beat over everybody else on the last arrests in this great manhunt, a great wrapup story all to myself, and I was being thwarted by this %$#@#$%! cop. I continued to protest that I wanted my office back so I could continue to do my job.

Belcher ignored my pleas and gave an order that I was to be arrested. As the other RCMP man drew his gun and started towards me, I ran out the door to the station platform. It was freezing out there. The policeman came out and ordered me back into the station.

I didn't go. I tramped up and down the station platform trying to avoid freezing while we all, inside and out, waited for the train that would take the prisoners back to the camp. I whiled away the time composing what I would write about this incident when I got back in.

Finally the train came, and police and guards and soldiers trooped aboard. I went back in to join my telegrapher.

"I sent a little stuff when you were out," he said.

"What?"

"Well, you know, all along the line down into the U.S., editors had got your first bulletin and were bombarding CP wanting to know where was the rest of the story. They were holding their morning editions for it. So just as you were running out of here CP sent a message saying, 'Hey, S.Y. what's going on up there?' (At CP, every staffer was known by his initials.)

"And I sent back that you couldn't answer right now, because the RCMP had burned your notes and tried to arrest you and a guy with a gun had just chased you out onto the station platform."

I certainly couldn't have bettered that myself as a tease for nervous editors.

The Mounties had at least left my typewriter behind. I sat down and wrote and wrote. The outcome was that when the other Toronto reporters got into Union Station the next morning, they could pick up newspapers with big stories under the Heron Bay CP dateline "Reporter Chased by Mountie with Drawn Gun," and it was cursing time again.

That same day, the RCMP's attack on press freedom was raised in the House of Commons. A day or two later, by which time I was back in Toronto, I was asked to come down to see an RCMP superintendent at his office in Union Station and answer a lot of questions, giving details, which I did.

Inspector Belcher weathered in good order all the freedom-of-the-press criticism that was thrown at him, and a few months later was promoted to Assistant Comissioner.

Meanwhile, Rassy and I were basking in my sudden fame. Basking, however, isn't always fun, repeating the same facts over and over. At a party a woman journalist I respected commented thoughtfully, "That is probably the most exciting experience you'll ever have!"

I thought, "Lady, what the hell are you talking about? I'm only twenty-three!"

A few days later the Toronto *Star* offered me a job at $47.50 a week, nearly double what I was making. I took it, but within a few months I found my assignments—fires in rag factories, drowsy luncheon speeches, features about two-headed chaps at the Canadian National Exhibition and so on—too trivial, so I quit and asked CP to take me back. I was making $52.50 at the *Star* by then. I didn't expect CP to match that, and they didn't: they gave me $37.50.

8

Going to the War:
1943-1944

I CAN'T REMEMBER WHEN Rassy and I decided to leave behind the screech of the Robina streetcar loop. Actually, I don't think we ever did make a real decision. It just happened, on one of my days off. I worked on the rewrite desk either days or nights eleven shifts out of every fourteen. The days off were our luxury, and we spent our time together, exploring the city, enjoying each other, not suspecting that some day we might recall those as some of the best and most carefree days of our life together.

One sunny spring weekend just before the prison camp adventure, we went downtown and took an eastbound Queen streetcar to Hammersmith, where CP's west wire editor, big, balding, witty Eric Dunn, off that day as well, had invited us for coffee. He lived a few houses from the lakeshore. Leaving the Dunns a little later we headed for the lake and strolled along the wide boardwalk. Waves were rolling in from a passing tugboat. Leaves were beginning to show along the well-treed stretch of grassy parkland between us and a row of solidly built duplexes. Kids were playing baseball and soccer. Somehow it wasn't at all like the Robina streetcar loop.

Near the east end of the boardwalk we turned and passed a three-storey apartment building called Hubbard Court. A sign read: Vacancy. As far as I can recall, the decision was made not in words but more like a meeting of eyes, no more. We went inside and found the janitor, who led us upstairs to a third-floor one-room apartment. There was a tiny bathroom in one corner and a kitchenette (fridge and stove) behind lattice doors near the entrance. But what captured us was the lake view, and all that action outside. We were sold even before the janitor gave his spiel.

The building, he informed us, was owned and administered by the city's property department, closed that day but open again Monday. First thing Monday I was at City Hall filling out the necessary forms. These mainly concerned my willingness to sign a one-year lease, which I did on the spot. One provision I scarcely noticed at the time, was that I could not sublet without City Hall approval.

Our time in the apartment was brief, however. Later that happy and carefree summer, Rassy became pregnant and we decided that with a baby we should have a home with a separate bedroom.

I checked with the man at the Property Department, who said it was okay as long as we found another tenant.

We advertised. An attractive young couple answered the ad and loved the place. We told them to go to the Property Department and do the paperwork. Certain that they would be considered perfect tenants and that the sublet would go through without problems, we went apartment-hunting once again and found a plain one-bedroom apartment in a building called Blythwood Manor in the north part of the city.

A day after we signed that new lease our new sublet tenant phoned to say that the Property Department had turned them down. At first I thought they might have changed their minds and were blaming it on City Hall, but he insisted that was not the case.

"We're heartbroken," he said.

"But what reason could they possibly give?" I asked.

"The man in the Property Department said he was sorry, and really didn't have to explain anything, but I insisted and it turns out it's because we're Jewish," he said.

I was shocked and offered to raise hell—even to write something for the paper on the lines that Hitler wasn't so far away after all.

"No, please don't," he said. "We don't want a fuss. Our families, our jobs. . . We have a line on something else and don't want to go there as the people who. . ."

I called the Property Department. The man there, when pressed, said—not apologetically at all—that in east Toronto, the Beaches area, there was an understanding about who could buy or rent, and that no Jews were allowed. The city Property Department could not go against the long-held will of the majority, he said. "You'll just have to find another tenant. Shouldn't be hard, but it's got to be someone we accept, as your lease says."

I knew the structure of the city's government, each department headed by a commissioner. I headed for City Hall again, found the property commissioner's office and insisted on seeing him personally. I felt somewhat hamstrung by the fact that my rejected sublet prospect had said clearly that he and his wife did not want to fight this discrimination publically—meaning, to me, in the newspapers. But even so, I thought I might just possibly fight dirty.

In the property commissioner's office I laid it on the line. "I'm a reporter for the Toronto *Star*," I said. "I think this might even make the front page, and not only in our paper."

"What do you mean?"

"This city, which has a substantial Jewish population who are taxpayers and voters, turns out to be enforcing its own form of anti-Semitism on city-owned property. I found a good tenant who you turned down for reasons that most citizens, I think, would find reprehensible. I don't accept any further responsibility for looking for another tenant."

He stared at me and I at him. He finally said, "Okay."

I still sometimes wish I had written it then. Some in Toronto certainly deserved an unmasking, including citizens who years later were still putting up signs reading "Gentiles Only" on Lake Simcoe beach property for sale or rent. But Toronto Jews at the time had enough to endure with Hitler running rampant in Europe.

The young Jewish couple must be old now, about my age, if they still live. I still keep them in mind when I see the throngs in the streets near the synagogues on the Jewish Sabbath in a much more human Toronto.

❧

Meanwhile, Rassy and I moved into our one-bedroom on North Yonge—just before Rassy's state of pregnancy might have caused the people who owned Blythwood Manor to turn us down. A lot of landlords simply preferred to rent to adults. Some who advertised vacancies wouldn't even answer the door when they saw a pregnant mother coming up the walk clutching a newspaper ad in one hand and a young child in the other.

Since the apartment came unfurnished, we had to buy furniture, and I decided to try some freelance magazine work to help pay for it.

Before submitting my first article, I showed it to my uncle Jack Paterson. It was called "Curling Town" and was about Glenboro when I was growing up and our curlers were winning everything in sight at the big Winnipeg bonspiels.

He took one run through the piece, then asked if I had any scissors. Rassy came up with some. Working on our bed because it had the space Jack needed, he cut the manuscript into more than a dozen segments.

Then he rearranged all the pieces so that, with some handwritten links, they told a more cohesive story. It was the kind of operation a computer could handle today without a pair of scissors in sight. I retyped it, and a few days later *Maclean's* bought it.

We got the cheque just in time to help celebrate the birth of our first child, son Robert Ragland Young, on April 27, 1942.

The day was to have historical significance as well as a personal one. Canada had been split on the issue of conscription for military service. To oversimplify, the split occurred basically because most English-speaking Canadians supported Britain and most French-speaking Canadians did not wish to be obliged by law to fight in what they considered British wars.

In 1942, when Canadians were dying in battle on land, sea and in the air, volunteers for military service overseas did not meet the projected demand. Thrice-wounded troops were being sent back into action while men who had refused to volunteer for overseas service stayed safely home.

On Bob's birthday, Canada had a non-binding referendum on the question. Since the referendum was the biggest civilian news story of the war from a Canadian standpoint, everybody at CP, coast to coast, was working long hours to cover both the run-up to the voting and the voting itself.

Two nights earlier, on April 25, Rassy had begun to experience heavy labour pains. She was admitted to St. Michael's Hospital, about three blocks from where I was toiling at the CP rewrite desk. At meal breaks, I would hurry up Victoria Street to spend a few minutes with her. She would swear and implore and sweat and squeeze my hand in the throes of pain that no man can understand. Sometimes I went back down Victoria Street closing my eyes and ricocheting off other pedestrians while I prayed that her ordeal would soon be over and that she'd be safe. All that night and the next day and another night and most of the third day, referendum day, there was still no birth. Then, while the polls closed and the early counting was showing exactly what everybody knew would happen—the huge yes vote in eight provinces and huge no vote in Quebec—I got a call from the hospital.

"Your baby is a boy," I was told.

I ran to the hospital to find my dear Rassy, pale and exhausted, barely conscious. I crouched beside her and tried to hold her without hurting her, two young people murmuring wrenched and torn endearments through their blending tears.

"I did it," she said. "I was beginning to think I never would. Oh, God, I'll tell you it's. . ." Then she fell asleep, damp black hair and pale exhaustion on the white pillow.

I got the full story on my next visit, a few hours later. Tired of waiting, determined to get it over with, she had gone to the toilet, stood on the seat, and jumped off. Bob was born a matter of minutes later.

Meanwhile, in my spare time at CP's rewrite desk I was certainly not giving birth to anything as interesting as a son, but had been assigned to write a daily piece called "Sports Snapshots." Not that such a mundane event would ever make anybody's great happenings of yesteryear, but I think it was the first sports column to go nationwide in this country. It did have something—a national perspective. Mainly I put it together by reading Canadian sports pages and picking the best bits from the columns of a lot of good sports columnists, thefts I acknowledged by using their names and publications, as in: "This one from Milt (Stratford *Beacon-Herald*) Dunnell" or "Herb (Winnipeg *Tribune*) Manning had this to say."

Other mainstays in this cut-and-splice effort included Andy (Toronto *Star*) Lytle, Baz (Montreal *Star*) O'Meara, Vern (Montreal *Gazette*) DeGeer and once in a while Eddie (Winnipeg *Free Press*) Armstrong or Dave (Regina *Leader-Post*) Dryburgh, plus Jim Coleman, Vince Leah, my young pal Trent (Winnipeg *Tribune*) Frayne and many others. I enjoyed doing it, and in a sense that experience led me into another CP job, putting together a national weekly news report. This I would cable overseas to CP's flagship London bureau to be printed there by Odham's Press in a skimpy newspaper for the Canadian Forces overseas called *Canadian Press News*.

One sidelight bonus in putting that paper together was that I worked on it at night once a week in a quiet and secluded office with the assistance of one of the most attractive women I ever met, then or later, the dark-haired, shapely and just plain beautiful Mildred Ogle. I figured later that someone in CP's character-testing detail must have sent Millie in to work with me on the grounds that if I could restrain myself from making a pass at her, I had real character and probably could handle any major challenge sent my way. For what it's worth, I won that one.

I was also going through other aspects of a fairly comprehensive training course at CP. I spent a stint or two with a new CP offshoot called Broadcast News, revising news reports off the CP wires to make them more easily readable for radio news staffs across the country.

In Broadcast News we had one senior editor from the Maritimes, Jack Tracy, to whom the Royal Navy was sacrosanct. He was also very easy to get a rise out of. In those bad weeks for the Royal Navy early in the Pacific war when the battleship *Prince of Wales* and heavy cruiser *Repulse* were sunk by the Japanese, Tracy really suffered. Those defeats were seen by him and many others as not only sad but shaming.

We all felt a pressing need to lighten up once in a while. As a result, I'm afraid, one morning finding myself with very little to do for a few minutes I coerced a teletype operator, my friend Eddie (Bombay) Baker (he always wanted to go to Bombay and the nickname stuck) into punching out an item that would land on news editor Tracy's desk looking as if it was in the normal run of news. Bombay had fixed things so that this would be just for us alone.

I wrote the item and Bombay punched it out, ready to go. Bombay then fixed the printer's bulletin bell to ring out and signal to editors that urgent news was coming up. When the bulletin bells sounded, Tracy jumped over to see what was coming in, and my piece began to rattle out on the news ticker, going something like this:

"The Royal Navy announced this morning that in the seas off Singapore two of our battleships, three heavy cruisers and six destroyers were lost when attacked by a hostile tribe in war canoes, using bows and arrows."

Oh, what a dirty trick. As Jack read the first few lines he wrung his hands and cried, "Oh, God, no. . ." and then arrived at the part about the hostile tribe, war canoes and bows and arrows and saw me and Bombay laughing. Yelling imprecations, he chased me from the room.

Bombay was too big, so Tracy let him be.

It took a while that morning for me to negotiate my return to my Broadcast News desk. Tracy never trusted me after that. Never.

It was not long after that escapade that there was a return to CP of an amazing man, Gillis Purcell, who during the 1930s had built CP into a first-rate news service. He had done so by demanding something more than 100 percent from everyone who worked for him. He was a legend of toughness. God alone knows how he managed it, but every line carried by CP, especially from its own staffers, was read by him.

Memos flew out of his office on everything from political pieces to sports, all signed G.P. "Good piece," he might write in his clear, neat handwriting on his copy of this or that CP story, a note to be treasured by the recipient. If he didn't like a piece, he'd either write a sharp note or call the writer in to take the heat in person. In CP, he was God, and no mistake. Earlier in the war Gen. A. G. L. McNaughton had been the closest thing to a military god, or at least national hero, that Canada had. Our dispatch of the first Canadian ground troops, the First Division, to Europe in December 1939, had focused Canadian attention on the likelihood that when the war in Europe heated up to real action, Canadians would be in the vanguard.

The original small coterie of Canadian war correspondents covered those first Canadian troops, and their colourful general, like a blanket. It became obvious that an experienced journalist should be along as the general's press officer, and Gil Purcell, general superintendent of CP, was invited. He eagerly accepted. When he left to join McNaughton, there were sighs of relief from those who had been his most frequent targets. One of these was Harry Eccles, a short and sandy-haired man whose suit-jacket pockets always bulged with newspapers to be read on the way home on the streetcar. For years he had been one of G.P.'s favourite targets—partly because Harry, whose typewriter sounded like a long burst from a machine-gun when he was hammering out his stories, was sometimes faster than he was good.

G.P.'s successor, Charlie Bruce, maintained the G.P. tradition in everything except acerbity. His time as general superintendent was marked by a special feeling for good writing partly because he was a fine writer himself. He ran a tight ship, too, but without G.P.'s shooting from the hip, making him, generally speaking, better liked by CP's rank and file than G.P. had been.

But like him or not, the whole of CP was shocked when a story came in one day that G.P. had been badly injured. The amplification of the story came soon after. He had been with the general and other senior

Canadian officers on an army exercise in England when a canister-carrying parachute failed to open and the canister plummeted down to where the group of the senior people was standing.

G.P. tried to dive out of the way. The canister struck him on an outstretched leg, which had to be amputated above the knee. A subsequent story from London noted that if the canister had hit him squarely, he would have been killed. It was a week or two before he was out of danger and the word went around that when he had recovered from the amputation surgery he would return to Canada. When he was physically ready to carry on his duties, he would return to his former job as general superintendent at CP.

That word went around the office with the speed of light. I happened to be standing by a printer reading this incoming story with Harry Eccles.

"Just think," Harry mused, "if that thing had missed him entirely, he wouldn't be coming back, and if it had hit him squarely, he'd be dead. A few inches either way, and we would have been all right."

That summer passed, and G.P. returned to work. His first artificial leg, which he called Barney, was a simple wooden peg with leather straps that held it in place on what was left of his thigh. Once he had reached his office he would remove Barney and stand it in a corner, using a crutch to move around the office. His legendary toughness reasserted itself immediately, and his army experience had given him an extra edge. By the spring and summer of 1942 he was back in full fighting form, with Charlie Bruce as second in command, and war stories cabled from CP London were mainstays for Canadian newspapers large and small, the material often even used by newspapers big enough to have their own correspondents overseas.

At CP, the London bureau represented the absolute cream. We were proud of it. The London staff list at that time, headed by longtime CP man Ernie Burritt and former Montreal *Gazette* news editor Alan Randal, included war correspondents Ross Munro, Doug Amaron and French-speaking Bill Stewart mainly covering the army, Louis Hunter as the specialist in the RCAF, and Foster Barclay. Soon other good men were scheduled to arrive.

One night in the autumn of 1942, Rassy and I were invited to the Purcells' home in the Toronto Leaside district along with our baby son, Bob, about six months old. G.P. was sitting in one corner, in his favourite chair. I was on a footstool beside him. I think Rassy and Gil's wife, her real name being Charlotte and her nickname archy—always spelled lowercase—were out of the room when he turned to me and said, "How long would it take you to get cleared up here and go to work in London?"

I had not been expecting this, and at first just stared. Rassy and I had the apartment and the baby, and I simply didn't know how long "clearing up" would take, or even what it meant—her going home to Winnipeg, staying on at the apartment, how my pay would be handled, what about our furniture. . .the questions raced through my mind, but finally I said, "Six weeks."

"*What?*"

"Six days," I amended, with a laugh.

"That's better!"

That was the moment when our lives changed again. Preparing did take a little more than six days, but not much. Rassy began packing to move herself and Bob into her parents' comfortable apartment in Winnipeg, at their brave invitation—they hadn't had an active child around for a while. Part of my pay would go directly to her. With injections of various kinds and my own packing, I remember little about our farewells except that Rassy took it all in her stride, as she had every move we made, then or later. She was going back to the many friends of her girlhood. I knew she would lean for companionship on her older sister, Lavinia (known as Toots) whose husband, Neil Hoogstraten, was an artist, and their children—and partings were part of life in wartime. Then the brief waiting period was over.

CP's top war correspondent, Ross Munro, had been in Canada for a few weeks at the time. The fast way to get overseas was by the RCAF's Ferry Command, which was in the business of flying bombers and crews from Canada to bases in England, occasionally carrying passengers who had to get to England on government or other priority business. CP had arranged for Ross Munro and me to make the next Ferry Command shuttle flight, Munro to get back into the field with the Canadian Army and me to help beef up other parts of the staff at CP London.

Within days, we were directed to report to a specific area in Dorval airport at a specific time but to keep our mouths shut about the arrangements. When the time came, we met in a dark room and were briefed on the use of oxygen masks, issued with flying suits, and instructed what to do if any emergency arose.

Among the eight or ten passengers, mostly British and Canadian, I knew no one except Ross Munro. The single American in our group, in the uniform of a U.S. Army captain, told me that his final destination would be Ireland. He further confided that he was a veterinarian from somewhere in the Midwest and had been in the army only a few days. The United States had some army personnel including a cavalry unit, complete with horses, stationed in Ireland. The call had gone out for a veterinarian, so they'd made the veterinarian into a captain and he was later to be responsible for one extremely memorable moment in the flight. All aboard and ready to go in our flying suits, we were conducted to the aircraft, seated on parachutes on metal benches along the walls of the unheated fuselage and strapped in. For each passenger there was an oxygen mask. The bomber's normal fighting armament had been removed, causing a multitude of draughts from the holes where guns had been. Within view at the tail end of the fuselage was a pile of life rafts and more parachutes.

Soon the four engines burst into deafening action. We rolled along the runway and into the air. Ross Munro had brought a book but when he tried to read his glasses fogged up badly around his oxygen mask. Discarding it seemed to help, so he did. A crew member warned him that breathing the thin air would leave him with a headache for days (which did happen). After an hour or two the pilot informed us by intercom that we'd reached our cruising altitude, ten thousand feet, and now were crossing the Gulf of St. Lawrence.

At that moment the U.S. captain-veterinarian, who had been looking uncomfortable during the bumpy flight, unhitched his seatbelt and stood up. He'd been hoping, he told us later, to relieve his nausea by stretching out on the parachutes and life rafts. He had taken a step or two when a major lurch of the aircraft caused him to lose his balance.

To steady himself, he grabbed what seemed to be an upright steel rod but really was a lever connected to the two long parallel sections that made up the floor of the bomb-bay. They creakingly parted wide open, one to each side. While the American hung on for dear life, the rest of us seated on the benches stared down at the brassy pitching water of the Gulf of St. Lawrence about two miles below.

We sat there stunned as the doors creaked back into the "bomb doors closed" position and the veterinarian sat down again and put his face in his hands.

Hours later, we landed at Prestwick in Scotland and scattered in various directions. Munro and I caught a train for London and were taken to the Savoy Hotel to eat and drink and sleep. The next day, still somewhat woozy, I reported to the CP office on the first floor of the Reuter building at 85 Fleet Street, a small office enclosed by a row of filing cabinets beyond which was the larger office of the U.S. Associated Press. Because it was nearly noon, pub opening time, Ernie Burritt and a couple of other CP men took me immediately around the corner to the pub called The Cogers for lunch and a restorative pint or two, after which, back at the office, I spent my first working shift in London reading the carbon copies of what CP London had been sending back home for the past few days. I hadn't really considered where I would stay, but Burritt said that while I found my way around I could bunk in with four other CP staffers.

Late that afternoon in a cab with two or three of my new colleagues and my meagre baggage, we stopped at a big block of flats called Fursecroft, which was to become my home away from home until I had my own place. There actually couldn't have been a better choice. The spacious CP flat there, a sublet well furnished even to Wedgwood beer mugs, I soon found was close to the Marble Arch tube station and handy buses on the Edgeware Road. The regulars in Fursecroft included Bill Stewart, Foster Barclay, Doug Amaron and Louis Hunter, but usually there were a few strays as well. This flat was well known not only in CP. Other Canadian correspondents and servicemen on leave often showed up looking for a place where everyone talked Canadian and drop-in visitors were the rule rather than the exception.

I found that out a few mornings later when I was on the morning tea detail. That was a homey arrangement by which each morning someone carried cups of tea around the flat, serving everyone present, known or unknown.

On my first tea detail, I found one man I didn't know. He had draped his RCAF uniform over a nearby chair and was asleep on a chesterfield in the living room. I gave him tea and he thanked me. When I wondered when he had arrived—he hadn't been around when we returned at closing time the night before from a nearby pub, I was told that the lock on our flat's front door was broken. This was known by a good number of Canadians who might arrive late in London with no place to stay and would head for Fursecroft and bed down wherever they could.

The beneficiaries of this arrangement included some Czechs from their government-in-exile quarters a few floors above. One morning I was wakened early by the low voice of a young woman saying, "Tea?" When she handed cups to me and Bill Stewart, a Fursecroft regular whose room I was in, I thanked her. When she left, I asked Bill, "Who's she?"

"One of the girls from the Czech embassy," he said sleepily. I found later that the Czechs, naturally very security conscious, locked their front door every night at eleven. After that nobody got in. Late arrivals knew there was no use knocking. But some of them knew that if they couldn't get into their own place, our door wasn't locked. A custom had come into being that if one of these Czech strays bedded down on our chesterfield, or whatever, and was first up, they'd do the morning tea.

Those first days in London had something magic about them. I quickly learned to find my way around Fleet Street and Chancery Lane and Fetter Lane, and through the city, chancing one day on the original of Dickens's Old Curiosity Shop.

That day I was on my way to find Odham's Press, where once a week I would be reminded of my earlier days in the Winnipeg *Free Press* composing room. At Odham's I would stand by the stone with a friendly Englishman, doing the makeup for the *Canadian Press News*, now that I was on the receiving end. In chatting one day he mentioned that his own home had been bombed flat causing me to remark sympathetically on the devastation caused in London's East End by heavy fire-bombing earlier in the war.

My partner in the composing room looked me in the eye and said quietly, "It was the best thing that could happen—when it's all rebuilt we'll have decent places to live."

I didn't stay at Fursecroft long. The CP flat was already fairly full, so I was there only long enough to find my way around London. I moved several times in the next few months, finally winding up in a nice small flat in Eaton Mews North, where I lived for the next year or so.

That mews flat was an adjunct to a larger and grander home owned by a Canadian officer in the Scots Guards, Capt. Billie Bull from the well-known Brampton Bull family headed by writer and politician Perkins Bull.

I was told that he and his brother Bartle had come to England before the war to take advantage of an arrangement by which they would receive commissions in the Scots Guards and at the same time qualify to run for the House of Commons in what were called rotten boroughs, meaning that any Tory who could put up the campaign money was sure of being elected, which both were.

All this time I was very lonely for Rassy and Bob. Earlier in the war some Canadians stationed in London had managed to have their wives join them. Very early on I started petitioning for permission to have my family join me in London.

I think I knew all along that it would never happen, which was the case, but for a year I kept trying. At the same time, I was not celibate. I almost wrote "entirely celibate," but I guess celibacy is a state that does not lend itself to the qualification. I was lonely, and sometimes things happened, unplanned, with women I met. I had a strange code to the effect that if I didn't plan such a liaison, I was not fully responsible for breaking my wedding vows. All that I can truthfully say is that I didn't go looking for trouble.

At the same time, I had one other frustration. There was an unwritten rule in CP that married staffers, as I was, would not be sent on the most perilous assignments. When we heard from RCAF headquarters in Lincoln's Inn Fields, a short walk from Fleet Street, that permission had been given for a CP man to fly with an RCAF bomber on a raid over Germany, I asked for the assignment. But Louis Hunter, unmarried and also CP's air-war specialist, got it and came home safely with the first eye-witness story of what it was like being harried by anti-aircraft fire, search-lights and night-fighters.

All the same, I did my best to make my mark on stories that could be covered after the fact; that is, without my being actually part of the actions I was writing about. One of my first trips outside London was to Liverpool, where two Canadian corvettes, *Ville de Québec* and *Dauphin*, had come in with two hundred survivors of a submarine attack on a convoy they were escorting. Several merchant ships had been torpedoed.

It was such assignments, living a few days with crews from such corvettes as the *Ville de Québec*, *Dauphin* and, another time, *Leaside*, and interviewing merchant marine survivors of submarine attacks, that gave me a sense of what the sea war was all about: corvettes sometimes standing by like sitting ducks in submarine-infested waters hauling dozens of survivors out of the sea. One corvette captain, the mighty former Ottawa football player Tiny Herman, was revered by his crewmen in *Leaside* for hauling survivors over the side two at a time, one on each strong arm, until survivors were stacked everywhere on the ship's decks.

When I travelled to Londonderry, exhausted Canadian navy men told me how exposed every escort group felt sailing into that northern Ireland port where, it was well known, German spies took advantage of Ireland's neutrality to watch from nearby hills and pass on information to their people about what ships were sailing in and out.

Sailors had a reputation of going on binges as soon as they reached shore. "Binge?" one sailor in Londonderry told me. "Mostly one drink does it. We come in weak from seasickness after eighteen or nineteen days in the North Atlantic and step ashore here in Derry or Liverpool or wherever and have one drink and in our weakened condition we're reeling, throwing up. That's where the drunken sailor idea comes from."

Since correspondents were seen as a link between the fighting men and their hometown newspapers, we were always welcome aboard, where we would listen to the men's stories, then retell them for Canadian readers. In this way the people back home learned the kind of lives their sons and husbands and brothers lived, minute to minute.

This didn't happen only in the ports. I also spent time with Canadian bomber or fighter squadrons.

In one fighter station I heard about the fate of my friend Paris Eakins, shot down a few months earlier during the disastrous raid on Dieppe. I went there to find out any details I could, so I could tell his family back home in Minnedosa, Manitoba, more than they had been told so far. I knew one man on that fighter station, a Toronto newspaperman and by then RCAF flight lieutenant, John Clare.

Partly because John and Paris had worked for newspapers, they had become close friends during the months before the Dieppe raid. John introduced me to other young Spitfire pilots who had been flying with Paris on Dieppe day. One told me of Paris's sombre last words during the Spitfire squadron's action against German aircraft hammering the Dieppe landings: "I saw him in bad trouble, engaging the enemy, hit, and then saying clearly on the intercom, 'I've had it, sir,' as his Spitfire plummeted toward the sea."

I had a few drinks with some pilots who had flown with Paris ever since they had come out of the Commonwealth Air Training Plan in Canada. The conversation was mainly about Paris as a person, their friend. It seemed he hadn't been a natural pilot. Everything came harder with him.

"Remember the Dornier bomber," one said, and they all laughed. "This was the real Paris. . . He and another pilot were on standby when some bombers came over, meaning they had to scramble to intercept the German bombers attacking the station. Through the clouds we could see Paris on the tail of a Dornier. We cheered as they went out of sight and then appeared again with this big clumsy Dornier on Paris's tail! How the hell they'd managed to get the position reversed. . . but anyway, he survived that one."

In a quieter moment, John Clare told me that he and Paris had spent their pre-Dieppe special leave together in London. They had no idea what was coming up, but since they'd all been given leave, they knew it was something big. On their last night in London, Clare said, Paris was very quiet, very down. After a brisk night in the pubs they were getting ready for bed in the room they shared when John asked Paris if something was bothering him, and Paris said that he had a feeling that next time in the air, he was going to die.

When I wrote to his family in Minnedosa to tell them what I had been able to find out about Paris's last days, I told them that he had been one of the best-liked men in the squadron, which was true. I left out the part about the Dornier but did tell them the bleak facts about when he was shot down and what he said when he knew he was finished.

Eventually it began to get to me: men about my own age, with as much back home to lose as I had, were in uniform and I was on the sidelines, writing about them and wishing I was part of them. Instead, all I was doing was trying to get their names and home towns spelled right and their stories to smack of truth. In short, I was becoming uneasy about my role as reporter. I no longer wanted to be in the war as a bystander; I wanted to return to Canada and join up. After a year in London during which I had missed the wedding of my brother and Merle Davis—"I got the good brother," Merle often said, as she and Rassy resumed their old time animosity—I told Gillis Purcell I wanted to come home and join up. An unmarried man could be sent to replace me and would have no limitation on what he could do, or where he could be sent. Finally, G. P. told me that he was making arrangements for me to come home, which I did on a troopship in the autumn of 1943 and made preparations to enlist.

There was a form of conscription in Canada by then, which I would be eligible for, but those conscripted could not be sent overseas unless they also volunteered for overseas service, which I would do. Rassy and I, with Bob, got happily reacquainted in a flat we rented on Denman Street in north Toronto. About the time I could have been drafted by the army, I enlisted in the navy as an ordinary seaman and soon was called in to begin my new entry training at the Canadian National Exhibition grounds, mostly with late teenagers to whom, at twenty-six, I was an old man.

I trained for about two months, most of the time being allowed to spend the nights at home as long as I was back in barracks by 7 a.m. When we passed out of that phase, mainly basics like marching in step and taking part in honour guards for visiting brass hats, and the occasional funeral, and a lot of being yelled at by our instructors, I was asked if I would stay on as an instructor. I declined.

Then with all the kids from our training division of seamen and stokers, we were shipped out by train to Cornwallis, Nova Scotia, for the next stage of training. Rassy and Bob went back west, this time to stay awhile with my mother and sister at Flin Flon. My dad had left again in 1942, landed with his mother at the old home farm near Cypress River, got a job in a drugstore, and never went back. Mother and Dorothy both worked in Flin Flon from then on.

At Cornwallis, I, Ordinary Seaman Young, number 80545, being paid $1.25 a day, wound up as sort of a senior member of dozens of youngsters, learning the workings of four-inch guns and depth-charge pistols, getting up every morning to run several miles before breakfast, learning the ropes, eating a lot, getting in better shape than I'd ever been, and thinking somewhat wistfully of the day when I would graduate as a trained seaman and be allowed into the wet canteen, where only trained seamen could drink.

As a trainee, however, I must have been doing all right. Having received good marks on tests and exams, I was put into an accelerated category—and would graduate to the trained seaman class in seven weeks instead of ten.

Our commanding officer called me in for an interview before a board of other officers to determine whether I had the stuff to be an officer candidate in the seagoing branch. I hadn't especially coveted being an officer candidate, but it could lead soon to promotion and a raise in pay (to $4.25 a day as a probationary sub-lieutenant).

Then—this, I believe, was in April 1944—the commanding officer called me in again, with what to me was bad news. He told me he'd been instructed by Ottawa that I was being transferred away form the trained seaman course I was taking in the seagoing, or Executive, branch to the Intelligence, or Special, branch, one of whose concerns was public relations. I didn't want that. I had been told by someone in authority even when I was still in London that if I wanted a Special Branch commission, it was mine for the asking—because it would make use of my writing and journalistic background. To me that kind of job was exactly what I had been doing as a civilian correspondent and would have kept me more or less on the sidelines of the war.

I put my position strongly to the commander and won his support.

He said he would send a signal to Ottawa saying that I was a very promising officer candidate in the Executive Branch and should stay there. I thought for a week or two that my appeal had been granted. Then the final blow fell. Ottawa refused to back off. I would be transferred to Special Branch whether I wanted it or not. With my journalistic training, I was needed in England. I learned later that this urgency was based on the upcoming invasion of Europe and increased requirement for navy combat reporters.

I still didn't give up. At the time Navy Information was headed by a civilian, Bert Howard of Montreal. I phoned him and explained my position.

"Look, Scott," he said, "we need someone we can send to England immediately in Special Branch, somebody who won't have to be trained in reporting or journalism or whatever. If you won't accept the commission, we can send you as an ordinary seaman, whether you agree or not."

Obviously, he had me. Did I go overseas as an officer or as an ordinary seaman? I gave in, except that I asked for the trained seaman rating that I had earned, got it, and made my first trip to the wet canteen. I was also given leave to go home to Winnipeg and see Rassy, buy a uniform, return to Halifax and be ready to sail with the next draft going overseas.

Meanwhile, D-Day had come and gone, and with many Canadian ships in the invasion force in support of Allied troops fighting their way through Normandy, I finally understood the urgency in transferring me to the Special Branch.

In Winnipeg I reclaimed my liquor ration book, which I had left for safekeeping, and illegal use, with my old boss Eddie Armstrong more than a year earlier before I went overseas with CP. I gave up my seaman's uniform reluctantly; I liked the bell-bottomed trousers and round rig hat. I kept my well-shined boots, bought an ill-fitting officer's uniform, couldn't find a proper officer's cap and had to settle for something less, and a few weeks later, after more farewells to my wife and our two-year-old son, I flew back to Halifax to sail for England.

9

Crossing the
Channel

W HEN I REPORTED TO Canadian naval headquarters in central
London, I had my duties spelled out by the officer who would be
my direct superior, Cmdr. Peter MacRitchie, RCNVR, a fierce Scot originally from the Hebrides but more recently from an assortment of senior jobs
in Canadian newspapers. We had known one another in Toronto and
apparently he'd been impressed with my work with CP London.

"When we could see that after the Normandy landing we'd need a lot
more people over here in Information, I suggested you and they found you
are already in the navy, which made it easy." He shot me a look from
under his big black eyebrows. "They tell me you tried to turn down this
Special Branch commission," he said.

"Yes, sir."

"Why?"

"I have a prejudice against being a PR man."

"That's selfish," he said, and seemed about to leave it at that, but
didn't. "We're very short of people who can interview, write and be
responsible in the field. You fill the bill. Don't let us down just because
you wanted to be Capt. Horatio Hornblower." My job, he said, was to sail
with Canadian ships wherever they were in action and report on their
exploits. My stories were to be directed to him in London. After being
passed by censors they would be handed either to the news services or to
naval headquarters in Ottawa, for general release to newspapers and magazines. Canadian sailors who'd been involved in the Normandy landings
were now working in the English Channel against enemy mines, surface

raiders, submarines and enemy aircraft. Their stories needed to be told by someone who knew what he was doing.

"That's you," MacRitchie said. "You know how to cover that kind of stuff. I also hear that you specifically told Bert Howard in Ottawa that you didn't want to wind up in a desk job."

"Right," I said.

He fixed me with those black eyes, this time with a glint of humour. "So let's get you started."

He handed me an envelope containing a travel warrant and orders to proceed forthwith to Sheerness on the Thames estuary. There I was to find HMCS *Mayflower*, one of the early Flower-class corvettes, and report to its captain, Lieut. Douglas S. (Pincher) Martin, ready to go to work.

I did as I was told and a day later was walking along a rainy jetty, past a dockside pub, asking directions at various gangways. At one point in my wandering, I came across what I thought was a scarecrow. When I got closer, I found that it was a dead-drunk navy lieutenant. The back of his greatcoat had been impaled on what seemed to be a meat hook hanging from a lamp post, the rest of him just hanging. As I didn't think this was the kind of you-are-there Canadian adventure that MacRitchie had in mind, I passed him by, figuring someone other than Probationary Sub-Lieutenant Young, S. A., RCNVR, should have this chance to be Good Samaritan. I asked another passerby and learned that he was duty officer on a ship enduring a long refit at Sheerness, and for several days had been trying to drink various other wardrooms dry. Finding him drunk and in danger of falling into the sea, another officer had hung him up on the lamp post and figured that the shore patrol would find him sooner or later.

I carried on and eventually found the *Mayflower*. Soon I was saluting the ensign, crossing the gangplank and being conducted into the captain's cabin. Lieut. Pincher Martin, RCNR, captain of *Mayflower,* was a slim and reserved Maritimer who in his pre-navy life had sailed in merchant ships, a matter signified by the initials after his name and rank—RCNR standing for Royal Canadian Naval Reserve. That meant that he had learned his seamanship in the merchant marine before being brought into the navy.

"We don't have an extra cabin for you," Pincher Martin told me. "Can you make do on one of the wardroom benches?"

That was where I slept that first night, while around me meals were served, and officers came off leave, roaming in and out for coffee or drinks.

Over the next day or so, still at Sheerness, Pincher Martin and I got to know one another better. I learned much about not only the ship but where it fitted in to the overall picture, and what its next job was. In the June 6 invasion of Normandy, the Allied plan included establishing on the French coast a number of huge prefabricated structures called Mulberry ports, intended to make up for the absence of established port facilities near the fighting front. The Mulberrys were built to precise plans. Old seagoing hulks were towed in and sunk to provide breakwaters. Barge-like concrete structures, styled like huge floating shoeboxes, were towed by tugs across the Channel and placed where they could be used for every normal port use. We were to sail for a Mulberry port in use but being improved, at Arromanches, on the coast of France about seventy miles across the Channel.

We sailed down the Thames estuary from Sheerness, our own ragtag and bobtail little armada. *Mayflower* was to provide protection against air and sea attacks. The biggest component of our little convoy was a Mulberry port section, towed by a tugboat, ploughing through the waves with mighty slaps and splashes.

Just leaving the Thames estuary, Pincher and I were on the bridge looking at a sea dotted with ships and boats large and small, slow and fast, and aircraft and the occasional German buzz-bomb overhead.

"How long is this trip going to take?" I asked.

"Waaaall," Pincher said, and then opined that our average speed would be about one mile an hour for the seventy miles. As it turned out he was almost dead on—the trip took a little more than three days.

Once we were in the open Channel the sounds of war were all around us: the booming of distant guns, passing aircraft occasionally drawing fire and the frequent unearthly clatter made by the flying bombs, nicknamed buzz-bombs, unmanned winged vehicles designed and built by the Germans for cross-channel attacks on Britain, with launching pads inland from the French coast. Each sounded like a thousand motorcycles going uphill. In a very short time they had an unholy reputation. Fighter planes would try to shoot them down, or even fly close enough to touch them and tip them off course to crash and explode short of their main target, London.

It seemed that first day out of Sheerness that we must be on sort of a buzz-bomb highway. Most were aimed at London but had to pass over us and cross southeast England to get there. So many went by and thundered into the distance towards London that those of us gathered on the bridge stopped paying close attention. Then one suddenly seemed headed towards us a lot lower than usual. We watched it through binoculars, feeling it was going to be too close for comfort.

However, flying lower and lower, it passed about a hundred yards above us. Then we saw something else. We'd noticed from time to time a small ship apparently at anchor between us and the Dover cliffs, also on the regular route of the passing buzz-bombs. We held our breaths when the bomb crashed into the sea and exploded. A great spume of water rose in the air, for a moment obscuring our view of the little ship, and we were silent, thinking it had been hit. Then suddenly there was another sight: the ship again, now increasingly visible as the water fell back around it. That was followed in a matter of seconds by another sight, the ship's anchor rising from the water at uncommon speed as it put on full power and got the hell out of there.

The explosion and the little ship's anchor clearing the water were so close to being simultaneous that all of us who had been raised on Disney cartoons laughed and cheered.

And kept on plodding along all that day.

I soon became familiar with another sound, common and constant, as if someone with a mighty hammer occasionally smashed it against the steel side of the ship. Those were the sounds of depth charges, from near or far. The sound travelled through the water and hit a ship's side with a boom like a distant drum.

The most memorable event of that trip began on the late afternoon of the second day, on the tugboat towing the Mulberry section. Although there was enough noise between the rumbling engines of the tug and the corvette to make communications difficult, there was also an understanding that anything that had to be said between the tug captain and the *Mayflower* should be done without breaking radio silence. Signal flags were used from the tugboat to summon *Mayflower* close enough to use megaphones. A pigeon had landed on the tugboat and apparently was either exhausted or did not fear the presence of men. The word came to Pincher, "It's just sitting there, sir."

A certain amount of jocularity then passed back and forth, such as asking if the pigeon appeared to be armed. Then a rather surprising word came back. One of the men on the tugboat was a pigeon fancier and had noticed that one leg carried a small object. The guesses began to fly. Because we were the navy, and the tugboat was not, it was felt that the pigeon and whatever it carried should be captured and passed to the *Mayflower* for examination. The pigeon hopped a few feet when approached, but did not attempt to fly.

Voice from a bystander: "I think that bird had been flying so long that from now on it's going to walk."

Accordingly, the bird was taken into custody and placed in a strong cotton bag of the type that ships carry in case of imminent capture, when by rule confidential books are placed in the bag, which is weighted and then dropped overboard to sink, against the danger of code books and other confidential papers falling into enemy hands. In this case, a line was fired accurately from *Mayflower* to the tugboat, and the bagged pigeon in its bag attached to a loop that could be hauled across the intervening sea and arrive safely aboard our ship.

Pincher Martin took the pigeon in its bag to the wardroom and removed the tiny canister from its leg. Inside was a tight roll of flimsy paper. With a few of us standing around rubbernecking, Pincher read a message in French. It gave details of some enemy troop movements, plus a fix on an enemy gun position in the tower of a village church. After some brief palaver, Pincher decided that this message should get to some higher authorities.

We were supposed to be keeping radio silence, but Pincher thought this rule could be broken as carefully as possible. He coded a message to be sent to intelligence headquarters in the south of England, reporting the surrender of the pigeon and that its message seemed to have some importance.

There was an hour or two of silence, presumably while the matter was debated by British Intelligence. Then we got a signal from England, saying that the message the pigeon had carried should not, repeat not, be sent anywhere, to anyone, by code or any other means, but that when *Mayflower* arrived at Arromanches the pigeon and its message should be delivered to the nearest intelligence headquarters for interpretation.

At the same time, we decided that the worst thing that could happen would be if the pigeon smothered in that cotton bag. Pincher made the humane decision to let the pigeon free, arranging a few curtains so that it would be confined to the wardroom. On its release, the pigeon looked around, then flew to a ledge by a porthole, where it perched for much of the next twenty-four hours, adding another element to the saga of the tired pigeon in that it seemed to be perfectly housebroken: we gave it food and drink, but what went down did not come out.

"That damn pigeon couldn't have had a crap since it took off from France," the engineer officer remarked at breakfast the next day. "You couldn't train a pigeon to act like that if you tried."

Pincher Martin was uneasy about this new development. His orders had been that when the Mulberry section was delivered and secured, *Mayflower* was to return immediately to England for another assignment. He worried about this alteration of plans and orders.

"Look, Scott," he said to me when we landed at Arromanches, "I don't like the idea of going by myself to find this intelligence headquarters and so on. It's out of my line. Would you come ashore with me and help out? I mean, you're better at talking and describing things than I am."

So, carrying the pigeon in its still clean bag, we walked along a completed section of the Mulberry dock and began asking people where we might find an intelligence officer. A tired sergeant pointed to a ruined house, one I was to see later in many a documentary about the earliest days of the Normandy landings. We walked up the steps into a small office where we found a harried-looking British army lieutenant.

"Yes, I have some orders about this," he said. "I've got the transport ready."

Soon we were in a jeep zooming along twisting roads, the verges laid with dozens or even hundreds of wires, part of the invasion's signals network. Maybe eight or ten miles later we pulled into the courtyard of what seemed like a small chateau, bristling with wary guards. We gave the password and were escorted into what originally must have been the building's dining room. I had insisted that Pincher carry the bag and its unnaturally quiet pigeon, so we stood there, two quite ill-at-ease Canadian officers being greeted effusively by a British army brigadier who told us to wait just a minute, his wingers from the Royal Navy and Royal Air Force would be right along.

During the wait, I stared with fascination at the walls, papered all over with huge maps of France divided into areas. Each area, besides names of towns and villages, carried the name of one or two local spies, along with editorial comments such as: "Pierre, usually useful," and "Armand, speaks fluent German, but unreliable," and "Albert has never given us anything useful."

The other officers arrived. One noted, accurately, that we probably didn't have much of an idea what this pigeon caper had been all about. He told us that many dozens of homing pigeons had been dropped over France in previous weeks, each with a canister attached, and a message reading, "*Vive la France!* If you are a patriot, please write on the attached paper troop movements and gun positions in your area, place the note in the canister and release the pigeon, which is of the homing variety and will carry your message back to us in England. Doing this well, you will be helping your country."

He told us that of the many pigeons dropped in France for this purpose, the one that landed on our tug was the only one heard from so far— "Not a great return for a massive and innovative effort, but one that gives us hope that others will report soon."

He turned to Pincher. "You have this pigeon in your bag? The message untouched? Could we have it, please?"

Pincher reached into the bag, manoeuvring a little to grasp the pigeon near its tail area, intending to bring the bird out of the bag upside down, which he did. As he turned the bird upright, its tail and hindquarters slipped into the sleeve of Pincher's uniform jacket. That manoeuvring, and perhaps the sight of that quite amazing room full of gaping brass hats, had a major effect on the pigeon. All that it had been holding back for nearly forty-eight hours flowed in one soft, hot, multicoloured blob into Pincher's sleeve, filling it from cuff to elbow. He instinctively swung his arm wildly away from himself and splattered all three senior officers, and all four map-covered walls, with pigeon shit.

We left soon after.

I didn't hear anybody laughing.

Never did hear of any abrupt turn in the war due to our, and the pigeon's, efforts.

Ours not to reason why.

I 0

In the
Mediterranean

W HEN I JOINED *Mayflower* and for more than a year thereafter, I worked almost every day writing a book. It is now residing, flaws and all, in the Trent University archives, and I'm told that it is considered in some ways to be a historic document, an unpublished personal eyewitness account of about one year of war. Because I was in the navy when the book was finished, it had to be passed by censor, so the manuscript has the naval censor's stamp and initials on most pages and blue pencilled cuts on others. The overall result so many years later is that there is some memory-straining that I don't have to do because here it is, what happened to me, and around me, and what I thought about it all in England, France, Italy, Corsica, Yugoslavia, Greece, Canada and Newfoundland (not then a part of Canada): two hundred typed, double-spaced, foolscap pages. It is the only book I ever wrote that remains unpublished.

I returned to England on *Mayflower* and reported again to my naval masters in London's Haymarket. I was told by MacRitchie that I was being hooked up with an officer I knew only slightly, Lieut. Gilbert A. Milne, RCNVR, formerly a news photographer mainly with the Toronto *Star*. We were to be a writer-photographer team and were to report forthwith (everything in the navy happens forthwith) to HMCS *Prince Henry* in Southampton, soon to sail for an unknown (to us) destination.

The *Henry's* most recent operation with its complement of assault landing craft had been the D-Day landings in Normandy. By the ship's very nature its next job likely would be another assault landing. Where, we wondered. The North African landings had happened almost two years earlier, the Sicily landings half that, Normandy only a few weeks back. The only clue we had was that we'd been advised to take tropical gear, probably meaning we were headed for the Mediterranean.

Gib Milne and I hurried through the blackout towards Victoria Station to catch a train to Southampton, where we found the *Henry* at its berth with six LCAs (Landing Craft Assault) and two larger LCMs (Landing Craft Mechanised) hanging from its davits—and for me there was a wonderful surprise. There at the gangway with his hand outstretched was a close friend, Ed McNally. Later he was to become an award-winning editorial cartoonist with the Montreal *Star*, but we had been at the Winnipeg *Free Press* together before the war, sharing a boarding-house room. I had been best man at Ed's wedding, and he at mine. And now there he was, the *Henry*'s assistant gunnery officer, and we did a lot of catching up. In Winnipeg, we had both worked nights, and used to come home about two or three in the morning, hungry. We would go down into the basement of the boarding house and chop wood, much to the horror of the rest of the household, and make sandwiches (our landlady hated us for supplementing her starvation diet that way). Then we would go up to our room, light a great hot fire of pine logs and sit and eat the sandwiches. Often we talked until five in the morning, about what we were going to do tomorrow, and ten years from tomorrow, and what we had done yesterday, and ten years from yesterday. But we never envisioned war.

For the next few days before we sailed, we resumed some of our old habits—such as drinking rather a lot together. As we knew one another so well in happy times, inevitably we talked things out that somehow had been skipped in the past, including our marriages, both of them happy then.

While the *Henry* took a wide swing into the rough seas of the south Atlantic to avoid the potentially unhealthy invasion-stimulated air and sea activity in the Bay of Biscay, I did encounter something new to me: seasickness. The *Mayflower*, like all corvettes, had rolled a lot but for some reason didn't produce quite the sensation of sailing on a bigger ship—one that pitched. It makes me a little seasick even to think of the way the *Henry*'s bow would ride up on a huge wave and then drop like a stone, taking my stomach with it. The only thing that made this seasickness bearable was that almost everyone was having the same trouble, even old salts who said they never had lost a meal at sea. It was a common sight to see people going to stand their watches carrying with them fire buckets, to be sick in.

The weather started to get better the night before we got to Gibraltar. There was the smell of summertime on the land breeze, and it made me homesick. It was also the smell of Spain—a soft, gentle, lazy smell.

The following day we dropped our hook in the harbour of Gibraltar, across a narrow revealing bay from La Linea, Spain, where we could be quite sure there were German spies watching us through their glasses.

I didn't go ashore in Gibraltar. I could have, but when the boat was pushing off I didn't have my identification card and didn't feel like sprinting to my cabin to get it. So I spent the afternoon in the wardroom with a few others, having a drink or two, which was not allowed at sea. An oiler came alongside, and we had her captain aboard and then visited him for a drink.

The oiler had a monkey as a pet, and a few people thought we should have one also, but McNally talked them out of it. When he was on the *Prince Robert*, he said, they had a monkey as a mascot. It would block passages with teeth bared and refuse to let anyone by. Finally it blocked one passage too many, and the quartermaster let the monkey have six shots between the eyes.

From Gibraltar to Naples took a little more than two days and gave us our first real experience of the Mediterranean's fantastic climate. The sun shone from sunrise to sunset without a break of any more than ninety seconds at any time. We lazed the days away on the quarterdeck. I worked a little, culling BBC broadcasts for world news, which I would read over the ship's loudspeaker at noon, but after lunch I would get a pillow and put on shorts and get out in the sun and read for pleasure.

We slept on the deck nights. Most of us had acquired camp cots before leaving Southampton, and by about ten or eleven every night the deck was crowded with officers and matelots alike seeking a cool place to sleep.

The war seemed very far away most of the time. I was listening to news every day for signs of a heavy and sustained bombing attack on any Mediterranean target, because that would give me an idea of what might be our target, but there was no such indication. Meanwhile, the occasional aircraft droned by, usually well away from us, and until it was identified, or flew out of sight, every one was at action stations. But we had no submarine contacts, and no reason to believe any of the several aircraft we saw every day were enemy. They certainly left us well enough alone. The only presence of war with us all the time was wondering about the job ahead. There were interminable and never uninteresting discussions about where the operation would be. Nobody knew, and the guesses ranged from one end of the Med to the other.

A veteran fighting man becomes a fatalist, because he sees so much death he knows it is not impossible for him to die, too. I thought of this one day when I was talking to Leading Stoker Bob Dowber, the engine maestro in an assault landing craft (LCA) commanded by tall and outspoken Jim Flynn, RCNVR. The action we were sure was coming up was to be Dowber's fifth assault landing.

"If they keep sending me in on these things, I'm bound to catch a packet some day, for sure," he said. "Hell, we had some pretty rough times on those first four, and some close misses, and we've always come out all right. But there must come a time when the number comes up. Then there's nothing you can do."

We were sitting in the sun on his landing craft, half lowered at its davits, while we talked. It seemed incredible, yet right, that we could sit there so peacefully in the craft that a few weeks later would take us into another bloody section of enemy-held territory, and talk about our chances of coming out of it. Dowber was a swarthy, muscular kid with a big grin and a wide knowledge of women from Glasgow to Oran and back again.

"Of all the shows I've been in," he mused, "Dieppe was the worst. It was my first, and there has been nothing like it since. But Normandy was next worst, and it was bloody close behind. Sicily was bad enough, and North Africa bad enough, but Dieppe was bloody awful and so was Normandy."

I looked out at the coast of Italy, a mile away.

"I wonder how the next one will be," I said.

He grinned at me. "I wonder."

❧

We got into Naples on a Monday morning, about eleven. The trip in was just like everything in the Mediterranean—slightly unreal. A few miles out we passed the Isle of Capri, with fine villas and hotels hanging perilously from its cliffs, and the sunshot blue of the Mediterranean licking its towering rocks and occasional sandy beaches. We spent all that morning on the bridge or the flag deck, watching Capri and Naples through glasses as we passed slowly in to our anchorage. We recognized a lot of our old marine friends lying around—HMCS *Prince Robert*, Canadian flak cruiser, going out; other ships of all shapes and sizes that had been in the Normandy show, too. Most were American. Two to every one of ours. We also had a good look at some of the Italian warships—ships with beautiful lines. The Royal Navy always thought in peacetime that next to the British navy, Italy's was one of the best in the world. It must have been poor leadership, or lack of heart in the fight, that made the Italian fleet so ineffective during its three years of war.

We all were hoping to get a few days in Naples, and maybe even get up to Rome. But there wasn't a good reliable buzz around the ship on how long we'd be there, so we had to be content with hoisting a few Collins in the wardroom with lemons that Gib Milne bought during his brief stay in Gibraltar. Then there was a boat going ashore, so a few of us piled in. The only two of us with no actual business to transact ashore were Bob Gilmer, a lieutenant from Victoria, B.C., and me.

Even before the boat touched the jetty everyone was talking about the women we could see walking along the shore promenade. But that's what comes from being at sea for a while and seeing nothing more feminine than a box of live ammunition.

The worst aspect of what we found ashore was the part small children played in the business of prostitution. On the first day, Gilmer and I strayed away form the beaten path early in the afternoon and spent the next seven hours drinking cognac, anisette, vino rosso, marsala, bernadetto and strega and eating melons and spaghetti in a part of the city we later learned was off limits to all Allied troops. Usually we had a couple of small boys as guides, and these youngsters always thought it very strange that we did not take advantage of their kind offers to conduct us to some girls, usually their sisters, if they were to be believed.

In a day or two, maybe more, we planned to get a jeep ashore and explore a little. Overnight orders wiped out that plan. We had a 7 a.m. sailing down the coast a few dozen miles to a village called Santa Maria di Castellabate, which was to be our base for subsequent training for what we now knew would be the invasion of southern France. We were not told that officially for a while yet, but two Royal Navy officers we had met had let us in on the plan. One, Capt. Taprell Dorling, I found had written several books of naval fiction under the pen name of Taffrail.

We became friends at least partly because I had read his books and liked them, and he became a lot more forthcoming about the operation to come than anyone on our own ship.

During the next few weeks my somewhat nebulous ideas about the Italian people crystallized considerably. My views until I went to Naples had been gathered mainly from what I had read or heard. Ralph Allen, my old Winnipeg newspaper friend and adversary, later war correspondent for the Toronto *Globe and Mail,* had told me how the Italian people seemed to him to have lost their self-respect and were—by their thieving, petty dishonesty and begging—the most aggravating people he had met. Ralph, a mild man, admitted that once, picking up a tommy-gun, he had chased an Italian for stealing rations. That impressed me. Anyone who stirred Allen to any kind of physical exertion had to be a considerable menace, indeed.

But in Santa Maria the Italians we dealt with were lighthearted, smiling, helpful and fairly honest. Occasionally as we walked along a street we would hear an outburst obviously directed against us, but we could not understand what it was and therefore did not care. More often we got smiles and waves from the people as we passed.

It was hard to rationalize my feelings about the Italians. Their entry into the war caused us thousands of casualties and the monumental hardships of years of desert war. But, as individuals, they seemed to be people like ourselves, not unhappy that their war had ended.

One day when we took a can of paint ashore to one old man who wanted to paint his house, and had been obliging in various matters, such as good cognac, we had a drink in his kitchen.

Half in jest, I raised my glass and said, "Viva Italia."

He raised his and said, "Viva Duce!" then, slowly and plainly, his entire English vocabulary: "Son of a beetch."

Still another told us he had a son fighting in the American army. There were many in Italy like him trying to make a connection, any connection.

The exercises we went through at this time were elementary, mainly concerned with getting our Canadian landing craft personnel used to towing the rubber boats we would use in the landing stage of our upcoming operation, practising loading them aboard the LCAs, and later stowing them on the ship's decks. We got acquainted with the mixed Canadian–U. S. Special Service Force people with whom we would be working for the next few weeks. I had had a reasonable amount of experience with soldiers but never met any who gave me such a feeling of confidence as these did. It was good to watch the way they handled themselves and their good equipment, and hear their laughter and banter as they went about the preliminaries to their job. And Jim Flynn told me that when they were in the boats and were supposed to be quiet, they were quiet—not a peep. He said they were the best soldiers he ever had seen, a proficiency that came from long experience.

They had been trained originally for an invasion of Norway that didn't come off, and in addition to taking regular Commando assault training had gone through stiff courses as ski and parachute troops. Early on, Kiska in the Aleutians had been their first operation, and there wasn't much to that. Then came their Italian fighting—an outstanding series of jobs around Cassino, when they were taking hills that then would be held by other troops while the SSF moved along the line to another particularly tough assignment. Following that came their eighty-nine days on the Anzio beachhead, south of Rome. They had heavy casualties all along. One told me that of the 250-man reinforcement unit he had been in when he joined the SSF just a few months before, there were only fifty men left. Only a smattering of the original ski-commando-paratroopers remained. Their commanding officer, Col. Edwin Walker, was one of them.

I was out with Jim Flynn one day on one of our elementary exercises when one of the troop-carrying rubber boats began deflating and soon was taking water, creating a terrific strain on the towline. Without hesitation, three of the SSF men leaped overboard. Had they stayed, the rubber craft probably would have been swamped and they would have been in danger of being run down by those following. That incident provided Flynn with an excuse to do something he had been wanting to do all day—go in swimming and cool off. As soon as he spotted a couple of helmet linings (fibre, and hard to replace) floating in the water after the men had clambered aboard another craft, Flynn slipped out of his clothes and dove overboard after them. That was Flynn—no telling another man to do a job he rather would do himself.

The bay at Santa Maria di Castellabate is beautiful. It is not particularly well protected, but the Mediterranean is such a peaceful old lady that

that doesn't make much difference. As far as I know, the bay had never been used by large ships to any extent, except when on a mission like ours. There never had been commercial shipping traffic there, except for a little fishing trade. There wasn't even a jetty to come alongside. We anchored out in the bay, and the fish boats were hauled up on the soft, fine sand in a little cove set in the centre of the village. It was in this cove that the children of the village swam. We occasionally brought our landing craft into the cove, when there was something to pick up from the town. Otherwise, we landed at a long, flat beach a few hundred yards away that separated Santa Maria and the next village, where there was more room and the water was cleaner than it was near the town: also fewer naked, screaming children. It was like the difference between a private lake and Coney Island.

All this time, the operation coming up was still the most popular topic aboard. Where would it be? The experts who had guessed as far afield as Crete were quiet now, and we all were sure it would be in the Italian end of the Mediterranean, and soon. The preliminary exercises had passed, and now our Combined Operations personnel and the Canadians and Americans of the SSF were working on advanced problems—night landings with full equipment. Our LCAs had no trouble picking up the knack of safely towing rubber boats filled with men and equipment and setting them loose in the right place. On my first sight of these rubber craft I had been slightly apprehensive of what would happen should we encounter bad weather for the operation, but I was reassured by the way they performed in medium swells.

One morning a buzz started around the ship that a big exercise was coming up. It seemed likely, because we had done all we could around Santa Maria, where all the landings so far had been made on flat, sandy beaches that wouldn't have presented a great problem for any breakfast food company's junior commandos, let alone these tough eggs. Then came word that we were to return to Naples for water and oil. On a Sunday we upped anchor and sailed, hoping like hell for mail, but not expecting any, which was just as well because there wasn't any.

I didn't go ashore in Naples that time, because I had several feature stories to do about the *Henry*'s workings, material that would be useful backup when our operation did happen and news editors would want everything they could get as background. That meant I should now get everything I had away to London. I was pretty sure that if I didn't, I would be too late.

Events seemed to be moving towards a climax rapidly. It is a strange thing, the hunches one gets in warfare. One day we were sitting in Santa Maria thinking the operation was remote—next week, or the one after, or next month—and suddenly everyone was sure it would be within a week. We had no specific information, but the tempo of everything was rising.

You may be thinking that I was not much of a war correspondent, not knowing all the intricate details of the plan. But none of the other war correspondents I knew hobnobbed with the great and near-great either. Ralph Allen, then writing for the Toronto *Globe and Mail,* once said that if he ever wrote a book about the war it would have to be called *The Autobiography of Mr. Uh, uh* because no matter how many times he talked to Montgomery, or any other brass hat, it was always: "Oh, how do you do, Mr. . .uh, uh." Wally Reyburn of the Montreal *Standard,* another honest debunker, said that it was his ambition to write: "Now it can be revealed that when the plans were laid for the last great attack on the such-and-such line, this correspondent was completely ignorant that any such attack was being planned."

In Naples, while I stayed aboard writing stories about the ship and its men Gib went ashore to see if he could dig any information out of our friend Captain Dorling about what was about to happen. We also needed more information on how we'd get our stories and pictures out after the operation. Allied Force Headquarters in Rome was the censor and communications centre, but we'd have to get there.

I sat around my cabin that afternoon in my underwear, working as hard as the heat would permit and occasionally going over to the porthole to look across the bay at steaming Naples. From a distance, I could see its possibilities of beauty, but I knew there was little beauty there: dirty people selling fruit, and little boys and girls and old men making their excretions in the streets where they stood. It was a city of rackets, with the worst black market in the world (among items for sale: a crated German fighter plane, an American jeep and everything down to C-ration beef stew), widespread prostitution, ten-year-old pimps, wealth and extreme poverty. There was always food for the rich, little for the poor. Troops took full advantage of the Neapolitan needs. Need a woman? Step into the street and wave a tin of bully beef or pilchards over your head. And set in the midst of the worst filth and poverty were little shops selling exquisite bracelets, necklaces and earrings of coral and cameo, the coral gleaned from the marine environs and the cameos usually carved on the premises.

The afternoon passed that way, split evenly between work and thoughts while looking across the mile of water at the city. Then Gib returned, and with him came confirmation that our target would be the south of France. That evening we sailed again for Santa Maria. The next morning the Special Service Force troops started to come aboard. The little harbour was busier than ever. There were several American assault ships—old four-stacker destroyers with the two after-stacks cut off and four assault boats hanging from the davits. There also were several modern destroyers, all American, and other landing ships like ourselves—the *Prince David*, *Princess Beatrix* and *Prince Baudouin*, the last two Royal Navy ships. All were to be with us on a big exercise that would precede the operation.

That afternoon, after we had been at sea about an hour, we were told that our objective was a small Italian island named Isola di Ponza and that the exercise would be a replica of the real operation. We passed Capri and the mouth of Naples harbour and continued north. Just after dark we swung hard to port around a little nest of islands and dropped our hooks.

As Flynn's LCA was to be headquarters for the exercise and subsequent operation, we were to carry General Jacob Devers, a couple of his staff officers and some naval observers as well as Colonel Walker, the SSF commander. H-hour for the exercise was midnight. When we were still aboard but preparing to leave the ship about eleven, our assault fleet was spread out on the sea around us, dark blobs in the black. Aboard, everything was being done in silence, except for an occasional murmured curse as our men, assisted by some soldiers, shoved, heaved and sweated the ungainly rubber boats into position on top of each landing craft. The soldiers piled into the landing craft first and got their heads below the gunwales while the rubber boats were loaded. Then the order would come quietly out of the darkness: "Lower away."

The LCAs went down into the water—some quietly, some noisily, depending on the condition of the davits. Immediately they hit the top of the first swell, all hands combined to push off the first rubber boat, then the second, third and fourth, until they all were in the water and the heavily laden soldiers had slipped into them from the landing craft. Paddles were taken from under the rubber thwarts and held ready. At a murmured order the soldiers paddled their craft out to assembly points a few dozen yards off the ship, LCAs alongside to rig the towing lines. Then, when all were ready, they set off.

All this could be seen dimly in the intense black. Flynn's craft was still slung in its davits until all else was in readiness. Finally a count was made, and officers who were to come with us were on hand.

From the beginning, our kind of trip could only happen to Flynn, and only Flynn could have come out of it without nervous prostration. In the first place, our LCA started an unaccustomed swinging while we were being lowered—lifting out about ten feet from the *Henry's* side and then coming in with a resounding crash. This happened three times, giving the assembled brass quite a shaking before we even got to the water. Then Colonel Walker, who nominally was in command of the LCA—at least, Flynn was asking him what he wanted to do—said he wanted to go to a PT boat lying astern of the *Henry*. We started off. That was about the only successful manoeuvre we made that night.

Through the dark we could see the rest of the LCAs and their troop-laden rubber craft lining up for the run into Ponza, as we pulled alongside the PT boat. There is always a certain amount of difficulty in identifying oneself in the middle of a black night on the Mediterranean, but eventually it was accomplished and Colonel Walker asked where a certain destroyer was lying. The voice came back through the nothingness from the PT boat: "Over there, behind you."

We couldn't see the destroyer, but Flynn started off in the direction indicated. After we had gone a few hundred yards, I smelled burning rubber. I was sitting on one of the ventilator pipes leading into the LCAs tiny stoke hold, so I figured that's where it must be coming from. I called to a seaman. He could smell it, too. He knocked on the hatch leading into the stoker's cramped quarters and called: "Hey, Jack, something burning down there?"

There was no reply.

"Hey, Jack," the seaman yelled, louder. "Open up."

By this time everybody in the craft was getting interested. General Devers, sitting next to me, with his feet hanging down inside of the landing craft, was watching with curiosity.

"What's the matter?" came a muffled voice.

"We can smell something burning. Put out your lights and open the hatch."

The hatch burst open, and the smell became stronger.

"You're goddamn right there's something burning," the stoker said. "The bloody generator is heating up." He gasped and took a deep breath. "There's no air down there at all. Good old carbon dioxide! Where we going?"

"Over to find a destroyer for the colonel," I said. "You think that generator will hold out all right?"

"Yeah," he replied. "I think so." He took one last deep breath, slipped back down through the hatch, and clanged the lid shut behind him.

By this time we were close to the destroyer. It was one of the converted four-stackers. There were rubber boats and landing craft all over the place. As we narrowly missed one line of rubber boats, I heard someone on the destroyer shouting, "Get that damn thing out of the way!" Maybe meaning us. Then came a lower voice: "Where's that craft from, off the starboard quarter?" That *was* us. Soon after, there was room to approach the destroyer.

A bell rang in the engine room, and simultaneously there was a muffled pop, the hatch flew open again, and steam rushed out around the stoker's head as he gasped for air.

"Goddamn it!" he said. "Goddamn it. If I ever take anybody else's craft out again you can kick my. . .Goddamn it!" Flynn had come running aft at the rush of steam, to see what was the matter.

The stoker beat him to it.

"A water line on the port engine's gone, sir," he said. "She's done for the night."

Flynn cursed vehemently as he strode forward, past all the brass hats. He addressed himself to Colonel Walker. "One of the bloody engines is gone, sir," he reported. "We'll have to get along on one."

The colonel was calm. "All right," he said. "Let's get in to this destroyer and see what is going on." Flynn gave the order to move in towards the destroyer.

The starboard motor revved, then died, and the stoker popped his head out again. His voice was hopeless this time. "There's something tangled around the port screw," he said.

During all this time, we had been towing one spare rubber boat—to be used to take the colonel and his staff in to the beach later. A seaman named Palmer had been trying to keep the towline free from the back of the LCA during the first part of our trip and had succeeded through judicious use of a boat hook. But when the port engine conked and we stopped, he had other things to do, and the rubber craft had been slapping against our stern while we sat there.

I yelled to Jim Flynn: "The line from the rubber boat is wound around the starboard screw."

"Jesus!" Jim shouted. "Come on, Palmer, let's get it loose."

They tried shaking the line and pushing the rubber boat away, but it was tangled hard. Palmer started to take his clothes off. So did Flynn. He walked naked along the catwalk on the side of the LCA, cursing luxuriantly and having a wonderful time. After borrowing a knife from one of the army officers, he dove over the side into the Mediterranean. Palmer went in beside him.

They came up, blew out some seawater, and in a couple of swift strokes were alongside again. Then Flynn went under. In a few seconds he came up and told the stoker to straighten out his screw. The stoker did so, and Flynn went under again. It took him and Palmer about five minutes to cut the line free, then they clambered aboard.

We nosed in towards the destroyer, going now on one engine and at no more than a couple of knots. Apparently we had been under observation all the time, undoubtedly rather astonished observation, because as soon as we moved an American voice came from the destroyer: "Who are you looking for?"

Colonel Walker replied: "This is Colonel Walker."

The voice came back: "He isn't here. He's over there somewhere."

"I know he is," Walker called back. "*I'm* Colonel Walker.

There was a silence while the voice figured that out, then Colonel Walker spoke again: "Is everything going all right?"

The voice replied dubiously: "Yes, sir."

We headed for the beach. Colonel Walker had wanted to get ashore about twelve-thirty, or just about half an hour after the landings, to see how things were going. Plugging along at two knots, we'd be lucky if we even came close to that time. On the way in the stoker popped his head up again and bitterly informed the world in general that a bearing was heating on his one good engine. He barely was out of sight before the towline broke on the rubber boat and we had to come about—with further cursing by all hands—to pick it up.

One American naval officer kept asking me if I would give the two seamen more line to make the rubber boat fast, and I kept assuring him they had enough. Flynn then came aft to see what was going on, and helped the seamen join the lines. Just at an inappropriate moment, when Flynn had banged his finger on something, the American officer really got heated.

"How about getting that damned thing fixed and getting out of here?" he called in an exasperated voice.

Flynn turned on him furiously. "Don't get your balls in a sweat!" he snapped, then added, as an afterthought, "Sir!" Just to add a final ignominious touch to what we had all hoped would be a smooth practice run, we had to get a PT boat to tow us back to the *Prince Henry*, after which we sailed for port again.

11
Going
Ashore

O N FRIDAY, AUGUST 11, we loaded our troops and sailed for Corsica, leaving Santa Maria di Castellabate silent and deserted.

The next afternoon, a few hours after our force had dropped anchor in a tiny bay on the west coast of Corsica, the final briefing for the force was given aboard the *Prince Henry*. Carrying the admiral, we were the force's flagship. Captains and senior officers of other ships trooped aboard between one and three, saluting our quarterdeck over which hung—for the first time on any ship of Britain or her Empire—the flag of an American admiral. Most boarding us were veterans of the sea, loaded with gold braid and an air of authority. But other officers were mere youngsters in com-parison—some of them commanders of the converted American four-stackers and other skippers of PT boats. Soon the admiral arrived, told us to be seated and announced that Captain Maynard would give the briefing.

Captain Maynard had a strong, resonant voice (and therefore was known as Whispering George.) He began by announcing that the army authorities had changed their designations for some of the beaches. For instance, what had been Purple beach in the exercise was to become Amber beach, because the purple signal light had not shown plainly enough in the night. He asked the officers present to make that amendment in the oper-ational orders they had been studying.

Then he confirmed what most of us already knew—that our zero-hour would be one-thirty in the morning of August 15, about six hours before H-hour for the main assault on the French mainland.

"The idea of our part of the operation is to land people on the islands of Port Cros and Levant to wipe out gun positions there which might menace the path of the main invasion force. Particularly we want the 120-millimetre guns on the eastern tip of Levant. They command the route the invasion force is to take, and must be in our hands by daylight.

"Shortly after dusk we can expect large formations of planes to go over us," the captain continued. "They will be friendly, going in to bomb the French coast and soften it up for the landings. It also may serve as a diversion. There also will be fighters, and eventually they'll be back, over us again." But whatever happened, he went on, at that point, "there must be no firing. Just because someone on shore starts firing, that doesn't mean they've seen you. They probably are jittery and have been hearing things for weeks. Let him fire! As soon as a gun crew opens up, it has lost its night vision—the men are practically blind in the night for minutes after."

Everyone in the wardroom was following every word. Some appeared relaxed, if you didn't look at their faces. They were smoking, legs crossed, and they occasionally shifted into more comfortable positions. But their faces were intent, and their eyes were all on the spare, wiry figure before them. British and Canadian officers, wearing our white short-sleeved shirts and shorts, looked reasonably comfortable in the heat. The Americans, with their regulation long khaki outfits, were much less so.

"I want to remind you to say a word to your coxswains on such things as breakdowns. Tell them to work everything out for themselves. They must not show lights, or break radio silence to tell their mother ships of any trouble, because the mother ships couldn't help them anyway and the enemy might find out we are near. Tell them to watch for people in trouble and help them out of it. And tell them above all to avoid accidents that can be avoided. We want no lines wound around screws, or things like that."

Jim Flynn looked at me and grinned.

Captain Maynard wound up then.

"Immediately after the operation, all troop-carrying craft except the *Prince Henry* will return to Ajaccio in Corsica. Your sailing time will be seven o'clock in the morning of D-Day. The *Henry* will stay around another few hours cleaning up any loose ends, recovering any assault craft that need recovering and picking up wounded. Any questions?"

The formal atmosphere dissolved. It could have been the last five minutes in a Rotary Club meeting back home, except that nobody slaps backs in the navy. The officers stood up, spoke to one another and started to disperse. On deck, the ones from each ship grouped together while the officer of the watch and the quartermaster summoned in turn the many boats waiting around our ship to take the officers back to their own. Back in the wardroom, the stewards methodically started moving the furniture back in place, and the bar steward began polishing glasses and setting out his bottles towards opening time.

The operation was two days away.

≈

While we sailed towards Corsica, Ben Malkin and I had had several long talks. He had gone overseas with the First Canadian Division in December 1939 and arrived in the midst of a cold and wet English winter at billets that hadn't been used since the Great War. Then training resumed, but they still weren't fully trained by early summer of that year when the First Division made a series of false fits and starts towards France, and finally stayed in England because it was too late for reinforcements to do any good in France. He helped man ack-ack defences on the coast all during the Battle of Britain, and then settled down for the three years of intensive training and exercises that ended with the invasion of Sicily in July 1943. Ben was there, with the artillery, leaving his newly acquired English wife behind while he started the first actual phase of the fight he had left Winnipeg to find nearly four years before.

He fought all through Sicily, went to Italy with the First Division and fought his way up through Italy in one of the worst winters on record until early in 1944, when he was doing an artillery shoot one cold spring day up near the front line. Commands were being given by loudspeaker system. At the gun site Ben and his gun crew were carrying out the firing orders, when a message interrupted: "Sergeant Malkin will report to Naples tomorrow to be discharged from the army. Fire four."

Ben claimed to be the first war correspondent who ever got a four-gun salute.

The *Free Press* had been casting around for a war correspondent to work the Italian front while Jam Cook, who had been in the Mediterranean with the Canadians since Sicily, returned to England to prepare to cover the opening of the Western Front in France. Ben was a logical choice. The editors knew he was a good newspaperman, even if he had been away from it for nearly five years, and he was on the spot. So they arranged for his discharge and he took over from Cook to cover various actions on the Italian front, which is how he happened across the New Zealand wine diviner. You know what a water diviner is—someone who uses a wand to indicate where a well should be dug. This New Zealand wine diviner, according to Ben, made his wine-divining reputation in the Eighth Army, always finding vino for the men in his artillery outfit, who like most soldiers really didn't need help except in the most difficult circumstances.

This *was* a difficult circumstance. The New Zealand battery had been moved into a front-line area to shell enemy positions, and near their gun sites found an abandoned house usable as a billet. On entering, the wine diviner stopped short, sniffed the air tentatively and announced: "There's wine here."

His friends were overjoyed, if slightly amazed. The place looked empty. They spread out through the house, looking for the wine they now knew must be there, but they could find nothing. The wine diviner, urged to be more explicit, ranged through the house until he came to a tiny room stacked full of firewood.

"It's in here," he said.

His mates began to remove the wood. Each log they picked up, they did so expecting to find wine beneath. They cleared the room, and found no wine. The wine diviner stepped inside. This had him slightly buffaloed. Suddenly, however, he pointed dramatically to the floor.

"There," he exclaimed.

So the New Zealand gunners went to work with pick-axes, digging up the concrete floor. And there it was—hundreds of gallons of wine stowed there for safekeeping when the Italian residents fled.

Two days later Ben arrived to do a story about New Zealand gunners. As he stepped into the house, he found himself ankle-deep in something. He reached down, stuck his finger in it and sucked thoughtfully. It was wine.

He went into the next room, battery headquarters. Officers, sergeants and gunners were all sitting on the floor, the wine lapping around their hip pockets. All had cups and were listening to an officer who was talking into a field telephone. As they listened, one or the other would casually reach down into the wine pool they were sitting in, scrape himself up a cup of wine, and sip.

The man at the phone was swaying slightly where he sat.

"How about another target?" he was saying. "Naw. We shot that target all up, all up. Itsh all gone, all gone." Then he listened awhile. "You got no more targets at preshent?" he asked sadly. "Oh, thatsh too bad, too bad. Call ush when you get one. Goodbye." He turned disconsolately to the assembly. "No more targetsh at preshent," he said morosely. "Too bad, too bad."

Ben also gave me instruction on the by then common use of the word *liberation*. U.S. president Roosevelt had requested that occupation of towns or areas in occupied territories was to be called not occupation but liberation. Soon it was the hardest-worked word in the vocabulary. A soldier didn't steal a pig, he liberated a pig. He also liberated eggs, vino, Italian weapons, a few Germans now and again, and occasionally a signorina. If some soldiers went on a party and broke up a wine shop, it was said of them the next day that "they sure liberated that joint last night." Later, I liberated some paper from an office in Rome that had been the Fascist propaganda agency, and some of my friends liberated a flat in Ancona, and one even was so lucky as to liberate a Fiat.

Sometimes the liberators signed for the things they liberated. One Italian presented himself to a Canadian town major with a chit. The Italian obviously was expecting payment of some kind. The major looked at the chit. It read simply: "This man's horse has been liberated." And it was signed, just as simply: "George."

Ben, like all Canadian First Division men, believed firmly that his was the best division in the world. That judgment could not have been far off the mark. I was told once that higher-ups in the Eighth Army always took Canadian First Division casualties to be the absolute minimum that could have been suffered in any given action. The Canadians were pretty good at generating offbeat war stories, as well. Once a small German night patrol picked up a couple of Canadians, also on patrol. The Germans were standing in a roadway, discussing how to get the Canadian captives to a rear area, when there was a polite cough behind them. It came from two more Canadians. They were from the Loyal Edmonton Regiment, noted for its scouts. The two Edmontons had come up so quietly that they were less than a foot away, listening with interest, during most of the conversation between the two Germans. Tables turned.

Germans who fought against Canadians through most of Italy were rather the same type of soldier, poised and brave. A Canadian in a one-man observation post was startled one day to look up from his binoculars and find a German standing a few feet away and regarding him with interest. The German turned and went away. The Canadian decided that either the German had looked right at him and hadn't seen him, or was just plain crazy. Just when he had reached this conclusion, he looked up. The German was back, his head poked around a bush. This time he spoke, in good English: "Just wanted to see if you were still here." Then he went away, and didn't come back.

≈

When the sun was high, we sailed for France.

There was no tension aboard, but there was more talking and joking about the jobs the men had to do and which beach would be the toughest, and how everybody else had the soft spots. They seemed eminently satisfied with the job ahead.

"I hope this is the last one," I heard one soldier say. "It should be, because they can't need many more around the Med once we get this thing going." That's the way everybody felt, and hoped.

I spent most of the morning getting my gear organized for landing. I had some elaborate web equipment that I was quite sure I wouldn't wear if I could help it, because it was too heavy. There was a water bottle, a long sharp sheath knife and a revolver and ammunition. I decided to stick one box of ammunition in my pocket, load the revolver, and let it go at that. If anyone shooting at me couldn't hit me by the time I fired off about thirty rounds from my forty-five, he should go home and work in a war plant. So one way or another, one box should be enough.

Once I saw Flynn. He was leaning over the starboard rail looking at the water rush by, and grunted to me when I came up.

"How're you feeling, James?" I asked.

"Fine. Except I've got a funny feeling in my stomach." He paused. "How do you feel?"

"The same," I said.

At dusk, according to plan, we were twenty-six miles from the objective.

There are many preparations men make just before going into battle—preparations quite apart from the normal procedure of testing weapons and checking equipment. I don't know what most of those preparations were, but almost everyone I knew who was going on the operation disappeared for a short time just before the hour the assault craft were to hit the water. Jim Flynn got his wallet, and some letters, pictures and small things that he would always want to have with him whatever happened, put them in a small bag and placed them in his LCA.

My preparation was entirely in my thoughts. I was sure nothing was going to happen to me, although psychology textbooks say that a man's first cry when he is shot in war is of surprise, not pain—surprise that he, who was so sure he could not be hurt or killed, actually had been hit. I looked over all my things for a few minutes. I had started my book, and I wondered if I should take what I had written. I decided not to.

The only other subject of serious consideration was the array of pictures of Rassy and Bob in my cabin. I looked at them for a long time, then waved them goodbye and went out of the cabin, thinking, "Ain't this melodramatic!"

I did all that by the light of a flashlight, because all the lights in the ship—except in the wardroom—had been cut off to preserve the night vision of men who had to be constantly moving from below decks to the main deck. Passageways were illuminated dimly by red lights, which do not interfere with night vision. Still, when I groped my way up the companionway to the main deck, I couldn't see a thing. There was no moon, and the sky was black with clouds. I stopped for a few minutes against the bulkhead and waited until my night vision came. Soon, dimly, I could make out shadowy blobs of blacker black moving through the darkness around me. Just then—it was sometime between nine and ten—the engines stopped. We were coasting the last mile.

Men about me were talking in low voices. The *Henry's* crew had been at action stations since dusk. Everything was ready so that in an emergency, such as a torpedo hit, the boats could be lowered and the troops put aboard them with a minimum of delay.

Then a quiet voice sounded over the loudspeaking system, telling soldiers to move to the embarkation positions. In two or three minutes they were filing out of the companionway entrance. I couldn't see them, but I could hear them just a little. They moved with scarcely a sound over the cluttered decks to the positions from which they would be lowered into the water. Soon seamen were manhandling rubber boats onto the tops of the LCAs. All around the ship the same process was going on. It was nearly eleven o'clock. I could see the rubber boats congregating about fifty yards from the ship. Some of the LCAs were in the water, too, moving out to the positions at which towlines would be rigged. Standing there, I realized that I had a comfortable feeling about the operation, as if I fully understood what was happening—which I really didn't. But with the Americans moving fast across Brittany and towards Paris, this could be the final blow to the Germans in France. Could be. Dreams can come true.

As the night wore on, the sky became lighter and the low outline of Levant rose into sharp relief against the sky. Our escorting PT boat left us, on schedule, about fifteen hundred yards offshore. The LCAs moved on alone. Then the colonel asked Flynn to move up closer to an LCA towing rubber boats. We did, riding directly behind it for the next five hundred yards. Then the LCAs—us, and all about us—drew to a gentle halt. Lines to the tow-rafts were cast off and paddles picked up. The rubber boats filled with troops began assembling in lines of their own.

Our colonel, who would go with them, called in a low voice to an officer in one of the nearby rubber boats. At first, the officer didn't hear. The colonel's voice was next thing to a whisper, because we were only a thousand yards off the enemy shore and voices carry well over water by night. Complete silence had been imposed on the men, and was being maintained. The colonel didn't want to risk anything louder than a murmur.

Finally the officer heard. A soldier heard him, too.

"It's the colonel," he explained in a whisper to the man in front of him, and the other men caught on. The rubber boat came close. The colonel poised himself on the LCA's catwalk, then lowered himself, one leg at a time, into the rubber boat with his men. His staff officers—I think there were just two of them—got into the rubber boats, too. It must have been heartening for those soldiers, going in on a glorified inner tube to a rocky shore defended by enemy troops, to have their commanding officer suddenly come down and sit on a rubber thwart beside them. Perhaps things like that were what made the Special Service Force the fighting outfit it was. Into the line of rubber boats, they pulled away. Soon we could see only black shadows bobbing along on the water, and finally they disappeared altogether in the black outline of the shore as the landings began. We sat and waited, straining our eyes and ears, but hearing and seeing nothing. I haven't the slightest idea

(Above) Marriage, Glenboro, Manitoba, September 1, 1917. My father is on Mother's right, with Grandpa Paterson fourth from the left, Grandma Paterson sixth from the left. My beloved Grandma Young is at my mother's elbow, near Grandpa Young (with mustache). All others are Patersons and Youngs.

(Right) Brother Bob, three, me, five, and Dad, in Glenboro photographer's studio.

A few years earlier, Baby Scott, 1919.

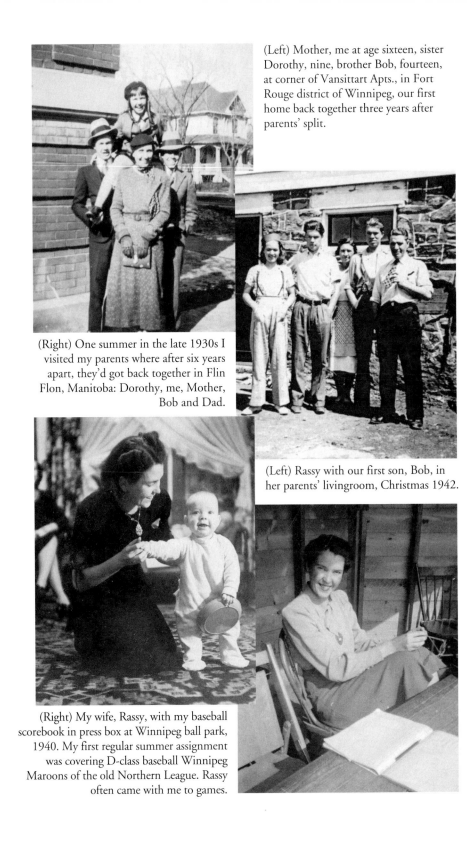

(Left) Mother, me at age sixteen, sister Dorothy, nine, brother Bob, fourteen, at corner of Vansittart Apts., in Fort Rouge district of Winnipeg, our first home back together three years after parents' split.

(Right) One summer in the late 1930s I visited my parents where after six years apart, they'd got back together in Flin Flon, Manitoba: Dorothy, me, Mother, Bob and Dad.

(Left) Rassy with our first son, Bob, in her parents' livingroom, Christmas 1942.

(Right) My wife, Rassy, with my baseball scorebook in press box at Winnipeg ball park, 1940. My first regular summer assignment was covering D-class baseball Winnipeg Maroons of the old Northern League. Rassy often came with me to games.

(Above) Granny Paterson and mother came to Toronto for Bob's christening, summer of 1942.

(Above) Bob, three, riding his tricycle around our living room in St. John's, Newfoundland, where I'd been posted as Chief Public Relations officer to Flag Officer, Newfoundland in the last few months of World War Two.

(Right) Son Neil, aged nine, 1954

(Left) From the bridge of HMCS *Prince Henry*, approaching Gibraltar en route to we know not where. It turned out to be the August 15 invasion of Southern France.

(Right) That's me, at left, having a few drinks with other officers in Santa Maria di Castellabate, August 1944, while we were doing workups for the Southern France invasion.

(Left) After Southern France I joined the 56th flotilla, Coastal Forces, in the Adriatic. This motor torpedo boat, commanded by Lieut. Cornelius Burke, had its stern blown off by a mine while on patrol north of Ancona, Italy.

(Right) Lieut. Corny Burke of Vancouver, my captain during 56th flotilla operations out of Vis island in the Dalmations, Marshal Tito's headquarters when his Partisans were terrorizing the Germans.

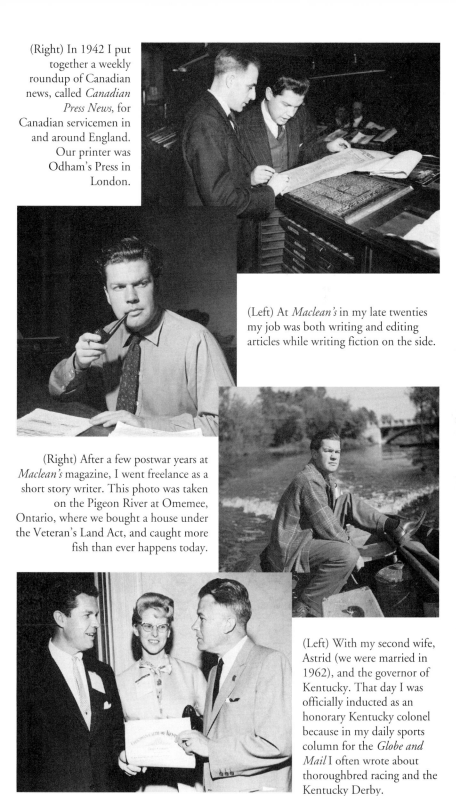

(Right) In 1942 I put together a weekly roundup of Canadian news, called *Canadian Press News*, for Canadian servicemen in and around England. Our printer was Odham's Press in London.

(Left) At *Maclean's* in my late twenties my job was both writing and editing articles while writing fiction on the side.

(Right) After a few postwar years at *Maclean's* magazine, I went freelance as a short story writer. This photo was taken on the Pigeon River at Omemee, Ontario, where we bought a house under the Veteran's Land Act, and caught more fish than ever happens today.

(Left) With my second wife, Astrid (we were married in 1962), and the governor of Kentucky. That day I was officially inducted as an honorary Kentucky colonel because in my daily sports column for the *Globe and Mail* I often wrote about thoroughbred racing and the Kentucky Derby.

With Premier Jean Lésage of Quebec and Premier John Robarts of Ontario. In 1963 I moved from sports to write of other things, including politics. This photo was taken at a seminar organized by The *Globe and Mail* and aimed at improving understanding between Quebec and the rest of Canada, which, as usual, didn't take.

Among books that Astrid and I produced was one called *O'Brien*, about the legendary early-Canadian railroad builder and contractor M.J. O'Brien. With us is M.J.'s grandson and then head of the Ottawa Football club, Barry O'Brien.

In 1969 I moved to the Toronto *Telegram* as general columnist and, later, sports editor.

At a book launch with sports writer Jim Coleman, Toronto Maple Leafs' coach Punch Imlach and *Globe* sports editor Jim Vipond.

(Right) In 1971 I was given the Eclipse Award for a column about thoroughbred racing. Here I am at the Waldorf in New York with winning rider Lafitte Pincay Jr. and winners in other Eclipse award categories.

(Left) For years as a news reporter and general columnist I was usually part of the *Globe*'s coverage of Royal tours. I think this was near Calgary, 1973.

In 1980 and 1985 in Moscow my wife, Margaret Hogan, and I spent a lot of time with Yuri Smirnov, who had translated three of my hockey books for Soviet publication. Yuri and his wife Katya Sipavina, an actress with the famous Moscow Puppet Theatre, became our favourite Moscow connections.

Nancy Southam, Jack McClelland, my brother and I at the Gzowski Golf Tournament in 1987, a major fund-raiser for the literacy programs of Frontier College.

(Right) I like the company — the great hockey people who are my fellow-members of the National Hockey League's Hockey Hall of Fame. We were all on hand for the opening of the Hall's new home in Toronto, 1992.

(Left) I never thought this would happen to me. My induction into The Hockey Hall of Fame, September, 1988.

Nor did I ever think that a school in Omemee, Ontario would be named after me. For the official opening in November 1993, my family from far and near turned out in force. Here are Neil and his wife Pegi, their children Ben and Amber, and Bob, outside the school the previous summer.

November 4, 1993, inside the school, Bob and Neil and I.

Margaret and I have travelled a lot together since we met in the mid 1970s, and after our marriage. This was in England in 1983 when I was researching my book *Neil and Me.*

Forty years earlier when I worked for CP and lived in London's Eaton Mews North through more than a few bombings, my favourite pub— my local — was The Antelope, near Sloane Square. It's still there.

(Left) The year *Neil and Me* was published, 1984, Amber Jean was born to Neil and Pegi, a lively sister for Ben.

One day in the summer of 1989 Neil and his family visited us at Omemee before his concert at the Canadian National Exhibition. Here we are on the front steps of the house where Rassy and Bob and Neil and I lived in Omemee: Ben, Neil's first son, Zeke, Amber, Neil and me.

(Left) My daughter Astrid, 1992, who writes and sings her own songs and sings and plays on some of Neil's albums. We were all together at her marriage to writer and musician Peter Jerumanis in California January 2, 1994, after which they headed for the snowbanks to spend their honeymoon at The Farm. Neil had ruled that anyone who marries into our family has to see Omemee.

(Right) My very supportive daughter Deirdre, who lived with me at The Farm for a while in the late 1970s when she was expecting her son David. She now lives with her husband and four children even farther north than Omemee — Iron Bridge.

My stepdaughters — Margaret's daughters — Maggie, Caitlin and Erin, have given me a great deal of happiness, and have taught me a lot about how close a family can be. They and Deirdre and Astrid are like sisters, and maybe that pleases me most of all. Caitlin's wedding, 1986.

(Right) Ever since I first landed in Omemee, some of my closest friends have been there, until death did some of us part. Dave Rea, former RCAF Bomber Command, and prisoner of war; Shirley Lowes, Helen Mansell, Christmas, 1986.

(Left) My good friends Edna Deyell, Berniece Hayes, Jay Hayes (with sunglasses)and Bob Hayes, 1986.

Longtime close friends Edna Deyell and Dave Rea are both gone now, but live on in a lot of memories of good times at Omemee.

One time around the middle 1980s Neil's Canadian tour included Winnipeg. My mother was well into her eighties and living in Flin Flon, Manitoba. "I'm going!" she said, and did. In a corridor Neil's archivist and photographer Joel Bernstein lined us up for this three generations' shot.

With Margaret, 1986.

how long it took, but every minute we expected to hear opening gunfire.

Finally, there was a burst of machine-gun fire over to the left. The assault troops carried as their main weapon an automatic carbine resembling the British and Canadian Sten gun. Its light rattle was easy to make out. Occasionally there was a burst of heavier stuff, which we could assume belonged to the Germans. Far to the left, we saw a burst of tracer.

Suddenly, Flynn turned and said excitedly: "What the hell's that?"

There had been a flash to seaward of us, and as we turned there was the low rumbling report of a heavy-gun salvo. Then we saw another flash, and in a few seconds the same low thunder of gunfire.

We couldn't tell what it was. By now the night was so light that we could make out the dim shapes of several ships out there, but the firing seemed to be farther out. From the flashes we could see, it seemed to be directed towards the shore. We thought some German warships might have attacked our force. As we faced seaward, ignoring the spasmodic fire ashore, suddenly the whole sea was lighted by a great flashing explosion. It was the first time I had seen a ship go up at sea. I thought it was in our armada because of the location. After that, the gunfire to seaward died down. We watched the flaming ship carefully for fifteen minutes, trying to catch a silhouette or something that would tell us what she had been. We saw nothing.

The shore fire had lessened. There was still a lot of machine-gun fire from the western end of the island, however, and the occasional crump of a mortar. That would make it tough for the troops ashore—mortars and heavy machine-guns against those light carbines. But from the area where the enemy's big guns were, our main objective, and the greatest single reason for our pre-landing operation, we heard nothing.

We were lying about five hundred yards offshore then, drifting in from west to east along the shore. Occasionally the stoker would start up the engines and we would move out a little. Then he would stop them, for silence, and we would drift in again.

There was still a glow to seaward where the explosion had been.

Jim turned wearily to the radio men for the dozenth time. "Hear anything about them getting those big guns?"

"Nothing at all, sir."

"Hear anything about anything?"

"Not a thing."

Flynn grunted and turned back to scanning the shoreline through his glasses. Everyone was tired. Flynn told some men to get some sleep. They huddled against the bulkhead under the catwalk. Two signalmen were hunched up in a sitting position, listening at their earphones to the crackle and rattle of nothingness. Some dozed. I was among them.

The radio man shook us all about dawn.

He put up his hand for silence, listening. Then, in the loud voice that people with earphones sometimes use, because they don't know how loud they're speaking, he said: "Main objective not taken, sir. They've just reported that from shore."

All night from the area of the main objective there had been almost no firing, after one long burst. Now it was getting lighter, and nobody was telling us what to do, or what to expect.

"Well, anyway," Flynn mused, looking at the shoreline getting plainer and plainer a few hundred yards away, "let's get the hell out of here!"

We pulled off to about twelve hundred yards, out of range of all but the biggest of automatic weapons (and, of course, big guns). We found most of the LCAs from the *Henry* were out at about the same distance. We waited there for about an hour, then we saw one craft go into a little cove. We moved in after it. The shoreline looked difficult. There were a few places where it rose in sheer cliffs, but it was mostly a shore of steep rocky outcroppings. All along the shoreline were scattered the rubber boats, which had just been left in the water when the troops scrambled ashore. Also, the water was dotted with hundreds of lifejackets. The troops had had them inflated while they were riding in the rubber boats, but had discarded them as soon as they touched down.

We listened. There was no firing at the eastern end of the island at all. Soon after, along a path of the cliff above came some soldiers with a line of German prisoners. One of the SSF officers said that they were mainly Poles and other nationals of occupied countries who had been pressed into the German army—or maybe they volunteered, for all any of us knew. But they weren't fighting men. Most of them, in Luftwaffe uniform, were ack-ack gunners.

Our sailors clambered ashore, and I was reminded of a saying in Italy that the Poles fight for hatred, the Gurkhas fight because they love fighting, and the Canadians fight for souvenirs. Everybody managed to pick up a helmet or a bayonet, or occasionally a German pistol. I didn't move off the shore, because I was too interested watching the German prisoners. Some were smoking, and each saluted briefly when given a cigarette. One soldier was acting the big shot, ordering them around. The rest of our troops—now that the enemy was in our hands—were polite, or ignored them. Some of the prisoners then volunteered to help unload the landing craft that by now were piling into the beach. When two LCMs came in with their great loads, the Germans formed a human chain to pass ammunition and stores ashore. I could detect very little feeling in their faces; they seemed simply apathetic.

Then we were told by radio what had happened to our main objective—the big guns on the eastern tip. They had fallen without a fight just after dawn—and the "big guns" that had shown unmistakably on dozens of reconnaissance photographs turned out to be an elaborate camouflage of two stove pipes, a log of wood and some painted cardboard!

The flip side was that despite the big guns turning out to be fakes, we'd been wrong about other matters—we had underestimated the strength of the Germans on the island. For every one who had laid down his arms in our vicinity, there were others at the western end of the island, all in good positions, with good heavy equipment. We were making no headway against them, and were losing men.

About nine o'clock one LCA was ready to go back to the *Henry*, and I was on it. When we climbed aboard, a big reception committee, almost every officer and seaman on the ship, fired questions at us. Finally I managed to get in one of my own—what ship got it last night? It had been a German corvette, and about fifty of the prisoners were aboard. They had been picked up by PT boats, all badly burned, and later transferred to the *Henry*. I walked into the wardroom. Over the operating table a surgeon was working rapidly, his arms bloody to the elbows. A dozen men were on stretchers on the floor, waiting their turn.

A big breakfast was waiting. I had bacon and eggs and toast and coffee. Fifteen feet away, an operation was finished and another man was moved to the operating table. He had a shattered leg, and it was going to have to be amputated.

I finished my breakfast and went to my cabin. "Hi," I said to the pictures of my wife and son, then I sat on my bunk, took off my shoes and slept.

When I wakened after a few hours' sleep, Jim Colyer, my cabin-mate, was standing by my bunk. The ship was moving, I imagined heading back to Corsica, which had been the plan.

"Thought I should wake you," Colyer said. "I know you want to write a lot before we land, so you can get it off. There's just been a funeral. One of the Germans, poor bastard. He was burned all to hell."

"How long have we been moving?"

"Since one o'clock. Get in to Corsica tomorrow morning."

"What then?"

"Don't know for sure, but the buzz is that we'll be picking up some French troops and bringing them back to occupy Levant after the SSF has taken it—if they ever do. They're still trying."

"Have you heard anything about the landings on the mainland?"

"They're said to be going well. Hardly any opposition."

"Good."

Colyer lit a cigarette.

"We got rid of those prisoners today—all the ones who weren't burned too badly. A PT boat took them away somewhere—probably to a prisoner-of-war place. They had one bastard of an officer with them. Gave the Nazi salute when he stepped aboard the PT boat."

"What else is going on?"

"Well, the doctors are still working like hell. Not one of them has stopped since early this morning, except for a cup of coffee or a sandwich. The wardroom is full of wounded, and so is the sick bay. The forward army mess decks are full of burned Germans. There's one American in the wardroom who's going to die, I think. They've given him several transfusions and they've been operating on him for an hour now. How about coming up for some tea? It's about time, you know."

"Okay," I said. I hopped down from my bunk and pulled on my shoes. I doused my face with cold water, which someone had left in the basin, thoughtfully enough, because at sea the fresh water is only on about four times a day, and this wasn't one of them. I followed Colyer down the corridor towards the wardroom and companionway.

"Jesus," he said in a low voice when we reached the top. "They're still operating on that guy."

I could see the man on the table, but not his face—just the top of his head. The American army surgeon, middle-aged, worked in shorts and an undershirt and with a steward standing behind him blotting the perspiration from his back. He was working over the man's abdomen.

"He got it on the western end of the island," Colyer said. "There were a bunch of them walking along a road. He's a sergeant in the medical corps. The Jerries opened up on this road with mortar fire, and they scattered to both ditches. They got by that first burst all right, and the sergeant was digging a foxhole for the captain when another stick of them came along and got him. A piece of shrapnel entered his abdomen just inside of his hip, cut through his intestines, stomach and lungs."

As we sat down to tea, the surgeon straightened and stood for long seconds looking down at the man he'd been working on. He wiped his hands and arms on a towel. Then he sloshed his hands in water and wiped them some more. All the time, he never took his eyes from his patient, until medical assistants gently lifted the man to a stretcher and placed him on the deck, over near a porthole. Then the surgeon walked slowly over to our table and sat down for a cup of coffee.

He was completely still for a minute. Then he suddenly seemed to waken. He took up his cup, gulped down the hot coffee, and pushed back his chair. He walked back over to the operating table, looked at the next case, an American sergeant, for a few seconds, then called for his instruments and went back to work.

I went out on deck. The Mediterranean sun, which shone all summer on blood, death, tears, groans of wounded, laughter, cheers, bravery, cowardice and joy, was nearing the horizon in a cloudless sky. Most of the combined operations men were asleep. There had been no casualties among our seamen. I looked in at the darkroom and found Gib Milne and Sully, the leading seaman photographer on the ship, hard at work. Gib came out on deck, sweat dripping from him.

"It's a hundred and thirty in there," he said. "What a place for a darkroom—right next to the stack!"

I went back to my cabin and wrote down everything I had on the landings. At dusk I went to dinner. Colyer came up as I was standing with Gib watching the doctors work on another wounded man.

"That American sergeant he was working on died," he said. "Anybody who passed him, he would say: 'Come over and sit down and talk, bud.' He died at sunset."

They buried the American about an hour later, just before the light failed. The padre spoke the service over him as he lay, swathed in an American flag, on a stretcher at the embarkation ramp from which I had stepped into Flynn's LCA about twenty hours before. They were many of us there, the American admiral, our captain and all the American officers who were left on board. Most of the Canadian officers were there, too, and in a little knot apart stood soldiers who had been wounded only slightly and were able to attend the service.

Some who had been with the sergeant were telling others about what happened after he was hit. After the firing died down, he had started back to the beaches with another couple of men. He had been given emergency first aid on the spot, and he was holding himself together. He walked almost half a mile before he turned to one of the others and asked in a mild voice if the other would mind if he put his hand on his shoulder, because it was hard walking. Then they had met one of the two jeeps we had put ashore, and he had piled into the back of that jeep and over the bumpy, rocky road, which must have meant excruciating pain for him. He had been taken to the beaches where a landing craft waited to take him off.

The padre finished his intonations, and the seamen standing by the flag-draped body on the stretcher stepped forward. They lifted the stretcher and tipped it slowly until the body slipped away. Thoughtful and intent on the service, none of us were prepared for the splash, the supreme finality of a burial at sea. Then, out over the silent waters rang three volleys from the rifles of the firing party, and the bugler's last post.

I went to the forward army mess decks, where the burned German prisoners were. They had been placed on the bunks used normally by troops we carried, the bare springs relieved only by a single rough army blanket. There were more than thirty of the Germans on the bunks. A surgeon was going among them, looking at their burns and their bandages. Over on two dining tables were several of the men with bad burns, being helped, if help was possible.

The sick bay was full, too, and the cases there needed constant attention. The bulk of the work on those horribly burned Germans was done by able seamen, ordinary seamen, stokers, cooks and stewards who served their regular watches and then came down to the army mess decks. There was no call sent out for volunteers; they just came.

An able seaman who had stood at action stations all the previous night, and couldn't have had any more than a couple of hours' sleep in the last forty, was working with a tiny pair of scissors, cutting dead strips of scorched skin from one German's hands. At another bunk, a stoker who spoke German was sitting by one of the worst burn cases, talking to him about things other than war, trying to cheer him up. In a few minutes, the German had fallen asleep and the stoker was just sitting there, thinking. When I left, our men were still toiling over the Germans, treating with extreme gentleness the men who had been sent out to kill them twenty-four hours before.

12

The New
Gunner

THE NEXT MORNING when we sailed into Ajaccio harbour, *Prince David* was lying at anchor. Doug How from CP had been on her for the landings. I wondered if he had got his copy away to Rome and if so, how? No news transmission facilities of any kind, telephone, telegraph or radio, existed for correspondents this side of the censor's office at Allied Force Headquarters in Rome. Everyone was itching to be first with the eyewitness accounts. Some had stayed on after handing me their stories on the landings. Homer Bigart of the New York *Herald Tribune* had come along in person to stand guard against anyone beating his stuff to Rome. The other two landing from *Henry* were Ben Malkin and Sgt. Howard Rutsey of the Canadian Forces newspaper, *Maple Leaf.*

It was nine, the sun well up, before we finally had our gangway down and five of us—Bigart, Malkin, Rutsey, Gib Milne and me—piled ashore. My information was that a Royal Navy lieutenant, Pochin Johnson, would arrange transport for our stories to Rome. We sought him out and found the transport situation not good. A plane was to leave later that day for Bastia, across the island, but it did not connect with the noon Rome plane. Pochin Johnson had a jeep, though, and he offered to drive across to Bastia to catch the Rome plane. Malkin, Rutsey and Doug How gave me their stories, and Gib gave me some pictures, so I had quite a parcel. Homer had decided to come along in the jeep. The others would follow us as soon as possible to Bastia and then fly to Rome.

Pochin Johnson drove like a wild man, trying to catch the noon plane. In the mountains, along narrow, rough roads dropping off hundreds of feet to sheer cliffs into the valleys below, we kept meeting convoys coming the other way, French soldiers in American uniforms, rolling towards Ajaccio to embark for their homeland. A couple of times we were forced to brake hard and crowd against a cliff or—more alarmingly—against the outer railing to let these big vehicles by.

Inland Corsica is a beautiful country of castles perched on hilltops, towns hung by some strange magic on the sides of steep hills, and vineyards. Italian prisoners were working on the roads around us, being driven hard. The French had no pity for the Italians, remembering that the Italians had had no pity for France in June 1940. Italians stood morosely beside rock piles swinging big hammers, crushing stone to be used in repairing roads.

As time wore on it became apparent that we weren't going to catch the noon plane to Rome. I wanted to stop for lunch. Bigart held out against it. He contended we could eat when we got to Bastia and could hunt for air transport. He was outvoted. We stopped at a small roadside bistro and had good wine and a little conversation with the excited French woman within. She'd had the radio on, she said, every minute since the first announcement that southern France had been invaded. She asked us for news, but we had little. She probably knew more about it than we did.

About two in the afternoon, after a four-hour trip of bucking big convoys going both ways, we arrived in Bastia to find that there was another plane going out that evening. It would be in Rome by eight o'clock. I booked a place on it, just in case we were still around later in the day. Then Bigart and I worked out a plan.

He had U.S. connections and was counting on them. I was counting more on hitching a ride. But two of us hunting together would be a waste of manpower so we left our parcel of news stories and photos at the desk of an officers' club and split up. First one to get a ride to Rome would pick up the parcel and take off. I sat around the airport for hours. Then in came a Mitchell bomber, going on to Rome almost immediately. I hailed a jeep, picked up the precious parcel, was shoehorned into where the tail gunner usually sat, and we took off.

An army jeep was waiting at the Rome airport. I climbed in with my parcel and rolled through the twilight into beautiful Rome for the first time.

As I was the first to return who actually had been ashore in any of the assault territory, I got quite a bit of attention. A few men had seen the invasion from bombardment ships, but otherwise nobody was back. I handed a couple of my stories to the Canadian Press and the United Press, delivered all the others to the censor, then found a services transit hotel and went to sleep.

In the next couple of days I cleaned up more stories, made a broadcast for the CBC and another for the BBC, and gave a press conference to about fifty correspondents at Allied Force press headquarters. The Canadian Navy got a major play in the world's press and radio for those first two days, not because our two ships there had been any great force but because I was the only person the backline correspondents could quote.

Then I settled down to enjoy Rome. There didn't seem to be much point in going back aboard the *Prince Henry* for a while to be a passenger while the ship ferried troops between Corsica and France, so I planned to rejoin her when she returned to Naples ten days later. Gib arrived in Rome the day after me with the first invasion photos to go by wirephoto to Britain and North America. We and our superiors were happy.

Then there was an angry hitch. Bigart had returned to Rome and found that my story had got the big first-from-the-invasion-beach play in New York. He sought me out at AFHQ and accused me of handing my story in first so that I would get all the first-eyewitness accolades. This angered me. I said I had put his story near the top of the pile, above mine. He didn't believe me. Then I remembered that when I'd handed all the stories in, they had been timed and numbered in the order that the censor took them off the pile. We marched through AFHQ to the censor's office and checked. Sure enough, Homer's story had been numbered ahead of mine, but delayed slightly because it required censor cuts. Mine moved faster, the censor said, because I seemed to understand security elements better than some others. As far as I can recall, Bigart didn't speak to me after that.

For my first days in Rome, I went around like a farm boy seeing his first skyscrapers. Nobody could be prepared for it, at first, after sinkholes like Naples and farther south. Rome had great broad streets and avenues, lined with trees, and—as a soldier once put it, succinctly—all the women wore shoes!

The Romans had seen very little of the war and had had no bombing except a few raids on rail junctions in the outskirts. Also, the Germans had been very careful with the city. They had wanted to make it a showplace for the way their troops could act in foreign countries, so they had imposed an eight-thirty curfew on their soldiers and ordered that none of them were to associate with Roman women. As a result, the reaction was terrific when the Allies first came. It was "liberation" to the nth degree. The overworked term *Roman holiday* applied in full. Allied soldiers went for the Roman women in a big way, and vice versa. One good hotel in Rome in the first days of liberation had doctors standing near the door to examine women entering, a prophylactic centre a little farther along the foyer, and no other restrictions.

When it seemed time to rejoin the *Henry* in Naples, I went straight to Santa Lucia jetty, bummed a ride out to the *Henry* on an American landing craft, and caught her just as she had hauled up her anchor and was preparing to leave. She wasn't going far—just down the coast about fifteen miles to Castellamare to have her boilers cleaned—a twenty-one day job. We moved to the *Prince David* in Naples until we got new orders—to hunt down a Royal Navy Coastal Forces flotilla of D-class torpedo boats and gun boats known as dogboats which had several Canadian officers and therefore was in our line of work. We hunted for these ships for a week, up and down the Adriatic coast, and finally found them in Ancona.

Two days later, in a flat calm, we made ready to leave Ancona for Vis Island in the Dalmatians, where the flotilla would be based, backing up Tito's Yugoslav Partisans. Assigned to a boat commanded by Lieut. Cornelius (Corny) Burke of Vancouver, we cruised eastward at about seventeen knots. Vis Island had been held by the Partisans all through the war. I had written about them often from London, when the world was in the process of finding out that the more-publicized Serb leader, Gen. Draja Mikhailovich, was not averse to dealing with the Germans and Italians and that the real fighting was being done by a far greater force led by a veteran of the International Brigade in the Spanish war, Marshal Tito. Tito had fought pretty well his own war for two years before the Allies started giving him full-scale aid, but it was only in 1944 that the Yugoslav government in London finally disowned Mikhailovich and his Chetniks and admitted Tito was the man doing the work. The Allied prejudice against Tito originally was his close connection with the Russians. All men, women and children who fought for Tito wore the Russian Red Star on their forage caps. Their fantastic deeds against the Germans had pinned down almost as many Fascist troops in Yugoslavia as the Allied armies in Italy and Sicily had been able to engage. Most of the Partisan fighting was with small arms, until Tito started to get real Allied aid.

We tied up that night alongside the jetty in a little town called Komiza, had a couple of drinks, played some blackjack and went to bed. Another flotilla, berthed there, was out that night. All through the night, along the jetty I could hear the voices of men and women and the quiet plodding of donkeys carrying their loads past our boat to old three-masted schooners that slipped out at night for other islands, carrying supplies and fighting units of men and women. I lay in my bunk listening to the subdued clink of rifle and bayonet and the low voices of fighters I couldn't see. This fight of the Partisans seemed something fundamental, more like fighting with fists. In a few hours, maybe still in the dark, they'd be stepping ashore on an island held by the Germans, to carry on with the unequal battle they had waged for years.

I was even more impressed in the morning. During the night the other coastal forces flotilla based on Vis had sunk three schooners filled with German troops. This had happened off the island of Brac, only a few miles from the Yugoslav mainland. The sunk schooners had carried either enemy reinforcements or troops being evacuated. I heard someone say that we probably would be going back to the same place that night to finish the job.

I went ashore with Corny Burke after breakfast to report my presence to the port's senior naval officer, headquartered about a hundred yards from our berth. Partisan soldiers guarded the jetty. Studying them, I thought at the time what a change from the Italians! Not that the Partisans were any bigger, built any better, better dressed or better armed. If anything, the only difference must have been that they were better armed spiritually. They had something in them that made their faces fighting faces, their walk a fighting walk. There were boys of seventeen, even some of fifteen or twelve, and men of fifty-five. Everyone I saw wore a uniform. And they all looked like fighters. There was a singleness of purpose about them that made a pleasant contrast to the discouraged-looking Italians, people who had been beaten, not liberated, no matter how many words of propaganda were written to the contrary. These Partisans never could be beaten, only killed. Without talking to any of them, because I didn't know their language, I respected the Partisans as much as I ever have respected anybody. I didn't respect the Italians, with their protestations of friendship and excuses that they hadn't wanted war with us, but now were fully on our side. And I felt that although the Partisans liked us now because their sole aim in life was to kill Germans, and we had shown, fighting beside them, that we could kill quite a few, too, they would fight just as hard against anyone who tried to tell them how to run their country. (Fifty years later, not much has changed except that the result was tragedy for the country.)

When we got to the operations room, we were told that we would indeed go out that night to Brac to patrol the short shore area the Germans still held, and make sure none were evacuated.

About half an hour before sailing time for my first operation with Corny, he and Steve Rendell and I went up to see Lieutenant-Commander Giles, R.N. commander of Coastal Forces working with Tito out of Vis. Giles pointed out to us on the map the large Yugoslav island of Brac, about three miles from the mainland, where there were heavy German shore batteries.

"The Germans right now are hemmed in there," he said, tapping the island's south tip. "We have been landing artillery about midway up the seaward side of the island for the last few days and now have quite a weight of stuff forcing the Jerries back. We also have been landing Partisans there for some time, and they are doing much of the fighting.

"Now, what I think you should do" – he turned to Corny – "is to go down and lie off the fighting area and keep a lookout for anything trying to evacuate soldiers to the mainland. It was here"—he pointed to a cove in the German-occupied territory—"that we hid out to catch three German schooners last night. You might do the same."

"How about a turn up the other side of the island?" Corny asked.

Giles looked doubtful. "Use your discretion on that. That would mean you would have to pass through this narrow channel between the island and the mainland, within easy range of the shore batteries. However, they may be trying to evacuate from that side, so it might be a good idea to go around there.

"Now, there will be a naval officer on Brac tonight with a portable radio set, so he will have our latest information. I'll put two men on your boat with a receiver, and they will try to get in touch with him. He just may possibly know of some shipping lying in the harbours around the hostile part of the island, and if he does he can tell you about it."

Ten minutes later we rounded the point out of Komiza harbour at about eighteen knots, Corny's boat leading and Steve's about five or six lengths back. Dogboats are a lovely sight at sea, with their bow-waves curling up in thin sheets of spray. The Adriatic close to sundown was a deep blue. We stood on the bridge and kept a watch and talked like men on a bus. Corny turned from a scan around the horizon to remark that the BBC that day said the Siegfried line had been cracked.

"Say," he asked, "just what constitutes an official crack, like that one in the Siegfried line?"

I recalled that in a censorship conference in Rome a couple of weeks earlier a crack in an enemy line had been defined as definite progress, but something that could be mended without too much trouble.

"Okay," said Corny, "then what is a pierce?"

I didn't know that one, but I said I thought it was about one degree better than a crack, which is like saying something is eleven-tenths of nothing at all.

"It all sounds very complicated to me," Rover Reynolds said. Being a Rover Scout is a high accomplishment, and Rover was only twenty. Corny said, "Let's wait until the damn line is broken. We know what broken means, anyway. War is a very technical matter." He looked around to make sure there was no other shipping in the vicinity and that we were clear of the island. "Let's test the guns."

He turned to me. "You, Sub-Lieutenant Young," he said, "are the new port Vickers gunner on His Majesty's MGB 658."

I'm sure I smiled. I was pleased. I checked the twin Vickers mounted on either side of the bridge. Both were loaded and ready for action, so I closed up to the port position, found out how the action and traverse worked, cocked them and got ready. As Ordinary Seaman Young, back in Cornwallis, I knew that gun.

"Guns," said Corny to Rover, "test your guns." Corny called Rover Guns when it was in connection with gunnery, and Number One otherwise. He also called any officer Flags if it was a question about communications, Scratch if it was about money, Captain's Sec if it was about correspondence, Pilot when it concerned navigation and other odd names when it was about playing checkers. Those are nicknames used for the officers filling those jobs on big ships, and although Corny had only two regular officers, he managed to work them all in at one time or another.

Rover had the loud-hailer system tested by then, and all the guns on the ship were manned—six-pounder aft, Bofors ahead of that, single Oerlikons at each side of the bridge, under the twin Vickers, and a twin Oerlikon forward. We all reported ready.

Rover gave the testing instructions—one-round test for the six-pounder, five for the Bofors, and bursts at will for the Oerlikons and Vickerses. At the order "Fire!" we all banged away, doubtless scaring hell out of any passing ducks, drakes or fish. Not far away, Steve's boat was testing, too. Because he carried torpedo tubes and didn't have quite the armament we did, his guns were loaded with star shells. The drill, should we go into action that night, would be that he would fire the star shells to illuminate the target and we would blaze away. Of course, for a big target he'd fire torpedoes.

Everything tested well, and we kept a close watch on the islands around us as we went by. All were held by Partisans, but it was likely we would be challenged as we went along. The Partisan challenge was to fire one rifle shot nearby, the job aboard being to figure out where the shot came from and give the recognition signal for the night. For about the first hour, or a little more, we would be passing through waters that had been friendly at last report. After about seven-thirty, we would be in waters where any shipping definitely would be hostile. We weren't worrying much about air attack, because the Germans were far too busy elsewhere to be doing anything in that line in Yugoslavia. This was a different kind of war. Already I liked it a lot better than a landing.

It was getting dark when we passed along Brac Island about eight o'clock. Suddenly there was a burst of tracer and some rifle and machine-gun fire well ahead of us, on the tip of the island.

"There's the war," Corny said happily. "Let's move in."

Darkness closed in fast. By the time we got to the firing area about eight-thirty the night was pretty black. There would be no moon, so we had a slight edge. At our operational conference we'd been told that if he got a chance the naval officer ashore would douse gasoline around and start a brush fire so we would have a better chance of silhouetting any passing shipping against the island. There was a fire burning on the tip of the island, too, but we didn't think it had been lit by the naval officer. It wasn't where we'd been told he'd be, and it was on the side of the island facing the mainland, where we were pretty sure our forces weren't.

Corny decided we should cruise around the end of the island and investigate the fires. We couldn't see them, but the glow was plain over the ridge topping the island. We were about a thousand yards offshore by this time, easing along at about twelve knots, when suddenly a bright light began flashing on the shoreward side. It was so low on the water, and so bright, that it could have been from a ship. Corny ordered a change of course to investigate. We had been at action stations for about an hour then.

We chased towards the light at good speed for about half a mile. The flashing seemed no closer, so we circled. Corny finally decided it was someone on the mainland shore signalling to Germans on the island. The stuff was coded, so we couldn't read it. Corny ordered a return to the original plan—to go around the tip of the island and investigate the fires.

I noticed then how clearly we were illuminated by the blazes ashore. There were three fires, all in the island's low brush. We could see every outline of Steve's boat, and he apparently could see ours. His voice came in over the inter-boat phone: "Corny, Corny, this is Steve, this is Steve. May I suggest that we look like sitting ducks against that fire? Over."

Corny called down the voice-pipe to the radio operator: "Make to Steve: Concur." But he didn't change his instructions.

We cruised slowly past the fires, but couldn't see anything moving or any fighting going on. There were occasional flashes of guns on the mainland—German coastal batteries firing over our heads in support of their forces on the island. Apparently they still hadn't seen us.

"Scott," Corny said. "From now on scan the mainland coast and try to catch one of those gun flashes and get a bearing on it." The object was to chart that gun position so we would know where it was next time any of us went by. I watched. No good. The gunners had stopped firing.

When we got away from the light of the fires and felt much less naked, Corny decided that we would buzz along to the German-held harbour town and see what we could see. That was precisely nothing. There was very little firing that we could see or hear. Corny then told Steve by loud-hailer that we would go closer. I was watching the shore through my glasses. Nothing. . . Then suddenly I took my glasses away, amazed. Almost fifty yards away was a jetty! Night light is deceptive, and we had come in very close and everyone saw it at the same time. Had Corny intended to go in that close? Maybe or maybe not. Did I yell? I don't

remember. Rover did. Corny said coolly to the helmsman, "Port thirty."
That's a sharp turn. We got out of there.

Soon after, we started to think about one (or more) of us going below
to get a little sleep. "This damn war seems almost over," murmured
Corny, scanning the coastline. "I think we'll go in and lie in a little cove,
up a little farther, and keep an eye on things." He told Steve. We started
up the coast. Close to the cove, Steve's voice came over the phone: "Corny,
this is Steve. Isn't this the same place where the little man was before?"

By "little man" he meant whoever had fired a random twenty-mil-
limetre tracer burst at us earlier. Corny didn't think it was the place, and
told Steve so. Then he found where he wanted to stop, and Steve came in
again: "May I reiterate that I think this is the place we were fired on
before." Corny still didn't think so, so he ordered the boat to stop, and
Steve's did likewise. We all looked around. Nothing. Then in about two
minutes there was a whine and the solid *phlopp!* a bullet makes when it hits
the water. We moved, fast. Rover's laugh could be heard in the black
when we were out of range.

"Steve'll be calling you up and saying, 'I told you so,'" he said to
Corny.

Corny just grinned. But Steve didn't call. I guess he figured his per-
spicacity already had been brought to our attention.

But there still was no shipping, and that was our business, to sink
ships. Corny sent the crew back to cruising stations, which meant about
half of them could snatch some shuteye. I went below and stretched out
on the wardroom settee. Other officers followed me in relays. I was called
about four o'clock by Rover, who told me the land war had started again.
I went up to see. We were lying directly off the little cove and harbour
now. Ashore a battle was certainly going on—mortars, lots of twenty-mil-
limetre stuff, heavy machine-guns, rifles stuttering away in the predawn
black. Just before dawn—so we would be away before the shore batteries
caught on to us—we pulled out.

Our seven-o'clock entry into harbour impressed me. Here we were,
two small wooden boats involved in an interesting war being waged practically in secret. We were putting into a tiny harbour filled with nothing
but Yugoslavs, a few old landing craft and another couple of boats like
ours. We had been out all night. But as we sailed in, up on the fo'c's'le
and back on the quarterdeck, our duty watch lined up in proper uniforms,

their battle dress and sweaters laid away again, and stood at attention while we entered harbour. As we neared the jetty, at a sharp order they turned smartly left, dismissed, and doubled to stations for coming alongside. The British Navy is the British Navy is the British Navy, even when it's part Canadian.

≈

I was in two more operations of note before I patted my twin Vickers farewell for the last time. One was a night patrol in Sulyet Channel, between Sulyet Island and Split on the Yugoslav mainland. In that one we sank three German lighters during an action that attracted the attention of heavy shore batteries at Split. Those German batterymen, apparently not wishing to fire because they did not know what had happened to their own ships there, kept signalling frantically to ask what was going on. They got no reply until Corny took over our signal lamp and, impersonating the silent Germans ashore, sent a signal that meant an answer was coming up. The German battery waited for it and from Corny then came the slow, deliberate message, "HEIL CHURCHILL!"

Then we got out of there.

The next morning Corny left for Ancona. A few days later, patrols either suspended or aborted because of the heavy winds of the Adriatic autumn storms, most of the boats returned to Italy. The best fighting season for dogboats was just about over, as was my time there. The war in Europe was going so well that the end seemed no more than months away. It was then I began thinking about the Pacific war.

I wanted to go, in one way, because I wanted to see the end of the war, and it would end in the Pacific. In another way, I didn't want to go—at least not before I had spent a month or two at home with my family. In short, my hopes and fears were like those of any other serviceman in the European theatre of operations—a desire to see the thing through, coupled with a strong and natural hope that history could pause long enough to let us have a few home-cooked meals, make a few snowmen with our children, and hold hands in the movies with our wives before we left again.

Like all other servicemen, too, I knew the decision wouldn't be mine. We would just go on about our business, and eventually we would be told.

13

Going Home Sick:
1945

⮑

I GOT BACK TO CANADA late that year by way of Ancona, Rome, Naples, Taranto, Piraeus (the port of Athens), Athens itself and finally Naples once again. Along the way—I'm not sure exactly when—I realized that I had a problem. Two problems, really. One was that now I was finally getting mail from home, Rassy's newsy offbeat letters filled my head with memories of happy love and explicit sex. Running them through my head didn't help me sleep. I had spent a lot of time when I was in London with CP thinking up ways to get us together again, but in my wildest dreams I couldn't even imagine how I could do the same from Italy.

I had one other concern. Picking up laundry that I had left here and there when I first travelled through Italy to Yugoslavia, I found that all my clothes were too big. I hadn't paid much attention to what I was eating on the dogboats, but I had no appetite for navy-issue tinned sausages and tinned bacon, dried eggs, dehydrated potatoes and dried peas so close to being indestructible that, when used as poker chips and accidentally dropped on the deck and walked on for weeks, they would suffer not a scratch. Peas that we cooked and ate after soaking them a couple of days were only marginally more scratchable. And of course, cooking on the dogboats was tricky—even with a lid and in light seas, a pot or pan had to be held on the stove burner by hand so it wouldn't upset. One day I wandered into a hotel in Rome that had a Turkish bath. When I stepped on scales there to weigh myself I couldn't believe it. At Cornwallis, as a twenty-six-year-old physically fit ordinary seaman, with hardly an ounce of fat on me, I had weighed 184 pounds. The scales in Rome assured me that I weighed 156. I dove into the cold water tub wondering what the hell?

A few days later at the urging of some other Canadian servicemen and correspondents I checked in to a Canadian Army hospital in Rome. One of the nurses, whom I'd known in England when I was with CP, gave me hell for not coming around sooner—"You've probably been drinking too much and chasing these Italian tarts, damn you! Canadian nurses like company, too, you know, with someone who knows what the hell we're talking about, and where Dauphin is, for God's sake! Or even Manitoba!" She was from Dauphin.

I was in hospital for only a few days. Finally, I couldn't stand being there among so many wound cases. So I checked myself out and travelled to Naples, where I reported to Capt. Taprell Dorling, who as far as I knew was still my commanding officer. Over a drink or two, this kindly man told me that *Prince Henry* had been assigned elsewhere. Meanwhile, I was to join HMCS *Prince David* in Taranto and sail in her to Greece carrying that country's former prime minister, George Papandreou, who had been in Britain since the fall of Greece in 1941 but now was to resume his prime ministerial duties. Two weeks later I was back in Naples, feeling sicker and sicker and still losing weight. Taprell Dorling thought I should go to hospital for a full checkup and after that apply for a convalescent leave back in Canada.

I had done nothing in that direction a day or two later when Taprell called me, in a hurry. A U.S. troopship now loading with medical and psychiatric cases was about to leave Naples for New York. If I could wangle the right kind of travel authority fast, maybe I could take leave at home in Canada.

"What kind of authority?"

"First, from the Americans, then I'll see what I can do with your people." I don't know what he did, but it must have involved cutting corners because my bosses seemed to know very little about what was happening except that when *Monticello* sailed I was on it.

Fifteen days later I was in New York having a huge spaghetti dinner with some CP staffers, then boarded a train that would stop in Niagara Falls. The navy or CP had told Rassy that I was on my way, and she met me there for a joyful reunion.

As I recall, perhaps faultily, from there I reported to a navy doctor at HMCS *York* in Toronto, who confirmed that I looked like the ghost of

Christmas past but thought spending Christmas and New Year's with family and in-laws in Manitoba might help. "After that you'll get a full examination in Ottawa," he told me.

I talked by phone to Mother and sister Dorothy in Flin Flon. They hadn't heard from Dad for a year or so. However, my Cypress River cousins told me by phone that Dad was working in a drugstore in western Manitoba, and if we visited Cypress River, he'd come to see us.

When we got to Cypress River, my cousins told me the bare bones of what had happened: "Your dad and your mother fought a lot, and a year or so ago he decided to take a holiday from his job there and from your mother, and once he got here he just didn't go back."

When Dad arrived a day later, we wound up out in the barn, talking, and I got a fuller account. In Flin Flon he'd thought he was having a breakdown, he told me. "I didn't know what to do. I couldn't stand all the fighting. When I got to Winnipeg I got a westbound bus, and it let me off at Landseer in the middle of the night and I set out to walk over here."

That walk of five or six miles on country roads in the dark took him back through many memories to the old home farm where he was born. The big house had burned more than a dozen years before, and had been replaced by a frame structure mainly consisting of two wooden granaries fitted together with an upstairs added. After Grandpa Young died, my grandma had lived there with her oldest son, my uncle Herb, who was farming the home place with his wife, Aunt Beatrice. It was late when Dad got there, and no lights were showing. The entrance was a screen door, not locked. He thought he would let himself in quietly, rather than wake the household. He opened the door and had just stepped inside when he heard a low voice from upstairs, the voice of his mother, whom he hadn't seen for years and who didn't know he was coming. But over the years she hadn't forgotten his step.

"Is that you, Percy?" she called.

First he helped around the farm, then looked for a job and found one in a drugstore farther west, and didn't go back to Flin Flon. Now, years later, I had found him again.

When the holidays were over, Rassy and Bob stayed in Winnipeg briefly. I returned to Toronto, and was sent directly to hospital in Ottawa where I spent the next few weeks being tested for what ailed me, which took a while. The tests revealed no identifiable medical problem, and in the end I was pronounced fit to return to duty, although with a cautionary recommendation to my superiors that until further notice I was not to be posted to an active war zone.

As I recovered over the next few weeks, with Rassy and Bob in the Lord Elgin Hotel in Ottawa, a job opened up in the information branch in St. John's, Newfoundland, as assistant to Clyde Gilmour, RCNVR (SB) lieutenant and chief public relations officer (CPRO) to the Flag Officer Newfoundland. Which is where in February 1945 Rassy and Bob and I rented an apartment in a tall old frame building on Gower Street, overlooking the harbour. Gales sweeping down the harbour past Signal Hill blew in through the cracks between the building's outer boards, making the living room linoleum pitch and roll like ocean waves. Bob, who had brought along his tricycle, pedalled up and down to flatten each linoleum bump.

I liked Newfoundland a lot, and still do; an exotic place, to me, fish and brewis, cod tongues, flipper pie, the lethal rum called Screech (before liquor boards tamed it). I also liked my easy working life, getting home at night, good food and drink. My duties were to cover anything I could find in the harbour or in corvettes or minesweepers that I visited by harbour craft, or that Lieutenant Gilmour, as precise about everything then as he was later in his popular CBC programs, wished me to do. I wrote local-interest stories for smaller newspapers, national-interest stories for the wire services, a few for magazines. Meanwhile, convoy escort duty in the Battle of the Atlantic wore down towards the end.

I was soon promoted to lieutenant (a raise in pay from $5 to $6 a day) and appointed to succeed Gilmour as CPRO-Newfoundland. After VE Day, one of my more interesting jobs, the first one of the peace, was to write about the surrender in Newfoundland of German submarine U190, one of many surfacing in the western Atlantic. That particular peril at sea was no more.

A few weeks after VE Day, having volunteered for service in the Pacific War, I was given what was called Pacific leave—several weeks in Canada until it was time to head for duty in the Pacific. I sailed to Quebec in a destroyer carrying others bound for Pacific leave. Rassy and Bob met me in Toronto. We were there, staying with friends, when the bomb was dropped at Hiroshima. A few days later a telegram from Ottawa told me that I was on leave until further notice, in effect ending my navy career.

One of my last contacts with the navy was an encounter with Bert Howard, civilian head of the information branch. More than a year earlier I had extracted from him the promise that my work in naval information would not tie me to a desk, that I'd always be posted where the action was. Sometimes I had wished I hadn't been so firm on that point.

"I guess I did my part, Scott," he said.

I 4

A New Beginning:
1945-1948

WHEN THE NAVY BADE ME FAREWELL, I badly needed a job. Rassy was pregnant, and we needed a place to live. But since I was still technically in the navy until my final discharge arrived, I couldn't take a full-time job. And then a temporary one came up.

At CP before my posting overseas, I'd written a lot about sports, mostly rewrite desk stuff but also some live coverage of baseball, hockey, golf and curling, especially curling, where my Manitoba curling-town background gave me an edge over reporters who didn't know what the game was about. When I covered the 1941 Canadian Curling Championship, then known as the Macdonald Brier, or simply the Brier, for me the experience was something like a baseball nut covering his first World Series. In those days the Brier usually was played in a posh and gentlemanly Toronto club, the Granite. A dozen or two spectators—always including my ninety-year-old great-uncle, Walter Scott of St. Catharines—was a big day at the gate. Pardon me for boasting (it's so rare), but the editor at CP told me that he'd never been able to work up the slightest interest in curling until I wrote up that Brier for CP, and sports editors nationwide sent similar signals.

And there was golf. I had started playing the game in the late 1930s, when I was given my first free membership at the Winnipeg Canoe Club. Since my father had taken his clubs with him to Flin Flon much earlier, I asked the trainer for the Winnipeg Maroons, a man who always haunted secondhand shops when we were on the road in the Northern League, if he would watch out for a secondhand set of left-handed clubs. A week later he produced an age-browned canvas bag, which held five clubs and a few balls. "The price was four dollars," he said. I still use some of them. A few years later the 3-wood, or spoon, broke when reporter Trent Frayne and I were playing at the old St. Andrews Club in north Toronto. As I shot, the club head flew off into an apple tree, which then rained apples and one club head, much to Frayne's delight. So I was (sort of) a golfer.

Also, before my assignment to the London bureau, CP had sent me to cover the 1942 Canadian Open Golf Championship at Mississauga, my first big-league golf experience. I wanted to do well. However, other reporters told me that the way tournaments were played there was no chance for one reporter to beat another in flashing the final result. I took that as a challenge. In the end I engineered a modest scoop for CP and our U.S. ally, AP, over the rival news service, United Press, the feat that all the golf writers had said was impossible.

Today, everyone gets the winner's name off the leader-board at the same time. But in 1942, with no radio coverage to speak of, competition to get that result in first, even by a few minutes, was fierce. The newspaper that got the news onto the street first garnered the biggest street sales. This was so important that in the States, AP and UP routinely issued bulletins to their member papers on busy sports days, naming the events, the winners and which news service led in flashing the final result. Newspapers across North America would hold their Saturday sports pages until late in the day, waiting for final scores from any major events.

You might ask, "In that kind of situation, how could one news service get enough of an edge over another to make a real difference in sales?" Well, this once at least, there was a way. On the final day of the 1942 Canadian Open, Craig Wood finished his round in midafternoon, in front of the pack—but with several players still on the course who theoretically might catch him. Most of the keen observers in the press tent had conceded the win to Craig Wood, but on the grounds that it ain't over until it's over, they had to wait until all close contenders were in before they tapped out on their typewriters, "Craig Wood today won the 1942 Canadian Open," etc., etc.

Sitting with a cold beer where I had my typewriter set up, I kept track of the last few contenders and wished there was some way to get the winner's name on the wires across the continent first.

Which is when I had an idea. There were birdies and bogeys and an occasional eagle out there as this golfer or that made a run at Craig Wood's top position. It occurred to me that among each of the contenders, there had to be a place where a shot would be missed and any reasonable person might say in the privacy of his own mind, "Scratch that guy. He can't possibly do it now."

With that thought, I decided that when each of the few contenders still on the course got to where he'd have to shoot birdies and eagles all the way in to tie Craig Wood, I could assume that he had shot his bolt. To get this information, I had to follow each contender shot by shot until in my opinion he was up against the impossible. Accordingly, I sent anyone I could find—friends, office boys, whoever—out on the course to report on each in the dwindling band of contenders, hole by hole, or even shot by shot.

When the last of my designated contenders reached and passed the point at which my system said he no longer had a chance, I handed a note to my telegrapher: "Craig Wood wins Canadian Open," followed by the pertinent details, which he tapped out on the Morse key.

It was funny waiting for the explosion. It was nearly ten minutes before my telegrapher, who could read other reporters' incoming messages as well as our own, said, "The UP guy is getting hell. Says AP is reporting Craig Wood as winner and what the hell are you guys doing, sound asleep?"

So Associated Press, taking its coverage from what I was doing for CP, won the marbles that week. Gil Purcell passed on to me the AP's cheery note to subscribers: "Hey, we murdered 'em this time."

That seems like small potatoes now, but three years later when my navy career was on standby until my final discharge, someone at CP remembered. That year, 1945, the Canadian Open was being played at Toronto's Thornhill Golf and Country Club. CP was hunting around its war-depleted staff for someone to cover it. Someone at CP called me and said, "How about it?" I was eager, but had to say no; I was still in the navy.

Then Russ Wheatley, CP's day editor, suggested I do it under another name, and he suggested one.

And so it was that under the name of Elwood Redding I covered the 1945 Canadian Open, providing running copy as well as features on the likes of Sam Snead and other golf greats of the time.

"Where did you get that name?" I asked Russ later.

Russ had grown up in the deep South, where he had an uncle who had a faithful black handyman whom Russ had always liked, named Elwood Redding.

~

While ol' Elwood was becoming a legend in his own time, Rassy and I were hunting in vain for a place to live.

"Go and see Oscar Burritt," Gil Purcell advised me. Oscar Burritt, the older brother of Ernie Burritt, my boss at CP London, was well connected in the housing business in Toronto. When I arrived at his office, Oscar had been primed with the facts: that I was an ex-serviceman, formerly CP, with a wife and family, needed a place to live, and was broke. In a few days Oscar called to say he'd found something that might suit us. It was a new three-bedroom bungalow in north Toronto, listed at $7,000. Apparently because of the Burritt connection, the builder had agreed to drop the price to $6,500, with a $500 down payment.

At that point Gil Purcell, so often there when I and others needed support, offered to stand security for a $500 bank loan. Which was how with Rassy due any day to give birth, we moved into the first home of our own.

At the same time I had sought, and got, a job as an assistant editor at *Maclean's* magazine. A few articles I had written for the magazine from London apparently had tipped the balance in my favour, plus (possibly) I was going cheap, at $4,000 a year. Whatever the case, Rassy and I were very happy, house of our own, baby on the way. We had no car, but our next-door neighbour, whom we hardly knew, Lloyd Zerbrigg, came over one day and said, "How is your wife going to get to the hospital?"

I hadn't thought of that. "Probably by cab."

"They're sometimes hard to get," he said. "Especially in bad weather. When it's time, call and I'll drive Rassy to the hospital."

When the time did come, we delivered Rassy to the hospital, then I went back home, thinking of the difficult time Rassy had had when Bob was born, and hoping it would be easier this time.

About eight the next morning, November 12, 1945, the phone rang and I was told that Neil (as he was to be named, after my brother-in-law Neil Hoogstraten in Winnipeg) had been born and that he and Rassy were fine. I went down Avenue Road on the old Hill Route bus and stopped in at the hospital on my way to work. I found Rassy pale and wan and happy, and baby Neil with a lot of black hair. We both wept a little. All this had happened within two months of my navy discharge. New home, new baby, new job. Things were working out.

Then came what seemed like a disaster—an unexpected income tax bill for more than a thousand dollars, covering the years I had been in England and thought CP was handling the income tax. We took it more or less in stride because we couldn't possibly pay it, anyway. Lloyd Zerbrigg's wife broke into tears when Rassy, laughing, told her. To me, it was just a sign that I had to work harder.

I try to remember what I was like as a father and husband in those days—I think maybe too driven, in debt, willing to do any job for whatever money I could extract. Bob found playmates and they skated away the cold days of winter. Neil, even before he walked and was spending most of his waking hours in his playpen, used to almost dance, sitting down, when we played his favourite records.

I had an old rolltop desk, obtained I don't know how, in what we called my study, a tiny room near the one that Bob and Neil shared, across the hall from where Rassy and I slept and did a good deal of plighting the troth. As my job at *Maclean's* kept me busy writing and editing articles, I started to write fiction in my spare time. That had always been my ambition, to write fiction for a living. Soon I did sell a short story. The income tax people seemed pleased that I was at least trying. From then on I allotted certain times each week for writing fiction: two hours each Tuesday and Thursday evening, the same each Saturday and Sunday morning.

Rassy typed my stories, and besides painting the house from one end to the other ("Boy, can I paint!" she would say then and in every one of the houses we owned later), she was the family's most dependable cheerleader. For the next two years, until early summer of 1948, I turned out short stories, all of which sold, at first in Canada and then to major magazines in the United States, *Collier's, Woman's Home Companion, Saturday Evening Post* (a story based on my wartime experience in Italy) and others, which soon produced more income than I was making at *Maclean's*.

I 5

Going Freelance:
1949-1953

From that time on I've always thought of myself as a writer of fiction: novels, books for young people, and most recently mysteries set in the Arctic. However, to many readers I am known principally as a sports writer, and specifically a no-holds-barred hockey writer.

My first brush with the powerful men who controlled the old six-team National Hockey League came in the late 1940s, soon after I joined *Maclean's*. The magazine wanted an article that took a critical line about hockey; the working title was "Hogtied Hockey," the thrust being that for all the colour and verve of the game on the ice, a reprehensible chattel system ruled the way teams were put together.

Every hockey bigwig that I approached got angry when he found out that my aim was to criticize the way club owners controlled players virtually from the cradle to the grave. Over the years the system had ensnared hundreds of young hockey players so starstruck by the game's place in public esteem that very few seemed to care what was happening off the ice. To them and most of their parents God was God, the Pope was the Pope, and hockey was hockey—hands off.

For example, one day in 1951 when Bobby Hull had just turned twelve, the chief scout for the Chicago Black Hawks, Bob Wilson, went to Belleville, Ontario, to look at a junior B team that Chicago sponsored. He arrived at the rink early and, to pass the time, watched a bantam game, where a burly fair-haired kid seemed to be in permanent control of the puck.

"Hey," he said to a bystander, "who's that kid?"

"Bobby Hull."

Wilson, instantly aware that any other scout who saw Hull in action would want to tie him up, promptly sent a telegram to NHL headquarters in Montreal to place the name of Robert Marvin Hull on Chicago's negotiation list. This simple act, costing a dollar or two, would by hockey's rules tie Hull to Chicago for life. Being placed on Chicago's negotiation list, without his consent and even without mentioning the matter to him, meant that as of that moment young Hull could not even be approached by another NHL team. From then on he was Chicago's property, to be moved around among other teams owned or sponsored by Chicago.

The result was that if he did turn out to be good enough to play in the NHL, it had to be with Chicago unless Chicago sold or traded his rights. As simple as that. Wilson, an excellent scout, had landed rights to a player who was going to dominate pro hockey for many years. Hull, or his parents, did not have to be consulted before that telegram was sent. Later that same day the scout did tell Bobby's parents, but that was not obligatory. The senior Hulls talked it over and decided that for the moment they wouldn't tell Bobby of the Chicago interest because, Mr. Hull once said, "we thought it might go to his head."

This method of controlling a boy's future forever (or until he was traded or sold) affected many hundreds of young players over the years. In Bobby's case he was moved away from home at age thirteen to board (and go to school and star at hockey), until at sixteen he was playing with St. Catharines in one of the country's top junior leagues. All his teams during those early times were in the Chicago system, the pay being room and board and a small cash allowance. At eighteen he was looking good enough to move up to Chicago's big team, the Black Hawks.

At the time there were virtually no public complaints about this system. It mattered not at all that a player tied to one team, and unable to move on his own, might have had a better career in a free market, or even might have had denied to him a lifelong ambition to play for some other team. There was no players' union. It was every man for himself. A stubborn owner might, and occasionally did, keep a particularly stubborn player tied up for years during which he couldn't play pro hockey at all unless he accepted the game's ultimate authority. Players were chattels, with everything that word implies. To players, and the public, it was just life, hockey style.

Many years earlier there had been money-based competition for players, and competition cost the owners money. The negotiation list had fixed that. If the system was questioned, however faintly, club owners contended, chaos would result, hockey itself would go down the drain.

When I started assembling the evidence, some alarm bells rang. I was asking questions the NHL didn't like. Conn Smythe, owner of the Toronto Maple Leafs, refused to discuss these matters with me, accusing me and *Maclean's* of nefarious anti-hockey intentions. He assured me that no other owners would talk to me, either, which was fairly accurate, unless you count threats. The president of the National Hockey League, Red Dutton, phoned me to promise that if I wrote that NHL rules were a form of bondage, the league would sue.

I wrote it. There was no suit. The article had no real effect, being treated more or less the way a horse treats a mosquito: when the mosquito flies away, the horse remains. There wasn't a whisper of public protest, no crowds of outraged citizens chanting, "Free our hockey players!"

However, the incident did rekindle my longtime interest in hockey, though at a different level. By the time the teapot tempest of "Hogtied Hockey" died down, I was beginning to write and sell short stories, some with team-sports backgrounds—football and baseball as well as hockey. I got my material by plain observation, and by getting to know the athletes and their private lives, and by enjoying their games, so that I could write about hockey as if from the inside. In doing this I had a lot of help from my past.

I first started writing hockey for the Winnipeg *Free Press*, riding the buses to or from Brandon or Portage la Prairie with junior teams, eating pregame meals with them, getting to know who could sing the best (Wally Koster and Syd May), who was the wittiest (Billy Reay), who was the worst skater and the best body-checker (Bill Juzda), best skater (Wally Stanowski) and so on. Most of the players were around my age, and became my friends. Not all of them landed in the NHL as players or coaches, but some did—among them Billy Reay, Wally Stanowski and Bill Juzda. Many of us were of an age. Billy Reay of the Canadiens and I were born the same year, 1918, as were Milt Schmidt of Boston, Punch Imlach and others.

When I wrote my first hockey short stories for *Collier's* and *American Magazine* in the late 1940s and early 1950s, I was always looking for real-life situations in hockey that I could use in fiction. I began by attending Leafs' training camps in St. Catharines. One day, Conn Smythe, the Leafs' tough-minded founder, owner and manager, was sitting high in the seats, and beckoned me over to sit with him. Our earlier encounter over "Hogtied Hockey" seemed to have been forgotten. Smythe had clear piercing blue eyes, had played the game and coached at many levels, and brooked no interference in anything he believed in. He would yell instructions once in a while, sometimes rather rudely, but when I mentioned that to Joe Primeau, Leafs' coach, he just laughed. "This is one of his easy days." When I mentioned once to Smythe that it was a wonder so many people he blasted publicly stuck with him, he turned those blue eyes on me. "They know that I'm trying to improve them no matter how good they are. I never met a good man yet who didn't know that he *could* be better." In wartime, many tough and unforgiving men forgave him a lot because of his directness and honesty. They called him simply "the major," and you knew who they meant.

I can give only a fragmentary impression of what those days at training camp chatting with Smythe meant to me as a fiction writer: it was a whole new, tough, forthright world I was now being welcomed into. Smythe mentioned approvingly one of my short stories once, one based on the coaching style of Dick Irvin when he worked for Smythe, coaching the Leafs, when his son, broadcasting's Dick Irvin, was a child. Maybe Smythe had liked having an audience. Anyway, I was in, with no strings. We might disagree, but I didn't at the time have a newspaper connection where I could continue any argument.

Smythe said he enjoyed those sessions with me, that sometimes I made him think. There was one other connection between Smythe and me, the armed services. He knew I had been in the navy in places he had not seen, and that I admired his record in the two major wars of our time: shot down and taken prisoner in World War One, badly shot up while leading his own army command in World War Two, his denunciations of political decisions that had sent wounded Canadian soldiers, some of whom I had known in Italy, back into the line time and again instead of conscripting and training other Canadians to share the load. Anyway, we got along. Sometimes years later when I needed his explanation or opinion on some major sports story, and he was booked up totally, he and his chauffeur would pick me up and I'd get my answers en route to wherever he was going. Near the end of his life he asked me to help him with his memoirs, I think because he felt I understood him, warts and all.

After 1948, when I quit *Maclean's* to concentrate on fiction, we moved around looking for a country place to live, and finally landed in Omemee, Ontario, a village of 750 people. Selling short stories supported us. About then my agent in New York, Willis Kingsley Wing, passed on a letter from the Boston publisher Little, Brown, asking if I would be interested in writing some sports novels aimed at young readers. That editor had been impressed with sports stories of mine (with football and baseball backgrounds as well as hockey) that had been published in *Collier's*, *American Magazine, Argosy* and others. He said that if I was interested in the book idea I could pick my own sport. Wing added his own note to the Little, Brown letter, urging that I give this idea serious thought. "The only way I know for a writer to get a pension is to write a good juvenile, because the good ones just keep on selling forever."

That suggestion resulted in my first books of fiction for young people. *Scrubs on Skates* (1952), *Boy on Defence* (1953) and *Boy at the Leafs' Camp* (1962) were based on hockey as I had known it in Winnipeg high schools and junior teams. Wing was right. Updated to allow for all the changes in hockey since the books were written—many of the changes concerning how pro hockey's dictatorial relationship to players had had to change— those three books still sell several thousand copies each year, half a lifetime after I wrote the first one. As Willis Wing had forecast, readers introduced to those books when they were boys buy them now for their own children, so they sell on.

Still, over the years I continued to receive offers to return to journalism—but at first I wasn't ready for that.

In 1951, after a Grey Cup column I had written for the *Globe and Mail* as a freelancer, Tommy Munns, the *Globe's* managing editor, had offered me the daily sports column. At the time I was still doing okay in my longtime ambition to write fiction for a living. My price had gone up to $1,500 a story for *Collier's, Saturday Evening Post, Ladies' Home Journal, Woman's Home Companion* and *American Magazine*, less from the top Canadian magazines. These stories often had a second-rights life (what fellow fiction writer John Clare called Basutoland rights), at much less money, in England, Germany and Italy, and eventually, with some hockey stories, in Russia. I liked that way of life. Taking a job, getting back into journalism's mainstream again would have been a retreat, moving back into the city. So I turned it down.

But a few years later when fiction-buying magazines in the U.S. were dying like flies, taking with them my main source of income, it was a different story.

16

Changes:
1954-1959

E VEN WITH WHAT TODAY WOULD BE a laughable mortgage, about $20 a
month, we were living on the edge financially. A life of watching for
cheques in the mail is hard on a marriage and, as I was to be told often
over the years, in times of financial stress I was not easy to live with. I was
writing fiction for a shrinking market, just scraping by, but over time rec-
ognizing that to make a living we had to give up the slow pace of Omemee
and return to the city. In 1955 Rassy and I first rented and then reluctantly sold the Omemee house and bought a small bungalow on two acres near
Pickering, then an overgrown village just east of Toronto. We were there
when I got a temporary new lease on life.

For years beginning during World War Two a British company whose
Canadian arm was based in Malton, near the toronto airport, had been in
the aircraft manufacturing business as A. V. Roe Canada. Its products
ranged from wartime Lancaster bombers to postwar CF100 fighters and
Orenda jet engines. Their senior public relations people, headed by a one-
time Toronto *Star* reporter, A. Ronald Williams, felt that the company's
first ten years in Canada called for recognition in print. Williams, who
knew my work, called to ask if I would do a book about those years, and for
how much. We settled on a flat fee of, I think, $2,000. As a result of that
book, entitled *The Way Up*, I immediately had two full-time job offers from
A. V. Roe companies, one to be assistant to the general manager of Avro
Aircraft, the other to hold a similar job and title with Orenda Engines.

It goes without saying that both were out of my line, but I needed
the job, any job, and each paid $10,000 a year. I chose the engine com-

pany, which employed about five thousand people. I sat on the management committee, ate in the management dining room, oversaw public relations and advertising, arranged plant tours and represented the company at big gatherings of aviation people. I studied hard so that I could talk the lingo. I was doing all right. My boss at Orenda was a truly likeable man, Walter McLachlan. Sometimes we were together at various air industry gatherings in Washington, San Francisco, New Orleans, Farnborough in England, and elsewhere. The pay was ample for our needs, allowing Rassy and Bob and Neil a cushion in the money line, the job a toehold in a field I came to like and that gave me useful insights into the aircraft industry.

The only trouble was that even working nights and early mornings at my typewriter in a basement room in our house, I wasn't producing much. In only a matter of weeks after I took the job, and would park my 1956 Volkswagen Beetle in the management parking lot among the big and expensive automobiles of other management people, I would get a serious headache every morning just walking through the door of the engine factory and thinking, what the hell am I doing here?

Apparently it showed, at least to my very perceptive boss. In 1956 he and I were in Victoria, B.C., at an Air Force Association convention. Late one night after the last seminar of the day the two of us went to dinner in an excellent Chinese restaurant, had a couple of drinks, and were talking hockey and politics and the chances of selling our engines to South Africa, Belgium and elsewhere.

He complimented me on a recent dinner in a private room at the Royal York Hotel for a Venezuelan general and his wife and entourage (they nearly bought some engines), then looked at me across the table and asked conversationally, "What are you going to do after you get the aviation industry figured out?"

In my nice new business suits and with my glib talk about jet engine thrust and research and development in the aviation world, plus my ability to represent him at plant openings and organize dinners for high-level people in the business, making sure the bar had everybody's favourite tipple in stock, I'd thought I had everybody fooled.

"What makes you think I'm not permanent here?"

"You strike me as basically a loner, not really comfortable in a teamwork situation, which ours has to be."

After a pause, I told him, "All I can say is that when I decide to leave, I'll give you lots of notice."

Which I did, a couple of months later. The *Globe and Mail* again had offered me a job writing some kind of column, the exact nature to be decided. I accepted, and my headaches stopped. Walter then was host at a management-level dinner at the Engineers Club in Toronto, made a nice speech about the good work I had done for Orenda, said they wished me well and were sorry I was leaving, and presented me with a fine double-barrelled shotgun to remember them by.

That prompted one of my friends, Jack Nesbitt, Orenda's industrial relations manager, to say to me later, laughing, "I wonder what they would have given you if you'd stayed around two years instead of one."

⬙

When I started at the *Globe* in early 1957, the best-read column in the paper was a lighthearted and sometimes funny one on the front page of the second section, which Bruce West had been writing for years. But West wanted to take a job in promotion that might have more executive future and be less demanding (a daily column *is* demanding). Harry C. Kimber, the head man at the paper, gave me the task of filling West's space, starting at $170 a week.

When Kimber retired a year or so later, several executives at the *Globe*, probably led by Tommy Munns, decided that I belonged in sport. The daily sports column was being written by sports editor Jim Vipond, a dedicated man, but his executive job didn't leave him as much time and energy as a good column requires. In the early summer of 1958 he had to take hospital leave to have an operation. I was asked to pinch-hit for him as sports columnist. In a couple of months I was given that column full-time, allowing Vipond to concentrate on the editor's job.

That began a good time for me, starting with my first World Series, the mighty Yankees of Yogi Berra, Mickey Mantle and Casey Stengel finally beating Milwaukee, whose main pitchers Johnny Sain and Warren Spahn made a good run during what became a famous pitching strategy under the title "Spahn, Sain and a Day of Rain." Trouble was, there wasn't quite enough rain to spell them off.

Then came early in 1959 the amazing weeks when Toronto hockey fans went mad as their Maple Leafs under new coach Punch Imlach rose from last place in the National Hockey League to make the playoffs on the final night of the season, win the semifinal with Boston, and then in the final, fall to Toe Blake's Montreal Canadiens with Rocket Richard, Jean Beliveau and other superstars.

For me, the months rolled on with no letup in exciting events: the Grey Cup, Kentucky Derby, Queen's Plate, Winter Olympics in Squaw Valley, championship fights in New York and Miami and Chicago featuring Sonny Liston, Floyd Patterson, George Chuvalo and Cassius Clay, before he changed his name to Muhammad Ali. He was still going by his original name before one Patterson-Liston fight in Chicago, when he confided in me and other sports writers that he could beat them both on the same night if he had to, which never was tried, but might have been true. Frank Mahovlich, one of the greatest hockey players ever, was with the Leafs, along with Bob Pulford, Dick Duff, Bert Olmstead, Carl Brewer, Dave Keon, Johnny Bower, Allan Stanley, Tim Horton, Bobby Baun and other great ones (one year Andy Bathgate) as they won four Stanley Cups under Imlach before the bottom fell out late in the 1960s.

Early in that time I worked on TV and radio hockey broadcasts, bringing me a kind of national recognition that in Canada few except hockey broadcasters ever experience. One autumn, covered in mud after a wet day shooting ducks in Saskatchewan, I stopped a sugar beet truck, equally muddy, to ask the way. The driver looked hard at me and said, "Say, I know you! It's that voice! Hockey broadcasts, right?"

At home on the Brock Road in Pickering, across from the Pickering Golf Club, son Bob had become one of Ontario's top junior golfers. Neil, then ten or eleven, had two main pursuits—listening to pop music on CHUM on a radio under his pillow and raising chickens to sell the eggs, which I delivered to regular customers in Toronto.

Once when I was making a Monday delivery in Don Mills, the woman there, who had a three-year-old son, said, "I've been waiting to tell you. On Saturday night our little boy came running into the kitchen all excited and yelled, 'Hey, Mom, come quick, our egg man's on television!'"

The downside of the sports job was that I was away from home more and more, leaving Rassy and the boys alone while I covered events across Canada and the States. Mainly because of too much driving to cover sports events, we sold our house in Pickering and bought another in north Toronto. I won the National Newspaper Award for sports writing in my first full year on that job, other awards for writing about football, and in a few years won a U.S. Eclipse

Award, for a horse racing column about a Canadian rider, Cricket Walford. But the *Globe* had other things in mind for me beyond sports.

The first indication had come late in 1959. The Queen and Prince Philip were touring the country, mostly in a media-filled royal train. I was pulled from sports for a while and left Rassy and the boys to join the *Globe*'s royal tour contingent. That was fun. I wasn't a mad royalist, but I liked those royals and people in their entourage. I had a lot of freedom on that assignment. It wasn't all "as the Queen spoke, the sun broke through" kind of thing. I was bemused by the people who turned out all along the way to greet the royals. The lineup along the station platform when the train stopped always included a troop of Brownies, little girls with socks at half mast marching, cheering, clapping, responding in whispers when the Queen asked a question.

These troops of Brownies looked so much alike that I decided they were really the same Brownies every time, flown across the country ahead of the train so they could meet the royals at stop after stop. When I was reporting on the crowds at Weyburn, Kindersley, Moose Jaw, Banff or wherever, I always included a good word for what I called the National Brownies, and their leader, Brown Owl. And reported that at Sicamous, B.C., where the Queen did a walkabout at the station, the mosquitoes were among the largest in the world, the only known site where a mosquito once had been haled into court by a turkey in a paternity suit.

One night that I treasured came when the train parked on a siding somewhere on the prairie not far from Brandon, Manitoba, and an announcement was made that the royals and the ink-stained wretches of the royal tour press corps would share a social hour, including a bar. I happened to be in one small group when a woman reporter was sympathizing with the Duke of Edinburgh about his gruelling lot.

"You must find it gha-a-a-a-astly," she sighed, "having to get out of the train time after time to meet all those aldermen and their wives and mayors and so on. Many of those people, I've talked to them myself, aren't they just gha-a-aastly?"

It was obviously a question calling for an answer. The Duke obliged. "On the contrary, madam," he said. "Most of them are no more ghastly than you are."

I also rather liked one of his sallies on another tour I covered. This was in Halifax where, as was the custom, city councillors and their wives lined up in a semicircle to be greeted by the royal couple. I noticed that the Duke said something to one group and everyone laughed. When I went to ask what he'd said, everybody clammed up, still laughing, but a Halifax *Herald* reporter with good connections among the aldermen, said she'd try to find out. It turned out that the Duke had stopped before a man who was standing alone. At the time the Queen's sister, Princess Margaret was much in the news because her marriage had broken up and she was considering other suitors. When the Duke asked jokingly why this man hadn't brought his wife along, he gazed heavenward and replied, "Well, sir, so far I have never been blessed in that way, to find someone who would have me."

"You should come over to England," the Duke replied. "I have this sister-in-law. . ."

That earlier tour, however, I remember best for something more personal. Each provincial government was in charge of its local segment of the national tour. On the night we arrived somewhere in interior British Columbia, the press room for the many dozens of correspondents from around the world, was managed by a slight and beautiful young woman, Astrid Mead. She ran the press room, taking messages, finding writers when their editors were on the phone, handing out daily schedules and press releases on what the Queen wore. Her job was keeping a wide variety of sometimes demanding people happy and being a link between the press and everybody else. Normally, she was the associate of a Victoria publicist, Gordon Root, in whose hands rested many of the press arrangements. Once in a while she and I had lunch or dinner or coffee, and soon became friends.

One night when the furore of a long day had died down and all the upright survivors were in bed or in the bar, we went for a walk in a little park. At one pause we happened to find ourselves in an ideal position to exchange a lighthearted embrace, and did so.

When we kissed, that very first time, I had a feeling that I was going, going, gone. It must have showed because when we moved apart she laughed and said, "Oh, don't look so serious."

But it was serious. Within a few days the die had been cast, as the saying goes. We had talked a lot in the spare moments. She had been born in Prince George, B.C., her father killed in a sawmill accident when she was five, her mother—not long out from Sweden, speaking little English—moving from place to place in the interior of B.C. as a house-

keeper trailing her two small children. Astrid later had worked as a telephone operator in Prince Rupert, married at eighteen to the handsome
Gavin Mead, several years her elder. He soon abandoned her and their
child, Deirdre, who was born in 1951. It helped greatly that they had
been befriended by Gavin's adoptive parents, the Meads, with whom
Astrid and Deirdre then lived. That was her life when we met. Gavin was
alive, but she didn't know where.

I told her that years earlier Rassy and I had separated but had patched
it up and were still together. I might have, probably did, give Astrid the
impression that the marriage with Rassy was close to being on the rocks,
and that our reunion after our one separation was probably a mistake,
which for some time I had believed to be the case. During the period after
that separation, I had had two or three mild or not so mild flirtations.
Astrid had had the same after her marriage ended.

As I moved back across the country on the royal train, we wrote letters almost every day. I had her picture stuck up on the mirror in my
roomette. I had a feeling this was for real, and maybe forever, but sometimes wondered if it all happened too fast.

What really made up my mind was that in Winnipeg, on the way
home, I called a woman friend. For many years she and I had felt a very
strong physical attraction for one another, even after long separations. She
was divorced and had a son. We went to a motel we'd used before. When I
took her home that night and returned by myself to the bed we had just
vacated, I was unhappy. I'd never really been a creature of one-night stands.
What pained me that night was cheating on both Astrid, whom I now felt I
did love, and Rassy, whom I had loved and who was still my wife.

Maybe it'll be different when I get home, I thought. There's always a
chance of rekindling. But it didn't happen. I was very tired, not only from
the trip but from what had happened to me emotionally. Within a few days,
Rassy and I found something to fight about. I don't remember where the
boys were that night. I packed a couple of bags and took a taxi to a hotel.

That was in September of 1959. A year later Astrid left Deirdre tem-
porarily with the very supportive Meads, who apparently approved of me,
and moved to Toronto. She found a job, and we bought a house in which
officially we didn't live together—I had a flat a few minutes' walk away.
Divorce papers were filed in 1960, when Rassy and Neil moved to
Winnipeg, and Bob stayed with me. The divorce came through in May

1961, and Astrid and I were married in a Victoria church and drove Astrid's TR3 full of wedding champagne back to Toronto.

Our attractive Toronto house was in Moore Park, a good district. Because Astrid was working, we engaged a German housekeeper, Mrs. Kleffman, whose daughter, Anne-Marie, was about Deirdre's age. We had an apartment finished in the basement for them. Deirdre and Anne-Marie went to the same school, Deer Park. Even with the alimony I was paying to Rassy, we were comfortable.

That first year of our married life was memorable, one part sad and the other glad, for two major events. That winter Astrid became pregnant and my father came to visit us around Christmas. He hadn't attended our wedding in Victoria so hadn't met Astrid. When I suggested he come to visit us, he decided on a time when the Christmas rush would have passed in the drugstore he managed in Melita, Manitoba.

Although I didn't know it until later, he was in ill health. The first evening he spent with us, we had a drink or two and all seemed well—but many times that night I heard him passing our bedroom door going to the bathroom. In the morning he said he must have had stomach flu. Later I learned that such symptoms sometimes are signs of an impending stroke.

At the end of the visit I took him to the old Toronto airport at Malton, and watched, with misgivings as he slowly and unsteadily walked out to the aircraft, seeming to drag one leg. Later, when he caught the bus to travel to Melita, he became confused, and when he left the bus, met by Florence Hall, with whom he had lived for some years, he did not know where he was. Florence took him home and called a doctor. She then called me to say that the doctor thought he had had a series of strokes and should be in hospital. My sister soon called to say that if I wanted to see him alive I should come. I was torn; my brother did go, but I wanted to remember my father as we had been just days before, rather than in a death-bed vigil. The next word was that he had died.

The funeral was in his old church at Cypress River. I met my brother and sister and our mother in Winnipeg and we drove out together, meeting at Uncle Milt's home just down the street from the church. I was rather proud of my mother. Astrid had felt that Mother, after twenty years of separation, shouldn't go, but when we walked into Uncle Milt's home and Mother looked around the room at all her in-laws and others she knew, she immediately saw the one person there she didn't know. She walked across the room with her hands out. "You must be Florence," she said in warm greeting. They talked a while and then Uncle Milt came to me and said, "Maybe your mother would like to go to the church to see your dad before the funeral."

I took Mother's arm and we walked along the slippery, icy streets to the church. The coffin was open. Mother stood silently for a few moments gazing down at him, then we walked back.

I thought that Florence, who had looked after him so well for nearly twenty years, might also want to go to the church, so I asked her, and took her arm for another walk along the icy road. I was thinking of Mother's silent farewell as I took Florence to the coffin. She sobbed my father's name and leaned into the coffin and held him and kissed his lips before sinking into one of the front pews and gazing at him. She touched his face silently once more, and we walked back together.

A day after the funeral service, Bob and I drove Florence home to Melita, and she gave us Dad's meagre belongings, including an envelope containing $5.65 in cash that Florence thought should go to me, as the oldest son. I still keep it, old coins and dollar bills, in my desk. I have been in touch with Florence each Christmas since.

I've sometimes thought that Dad would have enjoyed some aspects of the following summer as Astrid's pregnancy neared its term. It was very hot, and since we had no air conditioning, she had an exhausting time. Once I tried to cheer her up by promising that when the birth pains began in earnest we would drink cold champagne, her favourite drink, until we had to leave for the hospital.

By coincidence (I'm sure) she had several bouts of false labour pains. We drank nearly a case of champagne during these warmups until finally, on August 16, our daughter was born. I wanted to call her Astrid, after her mother, but it wasn't that simple. Deirdre's full name was Astrid Deirdre Mead Young. Her new baby sister, we decided, would be Vendela (her Swedish grandmother's name) Astrid Paterson Young, called Astrid.

She was a beautiful baby in all respects. To share the work of tending the new baby, I usually took the middle-of-the-night feedings, complete with bottle warmer, the two of us on a wicker rocker, and whether significant or not as an aid to lifetime bonding, we seem to have been on the same wavelength ever since, forgiving, supporting and above all understanding one another no matter what.

17
Covering the News:
1960-1969

I HAVE NEVER BEEN SURE, and am not to this day, whether I should have moved from job to job so often, more or less at the whim of others. I can't truthfully contend that I saw in each a challenge. Actually, I side with my friend John Clare on the use of that word. When our mutual friend Ralph Allen accepted the job as the *Star's* managing editor, a position that chewed up some pretty good men over the years, he happened to encounter Clare, then editor of the *Star Weekly*.

"What the hell are you trying to do, taking that job, Allen, kill yourself?" Clare said.

Ralph, probably drowning in congratulations at the time, was taken aback and mumbled something about it being a challenge.

"Challenge!" Clare barked. "You sound like a toilet seat salesman with a new territory."

So much for challenges. The truth is I really enjoyed the changes. I once recommended to Richard J. Doyle, managing editor, that every five years all columnists should be fired from the jobs they held and moved to some other column. There is nothing complicated about being a journalist, at least my kind of journalist, and by 1963 I was ready to leave sports.

The previous year, Pierre Berton had quit the Toronto *Star*, and his popular column space was about to become vacant. The *Star*, hunting for a replacement, called me. I turned up at the old *Star* building on King Street West to talk it over with Charles Templeton, a longtime friend and then a senior *Star* executive.

At first, the *Star* people didn't mention money, but when the subject came up I thought I might as well go for it. I asked for $26,000, about double what I was getting at the *Globe* (and, I learned later, more than Berton). In later dickering I came down to $24,000, and a few days later I was called into Templeton's office and told, with a distinct air that the matter had been settled, that the board of directors had authorized $20,000 a year.

Beland Honderich, head of the *Star* and a person I liked, came into the meeting at that point. I had the feeling that they felt they had me and anointment was next. But I still wanted the higher amount, and really liked the *Globe* and my role there, so the anointment did not take place and we mutually decided that was that. I was relieved.

The *Star* did well out of the exercise, however. After our negotiations foundered they hired Gary Lautens, not for the Berton job but mainly to give the paper some bench strength in the feature-writing side. Gary, a good friend from press boxes at Hamilton Tiger Cat football games, told me once that the *Star* started him at $8,000 a year. He was a first-rate journalist in all respects, including his ability to write some truly funny columns, and in time became one of the paper's greatest assets.

As for me, I went back to the *Globe* and told managing editor Doyle that I was staying.

"Good," he said, spoke briefly on the phone, and said that publisher Oakley Dalgleish wanted to see me in his office.

I walked upstairs. Nice big office. I'd never been there before.

Dalgleish said he was glad I wasn't leaving, and some other things, and I no doubt replied in kind, and he said that to show its happiness with my decision the *Globe* would raise my salary by about $5,000 a year, to $17,000, effective immediately.

I thanked him, and as there didn't seem to be an awful lot more to say, I was rising to leave when he said evenly, "I'll tell you one thing, Scott, I wouldn't pay you that much money to write sports." (That was the opposite of what John Bassett was to say to me seven years later when I left the *Globe* for Bassett's Toronto *Telegram.*) "What I want you to do is write a daily column on page six. There hasn't been a page-six column since J. V. McAree."

I forget what I said, but it wasn't no. McAree's editorial-page column had been a legend.

"First we'll have to get someone to replace you as sports columnist.

Give it some thought, and let Dic Doyle know who you think we should go after."

I immediately thought of Dick Beddoes, a flamboyant and sometimes outrageous Vancouver *Sun* columnist. He and I had become close friends during the 1960 Winter Olympics at Squaw Valley and later at other sports events. He dressed like a fashion model gone mad, wore outlandish ties, vests and jackets, and never was seen without a hat. In that, and in writing well with an unmistakably colourful style, he resembled another West Coast sports columnist whom I liked, Charlie (Hard-Hat) McCabe of San Francisco, although Hard-Hat always wore a derby, whereas Beddoes usually went for homburgs. Another difference between them was that Beddoes never missed, or gummed up, any sports event he was supposed to be covering. Hard-Hat had his own ways. The 1962 World Series (Yankees vs. San Francisco) he covered from his honeymoon bed in, I think, Reno, he and his bride watching the games on television. Beddoes and Hard-Hat had in common that they were afraid of nothing, except being unnoticed.

So, when Doyle asked for candidates to replace me in the *Globe* sports column, I said, "Dick Beddoes," and explained why. For thirty-odd years that I knew of, *Globe and Mail* sports columnists usually had been highly individual, a line including Ralph Allen, Vern DeGeer and Jim Coleman. "If you want to go again for somebody who will never be mistaken for anybody but himself, hire Beddoes."

A few days later I had a call from Beddoes. "Hey, I've just heard from the *Globe*, something about your job. I don't know whether to talk to them or not. What's going on? You going somewhere else?"

I told him what was up.

"Okay," he said, "I'll talk to them." In time he became a nationally known figure somewhat in the line of hockey TV's Don Cherry: loved or hated but never afraid to ride into danger, and for that and other reasons almost impossible to ignore. He wasn't particularly a womanizer as far as I knew, but when his wife, Margaret, who maybe knew better, changed the locks on their attractive house I was probably one of the few people unsurprised when Beddoes bought the house across the street so he wouldn't lose touch with their daughters.

When my move from the sports to the editorial page was announced by the *Globe*, Gil Purcell phoned and asked if I had been consulted and had agreed. I said I felt fine about it. He was not mollified. "My belief is that when you have something going well, you shouldn't change it."

Maybe he was right. I had built a readership on the sports-page, including many who were not regular sports page readers but did read my column, and others who, when I disappeared from sports, simply assumed that I had been assassinated.

On the other hand, I saw the change as a chance to explore new territory, especially politics. When people asked me, "How can you switch from sports to politics this way? You know sports! How can you throw away all those great connections?" I had several answers to the effect that by and large political figures were as easy to characterize as sports figures. The one I used most was to say, "In politics, once you figure out who is the Eddie Shack type and who are the Punch Imlach and Connie Smythe types, it's easy."

That was a flippant reply, but it had some truth in it. Writing sports or politics, the same techniques worked. In provincial politics I had fun with many, from solid and likeable Ontario Tory premier John Robarts to gadfly Liberals Elmer Sopha from Sudbury, Vern Singer of North York and Eddie Sargent of Owen Sound.

Sargent was most like Shack. When things got noisy in the Ontario legislature he would piercingly blow a referee's whistle to rouse the Speaker's ire and get things back on track. "'Oh, yeah,' people would say, 'Eddie Sargent, he's the guy who blows the whistle.'" There were also some unwittingly comic characters, including Ellis Morningstar, a huge Tory member known to my readers as Mighty Morningstar, who sometimes fell asleep as debates droned on. The well-fed row of cabinet ministers who flanked Robarts in the front row of that legislature I used to call the Beef Trust.

For a while I became somewhat addicted to the Ontario legislature and its people, its leadership conventions, its hidden currents. I don't wish to overstate the benefits that came to me as a reporter by building up these contacts, but they were there. At lunch one day, Treasurer John White arrived a little late, saying, "Can you stand two of us instead of one? I brought along the premier." I didn't make press conferences out of such accidents; I just liked the company, and might use the acquaintance some other time. Late in 1968 when I was writing a *Globe Magazine* piece on how the Tories had managed to stay in power in Ontario for twenty-five years, John Robarts would meet me for breakfast and help with his insider's view on his party's longevity.

All this showed in what I wrote, not only from an Ontario standpoint but in my pieces about major political events such as leadership conventions, both provincial and federal. My frequent sources included Liberals Judy LaMarsh and Keith Davey. Another was Tory Davie Fulton (through whom I came to know Joe Clark, one of Fulton's supporters in the 1967 Tory leadership convention); I thought of them all as friends.

Lunching with Joe Clark at the Lord Simcoe Hotel a day or two after that 1967 convention, which named Robert Stanfield as the man to succeed John Diefenbaker, I told him that I had some interesting information that I frankly didn't know how to handle. In that convention, voting machines were used for the first time in Canada. There were twenty such machines. I had come by a document listing the names of all who voted at each machine, and how the totals from each machine were split between the leadership candidates. Some lists I could see were of certain well-defined groups of delegates—senators, Quebeckers, westerners, Maritimers, longtime party stalwarts, former members of Parliament, and so on, but some were mixed, and most of the hundreds of names I didn't know at all, making impossible any accurate analysis of voting trends by machine.

In borrowing this list from a party official who was not supposed to let it out, but left me alone with it and did not object when he found it gone (just helping me get the facts, ma'am), I had hoped to be able to establish what particular elements of the Conservative party were responsible for electing Stanfield as their new leader.

"The trouble is," I told Joe, "I don't know most of the delegates' allegiances or backgrounds, so when I'm trying to analyze the voting patterns, I'm lost. But I've got to go back and figure them out as best I can."

Slight pause. From working for Fulton, Joe knew every delegate by name, background and likely voting allegiance. "Maybe I could help," he said.

We went across the street to my office. He read painstakingly through the lists and studied how each machine's votes were split. By that means he determined, for instance, that most Quebec delegates had supported Duff Roblin, the Manitoban, who spoke fluent French, and that in machines where most delegates were the Tory establishment—longtime party stalwarts, Maritimers, senators, defeated but loyal Tory members—

the majority vote had gone to Stanfield.

In the end we were able to determine which of the machines had swept Stanfield into heading the party, and what their voting makeup had been. Joe's analysis enabled me to write a story that clearly identified which segments of the party had elected the new Tory leader and made the point that with only a little better support outside Quebec, Roblin would have won. The *Globe* ran the story on the front page and basically told readers more than the voting figures alone could possibly reveal.

In the middle of the newsroom the next day Dic Doyle congratulated me on my enterprise. I said a lot of the credit was due to Joe Clark and that he should be thanked and maybe paid a consultant's fee.

Doyle agreed, and sent me a note saying that a cheque had gone out. A week later he stopped me in the newsroom and said Joe had sent back the cheque with a note to the effect that he had enjoyed the exercise and didn't want to accept a fee. As I was sure that without a steady job he could have used the money, I figured he was looking ahead to a time when his private papers might be interesting to others, in which case he didn't want one item to be a cheque from the *Globe and Mail.* He had more understanding than I did of how such a cheque might be interpreted as a political service to a particular newspaper, a label he didn't want on his record. Labels, as many a politician in Canada and elsewhere has learned the hard way, are easy to acquire and difficult to leave behind.

However, that connection, fleeting as it was, meant that after Joe became leader of the Conservative party and then prime minister, when we encountered one another we were somewhat more than ships that pass in the night. I happened to like him a lot. During one general election campaign Joe was fighting years later, hoping to regain the prime ministership he had lost a few months earlier, I was in the press box covering the Queen's Plate at Toronto's Woodbine racetrack, when Joe paid a visit. One of the entries in the Plate was a pretty good horse called The Liberal. Joe was being kidded by some of those present about The Liberal's chances.

"What'll you do if they come into the home stretch with The Liberal leading?" someone, perhaps I, asked.

"I'll run out on the track and grab the reins," he said.

◈

In the early stages of my 1963 move from sports, I had apparently been assigned the role of the man Doyle wanted in the front lines of major stories. He once wrote (not to me) that my "versatility and sensitivity never ceased to amaze" him. But sometimes being included in major stories seemed to me at least partly luck, just being there when something big happened. By luck, I was in the newsroom the day late in 1963 when President John F. Kennedy was assassinated. In an hour or so I caught a flight to Washington for the unforgettable gathering of world leaders there to pay homage. In the end, with my head full of the tragic images of those few days, I chose to wind up among the misty lights at Arlington National Cemetery on the night when the Kennedy family gathered for the burial, a sad and deeply touching scene, after which I went back to my hotel and tried all night to do it justice.

In 1964, when the Queen and Prince Philip visited Canada, landing in Quebec for a state dinner, I was assigned to oversee in a general way the strong *Globe* group covering this royal visit to what then was rather hostile territory. There was one really bad night when a state dinner for the Queen was in progress at the Château Frontenac. Angry anti-royalists thronged the streets, causing dozens of arrests and rough treatment by Quebec provincial police as demonstrators were clubbed and chased through downtown. That occasion is remembered in Quebec as *l'après midi des matraques* because of many anti-British demonstrators being clubbed during the arrests. Some of the English reporters the next day, meeting me in a corridor in Ottawa, hotly accused me of placing more importance than was warranted in my front-page story on those scenes, possibly feeling that overstatement was their private preserve and obviously knowing little of the long and often rabid nature of French–English feeling in Canada.

In 1965 I was sent to London to write about the last weeks of Winston Churchill, a death watch that lasted about a month and ended on a Sunday morning. On a hunch the day before his death, I had taken a train to Oxford, and stayed overnight at an inn near the churchyard where it was known he would be buried. My aim was to see the grave site with no crowds around. Very early the next morning when I called a cab to take me to morning service at that church, the BBC was on and the driver turned to me and said, "It just came on. The old man's dead."

Arriving early at the church, the only reporter present, I asked the pastor if he would show me Churchill's grave, which he did. After the service (the church was only half-full because not everyone had heard the news yet) I caught the first train to London. A week earlier I had written the lead for a story citing the major events of his amazing life, the story to be held in readiness so that it could be sent to the *Globe* immediately on the old titan's death.

Once again, as world leaders were arriving in London for the funeral service at St. Paul's Cathedral, I had a stroke of luck. I had tried in vain through Canada House and every other high-level source I could think of to find myself a place in St. Paul's for the service. Then I remembered from my CP days in London more than twenty years earlier a once-powerful organization called the Empire Press Union, through which press arrangements that affected all Commonwealth countries during the war had been handled.

I looked up the address on The Strand and found a small office in the charge of one middle-aged woman in a cardigan. "Yes?" she said, across the tiny wooden counter. I told her that I had been there many years earlier as a CP man, that I now represented the major national newspaper in Canada and asked if there was any way she could get me into St. Paul's for the funeral service. She looked in a drawer and came up with one ticket. Which is how I became, as far as I know, one of only two Canadian reporters, the other being from Southam News, in the crowded pews of St. Paul's while General de Gaulle and other world leaders walked past us down the aisle for the service.

When it was over and the throngs outside began to disperse, I met Astrid nearby at the *Globe* office in the London Times building to watch on television as Churchill's coffin was carried through the city and down the Thames. At some point I broke down and wept, remembering so much of what his life had meant to all of us in his domain when the future looked bleak and he was rallying the free world to keep the faith.

One of my concerns had been that when Churchill's service took place, the five-hour time difference with Canada meant that my firsthand account of the long funeral procession through the London streets could not be published in that Saturday morning's *Globe*. Instead I had obtained the route the procession would follow, then walked it and described in what would be a front-page story the pubs and other buildings that would be passed. This way, readers would be able to follow along when they watched the actual procession on TV.

I remember one light note from that time, peripherally involving the *Globe* publisher James Cooper, who had succeeded Oakley Dalgleish after his death in 1963. Cooper was English and a widely experienced journalist. Talking to Dic Doyle one day by telephone during the Churchill vigil, I mentioned that as I'd been away from home for a month I had persuaded Astrid to come and join me for a few days after the funeral.

"Good idea," he said. "Where are you staying?"

"Dorchester Hotel," I replied.

There was a pause. "I have to tell you," he said, "that Jimmy Cooper has told me that the one hotel in London he most admires is the Dorchester, but he has never been able to afford to stay there."

"Oh," I said, "I always stay at the Dorchester." Actually I had stayed at the Dorchester for some weeks ten years earlier when I was handling public relations for A. V. Roe Canada at the annual Farnborough air show, there to help promote our excellent line of CF-100 aircraft and Orenda engines.

Other guests at the Dorchester at the time of Churchill's funeral included Prime Minister Pearson and his wife, Maryon. I left a note with the hall porter asking if the Pearsons could meet Astrid and me for a drink or tea.

A note came back inviting us to visit their suite in the late afternoon after the funeral, which we did; it was a two-drink visit, both Pearsons in good form. That day, the Queen had taken advantage of the presence of so many visiting heads of Commonwealth countries by asking them all to lunch at Buckingham Palace after the funeral. One item of business was for the Queen to put her official stamp on the new Canadian flag, the one that has been flying over our country ever since. Small versions of the flag had been provided for all the other heads of Commonwealth states, who, Pearson said, had accepted it largely without comment "except that Ireland's Mr. de Valera grumbled that a real flag should have blood on it."

"I'm sure Mr. Diefenbaker would be glad to oblige," said Mrs. Pearson.

Our single maple leaf flag, incidentally, had won out over Pearson's original choice, which bore three maple leaves. The Queen had seen that one earlier. When she looked at our new flag, preparatory to the formality of accepting it, she murmured to Pearson, "Whatever happened to your design?"

As our conversation with the Pearsons went on, he merrily related a conversation he'd had with Ian Smith of Rhodesia, then in the intermediate stages of breaking with Britain, who had been invited to visit Number 10 Downing Street. It seemed to Pearson that Smith wanted to accept but was concerned about the effect at home if news photos showed him entering that much-photographed British prime ministerial address.

"Does Number 10 have a side entrance?" he had asked Pearson.

One morning at seven more than a year later our bedside phone rang.

"Are you listening to the radio?" Dic Doyle asked.

"No, why?"

"They've shot Bobby Kennedy in Los Angeles. I've checked Air Canada. There's a flight at nine o'clock."

"I'll be on it."

Within hours, I was outside the Los Angeles hospital where Bobby Kennedy lay unconscious, locating the nearest pay phones and telling the *Globe* that arrangements were being made across the street from the hospital to establish a press centre. I'd let them have the phone number as soon as I had it. The *Globe*, of course, at that point knew as much about Kennedy's condition as anyone. The wire services looked after that. My usual aim in such a widely covered situation was to assume that the paper would be keeping up with the hard news through the wire services. I worked on human-interest side issues—what the scene looked like and sounded like, the array of police, nearby streets blocked off.

At the end of the first long day I found a reporter with music connections who knew where I might find my son Neil, then in Los Angeles in the first wave of his eventual fame that began with the band called Buffalo Springfield.

I told Neil by phone where to find me. His box-like Mini was stopped at a barrier, but his explanation that his dad was in there somewhere got him through the police lines on foot. He took us to have hamburgers and beer. We hadn't seen one another for nearly three years, so there was a lot of catching up to do. When he and Rassy had gone to Winnipeg after our split, he had started putting bands together there, one being The Squires, playing for dances in community clubs and achieving some local fame before branching out into gigs elsewhere, mostly in Manitoba and Fort William, Ontario. I'd seen him mainly when I was in Winnipeg for football games and we'd usually have lunch together. Once he visited Astrid and me in Toronto and although he didn't stay long (he wanted to get back to his Winnipeg band) when he started playing on the road out of Winnipeg sometimes he would write letters. One I remember particularly was from Fort William, late in 1964: "Dear Daddy, Astrid, Deirdre and other Astrid: We leave for the Town and Country in Winnipeg on Sunday and we're coming back here in two weeks. I will try to get us lined up in the East so that the chances of dropping in on you will be better."

A few weeks later he wrote a three-page letter. "Here I am in the scenic Lakehead at the Flamingo again. We've been here a week and I haven't found the time to write anyone. However, it's three a.m. and I have found time. This is a good booking, $350 a week plus food, a $25 raise from the first time. I'm not particularly worried about where we go right now as long as we get paid and improve ourselves. I'm trying to save enough money to buy a secondhand car. I'm learning more about the entertainment business every day. I have a feeling we'll be seeing you soon but no concrete reason for having that feeling. However, here's hoping! Love, Neil.

"P.S. Thursday will be my first birthday away from home. When was yours?"

And a second P.S.: "One of the guys just said all he wants is a Corvette with a telephone in it. Good grief! I look around and I haven't even a phone in my room!"

As I wrote years later in the book *Neil and Me*, I have often thought of the contrast between the jaunty tone of that letter and the wistfulness of one of his classic songs, "Sugar Mountain," which he wrote a few days later on that nineteenth birthday, the last verse going:

> "Now you say you're leavin' home
> 'Cause you want to be alone.
> Ain't it funny how you feel
> When you're findin' out it's real."

In another few months he had his car, a secondhand hearse, and was heading east with his band, but the hearse broke down at Blind River, Ontario, and the band had to walk and hitchhike most of the rest of the way to Toronto. He had told the band our Toronto address and for days thereafter the doorbell would ring and one or two of his band would be standing there, and we'd look after them. Neil was the last to arrive.

Hitchhiking out of Sudbury, he'd been picked up by a carload of teenagers who told him they hated hippies like him. They drove him miles along a country road and then hit him a few times and pushed him out into a ditch. He didn't know where he was. He walked all night before he found the highway again, and a more friendly ride. We had the whole band off and on for a few weeks. But after rehearsing in a rented studio downtown, Neil decided that the band wasn't good enough, broke it up and started looking for a job that would support him a while.

One day he came to me and asked where I got my hair cut. "When I go for a job they take a look at my long hair and it's no go. Yours always looks long enough, but neat."

I took him to my barber, whose place on Yonge Street was called Mister Ivan's, and paid $4, the going rate, to save as much of Neil's hair as he could but still leave him looking neat. Neil came out of the chair and walked up Yonge Street and got a job at $50 a week as a stockroom boy at Coles' Charles and Yonge bookstore. That didn't last long because suddenly Neil was in demand, getting all the playing he could handle with a band called The Mynah Birds, but hardly any sleep. Coles let him go after he'd been late for work several times. Once when I was away he called Astrid saying he was very sick, didn't know what was the matter. She told him to stay where he was, she'd pick him up, which she did in her little TR3. She told me later he slept for two days, hardly moved, then ate ravenously and was all right again. Not long after that, living in a rooming house in downtown Toronto and deciding that he wanted to move on, he bought another hearse, filled it with musicians and girlfriends and headed for California, where by chance he found another good musician, Stephen Stills, whom he'd met at Fort William. Stills was trying to put together a band, which instantly included Neil and one of his hearse passengers, bassist Bruce Palmer. That became Buffalo Springfield, which in a few weeks became much in demand for concert dates and TV shows, and was recording songs by Neil and Steve Stills, the band's main players, songwriters and performers. He was on his way.

But back to the night when Neil and I met and Bobby Kennedy was dying. Neil and I made a date for the next morning that didn't work out. By that time Kennedy was dead and the press people on the story, including me, were being flooded with instructions on flights east, cautions that from here on we would need special police credentials, and other bits and pieces preparatory to catching an aircraft back east for his funeral. We survived, and that memory of the night with Neil always warms me, a personal footnote to an otherwise sad assignment.

☙

As far as I know, I've had only one friend who possibly was a murderer. We never met until 1965, but his name, Wayne Lonergan, and the crime with which he'd been charged, had been known to me since late in 1943. I was back from my stint with CP London then and working on CP Toronto's rewrite desk awaiting induction into the navy when Lonergan, a Canadian in an RCAF training course at the University of Toronto, became a suspect in the murder of his wife, Patricia, an American heiress. They had met in New York a few years earlier when Lonergan, tall and handsome, took a job as an attendant to her father, who used a wheelchair. They married, split up, and when Wayne joined the RCAF she stayed in New York with their infant son. Lonergan had been on a weekend leave in New York when she was murdered, but had returned to Toronto before her body was discovered in her apartment. She had been bludgeoned to death, possibly with a heavy candlestick.

Lonergan, when first questioned by two New York detectives who flew to Toronto for that purpose, admitted that he had seen her and they had argued heatedly, after which he stayed overnight with a male friend.

The New York detectives then pulled a fast one. They persuaded Lonergan that he should return to New York for his wife's funeral, see his father-in-law and arrange care for his baby son. Lonergan fell for it. He and the detectives travelled to Buffalo, Lonergan still believing that he was not under arrest. But when they checked into a Buffalo hotel he was handcuffed to a bed, well and thoroughly double-crossed. There had been no extradition, no nothing. The New York papers then painted him as a homosexual well known in high society, indeed did such a job on him that when a district attorney assured him that if he pleaded guilty to the lesser charge of third-degree murder, he would be out in two or three years, Lonergan accepted that.

Instead, he was double-crossed again. When he got to court, on the basis of what he thought was a limited guilty plea he was convicted of first-degree murder and spent the next twenty-two years in heavy-duty prisons, one being Sing Sing.

As a CP rewrite man in 1943, I'd worked on Canadian aspects of the story, thought of it occasionally over the years until, in 1965, I noticed a brief item in a New York newspaper that he had sought and got the right to appeal in what was called a Huntley hearing, a legal precedent establishing that if a prisoner could claim to have been coerced into a confession, he might appeal.

I went to Dic Doyle with the clipping and told him this could be a juicy hearing and I would like to cover it, and he gave his okay. I then spent some time in the New York courtroom, writing a lot about the background while the appeal was heard. Other Toronto papers were interested by then. He lost the appeal, but as he had served twenty-two years and the case still had some doubtful elements, the court ordered him deported. I found out when this was to take place and drove to Clinton prison in New York State hoping to see him. On the morning when he was conducted by two officers from the big prison gates, I followed close behind. He was to be still in custody until he reached the Canadian border, and across to St. Johns, Quebec, also known as St. Jean, where he was dropped in the street by the bus terminal.

The Toronto *Star* had a reporter and photographer on the scene as well, but I had been a distance ahead when the U.S. officers were driving away. I approached Lonergan and introduced myself.

"Oh, yes," he said in a friendly way, "I remember seeing you at the Huntley hearing. I used to get your paper in prison. Read everything you wrote about my case. You were pretty accurate. Thanks."

"Where are you going?" I asked.

"I guess Toronto." He had been given a bus ticket.

"I'm going back there. I'll drive you, if you want."

At that point the *Star* people arrived. They offered to take him to Montreal for total seclusion in a hotel suite, all expenses paid, with no other reporters until they had the story. Lonergan said no, he'd come with me. I invited Ron Lowman, an excellent *Star* reporter, to ride with us so that, in effect, we could both talk to him, Ron in the back seat, Lonergan and me in the front.

Why such charity? It was nearly noon. I reasoned that I could interview Lonergan and have the full story in the *Globe's* early editions that evening. As for Lowman, well, I hated to do it (of course) but I did not stop, even for food, until late afternoon when Lonergan was hungry and I felt that the most Lowman could do was phone in a few paragraphs for the *Star's* final edition that day.

We reached the eastern outskirts of Toronto in early evening. I stopped for gas and to phone the *Globe* to say that we would arrive soon at the Royal York Hotel, where Lonergan intended to stay, and that the *Globe* should have a photographer on hand to greet us.

When we pulled up at the Royal York, I decided to go in to watch while Lonergan registered. That would be the end of my story, seeing the desk clerk's reaction when he heard who was checking in. Several photographers waiting in front of the hotel followed us up the steps, flashbulbs popping. When Lonergan and I turned towards the desk down at the other end of the lobby, I saw Phil Givens, the Toronto mayor, a man who reacted to flashbulbs like moth to a flame. He was staring our way, interested in who could be the focus of all that attention. Then he started walking towards us.

"This is going to be good," I said to Lonergan. "Here comes the mayor..."

"Hey, Scott," Givens said. "What's all this about?"

"Mr. Mayor," I said, as the photographers closed in, "I'd like you to meet—" The mayor had his hand out, Lonergan also reaching for the handshake, flashbulbs popping, as I added, "Wayne Lonergan."

The mayor dropped Lonergan's hand like a hot brick and turned to me. "You son of a bitch!" he said and got out of there.

The next day, Ralph Allen, managing editor at the *Star,* phoned me at the *Globe.* Oddly enough, his greeting to his old sportswriting buddy from Winnipeg was exactly the same as the mayor's, except longer. "You son of a bitch!" he said. "We spent hours with razor blades trying to cut you out of the goddamn picture, but it couldn't be done and still show Givens shaking hands with Lonergan."

So the *Star's* front-page picture that day showed Lonergan at the left, the mayor at the right, both identified in the cutlines, and me between them, laughing, and not identified—which I thought was very parochial of Allen.

The *Globe* did not use that photo on the first night, or anytime else. As soon as I arrived at the office from the Royal York, before I'd even started to write, I found Doyle and managing editor Clark Davey. I said, 'We've got a great picture of Givens shaking hands with Lonergan, but I played a real dirty trick on the mayor to get it. In fairness, I don't think we should run it." Which we didn't.

One other paper besides the *Star* did use it. The old New York *Herald Tribune* had brought it in by wirephoto and gave it a good play, I think on page two or three, over a caption that read, "Toronto mayor greets convicted murderer."

As part of the aftermath, I was asked to appear with Lonergan on the celebrated CBC-TV program *This Hour Has Seven Days*. Lonergan and I were in a studio waiting for the camera lights to go on when I heard in my earpiece the producer say, "Right off the top ask him, 'Did you murder your wife?'"

I didn't do it. I had my own ways of interviewing, and I didn't like that sledgehammer approach. Lonergan had been at our house for family dinners. I didn't feel like harassing him. Besides, I knew what a complicated answer would be required to get even close to the truth. The producer asked the question himself and got nothing new. Is a man who has spent twenty-two years in jail going to spill his guts just because the camera lights are on? I suppose that's the TV theory. I never regretted the decision I had made in that split second to stay out of the interview.

In later years Lonergan was quite well-known around Toronto, tall, handsome, well spoken, intelligent, often seen at parties. He went to England for a while, partly to visit a friend who might have known more than anyone except Lonergan about what happened on the fatal night in 1943. Someone, at any rate, had kept him supplied in jail with books, newspapers and magazines. And he always had a radio. Once I asked him how he had kept such good pace with what was going on in the world, with stock markets, politics, sports, sometimes startling arcane facts.

He answered, "When you're lying there in the dark with a radio, you can be anywhere—New York, Rome, London, Paris, the World Series, anywhere. You hear the musicals, the political debates. . ."

For years before his death he lived with actress Barbara Hamilton, a great woman whose off-stage style was very much like her on-stage style: straight to the point. Once, not long after Wayne died, singer Betty Robertson asked Barbara, "Do you think Wayne killed his wife?"

"Absolutely not!" Barbara said. "If he could live with me for twelve years and not kill me, he couldn't kill anybody."

1 8
Leaving the Globe - Twice:
1969 and 1980

OR SOME YEARS I had been preoccupied with what was happening
between Quebec and the rest of Canada. I liked Quebec and
Quebeckers, and the ones I knew through hockey seemed to understand
that. I took one-on-one French lessons at Berlitz twice a week so I could
make a speech or interview in limping French and could understand the
printed language. The *Globe* often sent me to conferences on what was to
happen between Quebec and the rest of Canada.

During royal tours (I covered them all from 1959 to 1976) I would
often read *Le Devoir* or *Le Soleil* to check my own impressions, once interviewed college hockey players in French on TV without disaster, made
friends with Quebec newspaper people—but, I guess, never really built
much of a bridge. At lunch one day, I was sitting next to René Lévesque at
a conference of newspaper people called in Montreal by George Ferguson,
editor of the Montreal *Star* (the same one who, as managing editor of the
Winnipeg *Free Press*, had told me I'd never be worth more than $25 a week
to his paper). I made some remark to Lévesque that caused him to snap at
me, "Don't treat me like your little brother!" What had I said? I didn't
know, couldn't figure it out, but in common with most earnest Anglos of
my type, determined not to make the same mistake again—whatever it
was.

At a similar conference called in Toronto by the *Globe*, another try at
improving French–English understanding through journalism, I made a
suggestion that still seems to me realistic (or would have been when I made
it, thirty years ago): that the editorial boards of leading French and English

newspapers should trade editorial writers on one-year shifts to sit in on editorial conferences, write editorials and thereby greatly improve mutual understanding of each other's editorial attitudes. I volunteered to be in the first wave of such a trade. With a little bit of luck, it could become a media event—"*Globe* and *Le Devoir* Trade Editors and Draft Choices."

When I made that proposal, a deep silence settled over the conference. What? Actually *do* something? No takers.

Throughout the 1960s, after my mild and aborted flirtation with the *Star*, I was what I could class, even now, as a loyal *Globe and Mail* employee. I never even considered leaving the paper. There were only the three Toronto dailies at the time. I had rejected one chance to go to the *Star*. John Bassett of the *Telegram* had asked once, in 1966, offering me $35,000 a year to be the *Tely's* sports editor. But I turned it down. One reason was that by then I couldn't imagine any better situation in journalism than the one I had at the *Globe,* partly due to managing editor Dic Doyle seeing so many major news stories as being up my alley.

Besides that prime position, I had a lot of freedom. I could take my family to Florida and write my columns from there. There were no quibbles about outside work on books or broadcasting, even when such pursuits took me away from Toronto, such as when I researched and wrote a CBC-TV show on the Mackenzie River for a *Rivers of Canada* series. I was away for many weeks, going down the river from Hay River 1,100 miles to the Arctic on a Northern Transportation tugboat, my daily columns from Fort Smith, Norman Wells, Inuvik and other northern settlements, whetting my longtime interest in the North. My first work there was as a freelancer, when *Sports Illustrated* assigned me in the middle of the 1950s to write about what was seen as the vanishing caribou, a story that never was printed because the caribou, for their own unfathomable reasons, made a tremendous comeback. On that job I had flown over much tundra in small aircraft while Canadian Wildlife Service biologists counted caribou. I had slept on the floor of a Mountie detachment's cabin at Fort Reliance and thus learned much about the RCMP's role in the North; had been involved in the pickup by air of a trapper who had been stranded with his winter's bales of fur when the ice broke up. All this experience was translated into columns and *Globe Magazine* articles, mostly not costing the *Globe* a penny in expenses. During trips to Russia on a CBC-TV assignment to write about Soviet hockey before it had been seen in a major way in North America, I had studied because of my own interests the way the Soviets dealt with their North much more successfully than Canada did. Another year I flew east to west across our North in a small press group with Governor General Roland Michener. On that trip, I was representing the *Globe* but also was building up a host of impressions that enhanced what I would write in the future, in both fact and fiction, about that vast part of our country and its peoples.

In addition, I wrote books at the rate of close to one a year throughout the 1960s and into the 1970s, adding by large or small degree to my income—ranging from such titles as Punch Imlach's *Hockey Is a Battle*, *War on Ice* (the early years of Soviet–Canada hockey) and *The Leafs I Knew*, about my early hockey-writing years with the Leafs. I'd been happy with two books on early Canadiana, *O'Brien* (about M. J. O'Brien, Renfrew timber baron and railroad builder) and *Silent Frank Cochrane* (the North's first major politician, a powerful minister in both Ontario and federal governments). O'Brien and Cochrane were little-known Canadians whom I particularly enjoyed writing about, my wife, Astrid, helping powerfully in the research for both, and sharing the bylines. So I was busy, and fulfilled. And then in 1969 came an unexpected crisis with the *Globe*.

The book I had written with Punch Imlach, *Hockey Is a Battle*, came just after he had been fired by the Leafs and was willing to talk freely, which he did. What he said was Topic A in the hockey world. Readers couldn't get enough of what had happened to the Leafs, rising from last place to four Stanley Cups under Imlach and then back to also-rans inside of ten years. The book being hot inside stuff, I figured, loyally, that my employer should get first crack at publishing excerpts, but the *Globe* ignored my offer entirely. The book's publisher therefore offered the serial rights around, drawing bids from both the *Telegram* and the *Star*. The *Star*'s offer was a few thousand dollars lower than the *Telegram*'s, which came from its publisher, John Bassett, by phone to our farm one Saturday morning. He offered $7,500 for five one thousand-word excerpts to be published in his paper and one two thousand five hundred-word piece to go in *Weekend Magazine*, which the *Telegram* carried on Saturdays.

"I know there are others after it," he said, "but I don't want to dicker. Just yes or no."

I said yes. The *Star* complained bitterly, but had had its chance and blew it.

But the *Globe* came to life again. They said that under my union con-tract I was forbidden to write for any competing newspaper, ignoring the fact that the paper had not exercised this veto when a sports book by *Globe and Mail* sports columnist Dick Beddoes had recently been excerpted in the *Star*. I argued as best I could. I even offered to have my name taken off the book excerpts so that they would appear simply as "By Punch Imlach." The *Globe* replied that the union embargo covered anything, under whatever byline, that I had written being published by an opposi-tion publication.

An unspoken factor in the *Globe's* embargo, I was later convinced, was that publishers of the *Globe* and *Telegram* had a long-running antagonism into which Imlach and I had unwittingly stumbled. The only thing I could do, I felt, was quit the *Globe*, rather than do Imlach out of his just share of the serial rights money. (Later Dic Doyle, in his book *Hurly-Burly*, said that I had left the *Globe* in 1969 "over a simple matter of dollars and cents," which was oversimplifying to a ridiculous degree.) When Bassett heard this, he phoned me and said that he didn't like me ending my years at the *Globe* over this matter and would release me entirely from our spoken agreement as long as the book was not published by another Toronto paper. But I declined. I had made a deal in good faith and was sticking to it. Which was when he made his second offer that I move to the *Telegram* as sports editor: "Why don't you quit that stupid outfit you work for and come over to a real newspaper?"

His adjective *stupid* pretty well agreed with what I was feeling about the *Globe* right then. I asked what he had in mind as salary.

"Thirty thousand a year," he said. "That would include some work at CFTO, too." That was his TV station.

"Have I gone back that much in only three years?" I asked.

"What do you mean?"

"The last time, you offered me $35,000."

He laughed. "Did I? Okay, thirty-five. And I want you writing sports, not that folksy country stuff you've been writing a lot of at the *Globe*."

I said okay, somewhat amused that he wanted me in sports. However, Bassett's senior adviser, J. D. MacFarlane, contended that the paper already had an overload in sports. So instead I wrote a general column for a while, then was appointed sports editor, my column carrying that title but the actual executive work being done by Chick McGregor and George Gross, then Chick's associate sports editor.

Two years after I joined the *Tely*, whose atmosphere I thoroughly enjoyed, it folded (which I regard as a coincidence), and George Gross went on to be the best-informed and richest sports editor in town as a founding member among the orphaned *Tely* people who started the Toronto *Sun*. I might have been one of that group, except that in the one organization meeting that I attended, it was agreed that to start the *Sun* everybody, regardless of position, would accept a nominal salary. I figured it out. After paying Rassy's alimony, Astrid and I wouldn't have much to live on. Goodbye, *Sun*. Dic Doyle called from the *Globe and Mail* and asked me to come back.

I jump ahead here, a few years, to 1980. Conn Smythe was having trouble writing his memoirs. He called me one day at the *Globe* office and asked in that rasping voice, "Scott, will you help me with my book?"

I knew that he'd tried one or two other writers but had felt he wasn't getting anywhere. One was Dick Beddoes, a good friend of mine but with a style as much his own as Smythe's was *his* own. I said we had better meet and talk about what was involved.

Smythe's call was lucky for me. I had just quit the *Globe and Mail* for the second and final time, mainly because of what seemed to me a *Globe* policy (or lack of policy) that had made Punch Imlach, in his second go-round as Leafs coach and general manager the target of a vendetta by some players. He was trying to run the Leafs the way he had in the 1960s, and the 1970s, but players wouldn't stand for it. The players had a media mouthpiece to whom they fed inside "stories," the source never identified (an easy way to get slander into print). These had been written by another *Globe* sports writer. I protested to the *Globe's* editor-in-chief the first time it happened, saying that if this sort of thing wasn't stopped, some day it would cost the paper a million dollars. It had happened again, so I quit. I had no job to go to and flatly declined the *Globe's* invitation to come back. Then Smythe phoned.

A couple of days later he and I met to talk it over. I was excited. I had been along for the ride in much of his long and colourful life in hockey, business and horse-racing, so had the head start. He had led fighting men in action in two wars, been a prisoner-of-war in one of them, was badly wounded in the other, had earned the lasting enmity of the Liberal Party of Canada because of his attacks on the government over its wartime foot-dragging on conscription policy. As a result, and meanly, he was never offered an Order of Canada.

Heavy research would be called for on my part so that he could have his final word on events whose details might have become dimmed in his memory. I knew all that when Conn and I sat down in his office one day to discuss his book.

"I'm not going to live much longer, Scott," he said. "I figure I've got just this one shot to set a lot of records straight."

We talked about what had to be done, and how—prompting him with questions, taping answers, organizing sensitive historical material, making a deal with a publisher, gathering photos, and completing all this in a matter of a few months. I said it could be done if I worked full time, as I could, being otherwise at liberty—or broke and unemployed to put it another way. What would I need as a retainer, he asked. I had thought this over and reached a number I thought was high enough. "Fifty thousand. And a fifty-fifty split on the royalties."

He picked up a pen, looked at me with a grin, blue eyes flashing. "Prices are sure going up," he said. "Okay, you got it."

Then came a moment I cherish. He had become thoughtful, and said, "I'm planning to turn over my share of the royalties to the Crippled Children." This had been for years his favourite charity. "How much can I count on for the fund from my book?"

I said that if it sold really well, the total royalties might reach $30,000 or $35,000.

He was surprised. Even shocked. Some people tend to think that writing is an easy way to make a fortune. "You mean I might get only fifteen or sixteen Gs for charity? Geez, I can give that much out of my own pocket, without doing a book!"

I said, "Well, maybe we could negotiate on the royalties split."

"What do you mean, negotiate?"

I don't know and never will know where my answer came from. "I'll throw my royalties split in for the Crippled Children along with yours."

His eyes filled with tears! "And I always thought you goddamn sports writers didn't have a heart," he said.

It might just have been a coincidence, but he was a sentimental man and from that moment on everything I did in the subsequent research and writing, even sometimes when we disagreed on a fact, a date or a person, he accepted.

But lest anyone think he'd reined in some of his legendary toughness, I sometimes think of how quite often during my subsequent research he would acidly criticize Punch Imlach, whose Leafs this time were in disarray, and then watch for my reaction. His dislike of Imlach was at least in part a family bias. Imlach and Stafford Smythe, Conn's son, had been at daggers drawn just about forever, Imlach as coach and general manager and Stafford, also tough, insisting that he, as an owner, had the ultimate right to call the shots.

Finally one day Conn and I and the tape recorder were at his home in Caledon, and he was blasting away at something Imlach had done or was doing or might do, when he looked at me keenly for a reaction. I didn't react.

"Damn it," he ground out, "every time I say something rough about Imlach, you just sit there. Never say anything, never even *look* anything, just sit there! Why?"

"Imlach is my friend," I said. "When you criticize him that's your business, but when you do I'm not going to even look as if I agree with you."

He stared at me for several seconds. "So you're Imlach's friend, eh?"

"Yes."

"Good! He *needs* a friend."

❦

While writing that line about the late Punch Imlach needing a friend, it occurred to me that friendship can reverse itself unpredictably. One evening in 1994 I was invited to speak about sports writing at Trent University. A friend I arrived with jerked his head at a bald and burly man in the upper rows. "Isn't that Carl Brewer up there?"

He was right—there sat one of my all-time favourite hockey players but also a man who was often on Punch's shit-list. Brewer was an all-star defenceman with the Leafs when they (under Punch) were winning Stanley Cups. I headed towards him. Brewer was with his daughter, a Trent student. We talked for a while, and one of the things I remember out of that conversation was Brewer telling someone that he and I had always been friends "even though Scott is also a friend of Punch Imlach and Alan Eagleson."

Well, so? What Brewer knew from the first was that Imlach and I were close friends and wrote books together. What he *assumed* was that I must also be a friend of Eagleson's, because I had helped Eagleson with his memoirs just before the roof fell in on his career as hockey's most powerful individual (an event that crippled sales of his memoirs, I might add—ruefully, because he and I shared the royalties fifty-fifty). The Eagleson connection, however, had not been because we were longtime friends. It was because he had helped hockey players get their status raised. In early years I had been nasty to him in print more than once when I was sports editor of the *Telegram*. Once, after I had been rather acid about his behaviour as a member of the Ontario legislature, he told *Telegram* hockey writer Paul Dulmage that if he caught me he'd punch me on the nose. Which he might have; he'd done it to others who riled him.

But he had supported me sometimes when it counted. He called after I quit the *Globe* in 1980 to protest the newspaper printing a story involving Imlach that I felt was untrue.

"Congratulations," he said.

"What about?"

"It's about time somebody took on that poisonous little bastard," he said, referring to the reporter whose stories I had quit in protest over.

"I thought you'd be in favour of anybody who took a crack at Imlach."

"Not in this case," he said. "You got it right. Darryl Sittler"—the Leafs captain—"phoned me as soon as he saw the paper to tell me that the quotes attributed to him had been manufactured, never made."

Eagleson was like that, impulsively taking a side in support of a man he'd been in conflict with. Anyway, in time we two more or less buried the hatchet. After Imlach's death when there was wide interest among publishers in an Eagleson book, I was interested in writing it. The idea fitted with one of my beliefs—that anyone who had achieved much, and was almost constantly under attack, deserved to tell his story in his own way.

Very early in working on such a book, Eagleson asked me, "Why didn't you do this as a biography?"

I said that in doing his biography I would have to balance what he believed of his own life and achievements against what his many enemies wanted to say in rebuttal. In effect, a biography would mean setting myself up as the judge and jury of his rightness and wrongness. My preferred method was to let him have his say, after which, whatever I did, his critics would have their say. That turned out to be true. When the critics swarmed him, sometimes fairly and often not, the facts of his achievements were ignored. But they are there in his book. Other books I have written about controversial people, Conn Smythe, Leo Cahill, Gordon Sinclair, also flushed out a good deal of resentment, which either died away or didn't, but never came before the courts, as the Eagleson career eventually did.

In all cases, I would do the same thing again.

A lot of my Eagleson memoirs contradict what happened later. I remember the first time I met Bobby Orr, then a teenaged junior star. It happened on a staircase at Toronto International Airport. He was with Brewer, who introduced us and said something like, "I've been telling Bobby that he should have an agent working for him, and he should talk to Al Eagleson." Subsequently, Orr went on to his great achievements in the game, the business side for years guided by Eagleson, until their relationship soured and Orr, from being the green kid who Brewer had thought needed guidance, became Eagleson's implacable enemy, as did Brewer, and some others.

The funniest outcome came years after my Brewer–Orr meeting when Brewer, long out of organized hockey, played in an NHL oldtimers game. Imlach thought he looked better than some of the defencemen then playing for him with the Leafs. As a result, Imlach offered Brewer a short-term contract to play again with the Leafs.

This didn't work well because some Leafs—Tiger Williams and others—distrusted him. They contended that Imlach had hired Brewer only as a mole to keep him informed on what went on in the Leafs' dressing room.

Brewer a mole for Imlach! Times do change, but not that much.

That winter Imlach flew in a team charter back from a Montreal game and found that his car, parked with the others owned by Leaf players, had a dead battery. In Tiger Williams's frank and revealing book, *Tiger*, he related that when the team had left Toronto for Montreal a few hours earlier, some players noted that Imlach had left his lights on. Some said, "Don't tell the bastard! Piss on it." When they got back from Montreal, Tiger related, the players sat in their own cars laughing because Imlach's car wouldn't start.

Brewer, who was riding with Imlach, the only ride he'd been offered because of the antagonism of other players, ran over to ask some of the others for booster cables. Instead, they roared their own engines and drove off, one player waving a set of booster cables out of his car window.

To me, that childish incident took a lot of the steam out of the contention by some players that Imlach treated *them* like children. Whatever the details, Imlach's go-around with that set of Leafs was an obvious failure, and is remembered by some more than his successes in winning four Stanley Cups in the 1960s with players who, by and large, responded positively to the same kind of hockey thinking that spelled his demise the second time around.

Still, talking with Brewer at Trent years later, he and I left all those old bones unstirred. Brewer was one of the best hockey players of my time and his enemy, Imlach, a man equally good at his job, one of the best coaches and managers.

Another time I was involved between the Leafs and a star player was in 1962 when Frank Mahovlich, one of the most gifted players and straightest human beings I ever saw or hope to see, was being sought by Chicago with an offer to the Leafs of a million dollars. The story had been front-page stuff for some weeks one autumn while I was in California covering baseball playoffs and the early games in the World Series between San Francisco and the New York Yankees. In mid-series, when the teams moved to New York, I landed in Toronto briefly when the three men who then ran the Leafs, John Bassett, Stafford Smythe and Harold Ballard, were being quoted every day on whether or not to sell Mahovlich.

I was at the *Globe and Mail* office writing my next day's column when Stafford Smythe phoned me to say that he and his partners had decided not to sell Mahovlich. At the same moment, the afternoon edition of Bassett's *Telegram* arrived on my desk. The front-page banner headline quoted Bassett as saying that he and his partners *would* sell Mahovlich. It was late in the day. I was to leave for New York and had a column to write. In it I quoted Stafford Smythe on the no-sale decision and pointed out that at the same time Bassett was saying the opposite. To this I added the fateful (but I thought justified) line, "Doesn't John Bassett know that vaudeville is dead?" What I didn't know at the time was that when Smythe had announced the no-sale decision, Bassett had not been part of it. Stafford had acted on impulse, partly because his father, Conn Smythe, had told him, "End it right now. . .don't sell."

As a result, my column made Bassett so angry that a few days later he called a meeting in the boardroom of Imperial Oil, the main sponsor for TV's *Hockey Night in Canada*, on which I had a job as intermission host. Bassett demanded that MacLaren Advertising fire me or he would find another network to carry hockey, and another sponsor, and another ad agency. All this over a guy making $5,000 a year for that *Hockey Night* job. (Dollars bought more in those days.) It wasn't hard to determine what the decision would be. The story that went into hockey folklore was that Bassett had caused me to be fired by TV and banned from Maple Leaf Gardens. That was not the case at all. I lost the TV job, but I kept everything else I was doing, including my job as a panelist on radio's popular between-periods show, the "Hot Stove League". And I never missed a game.

The publicity didn't hurt. It increased my reputation as a guy who plunged bravely into areas where angels feared to tread. In the beer parlours I had become the sort of folk hero who stood up to the hockey bigwigs and suffered for it. In the Gardens press room there would be indrawn breaths when Bassett walked in and there I was, the poor lamb. He and I would chat as if nothing had happened, while everybody would watch for the fireworks to begin. They never did. But the myth has persisted. To this day, I'm often introduced, more than thirty years later, as "the guy who was banned from Maple Leaf Gardens for just doing his job."

I 9

The
Farm

❧

B ACK IN 1969, Astrid dealt calmly with my decision to bid the *Globe* farewell, although I imagine it was at this stage that she began to wish for more security in her life.

My way of dealing with this was to drive west, taking the whole family, with the intention of researching a book tentatively entitled *My Manitoba*, in the end never to be finished.

"Look, Scott," Astrid said as we were rattling over Manitoba's highways heading for Flin Flon, "tell me where we're going to live when we get back."

"We'll rent something eventually," I said, or words to that effect, "but we'll take our time deciding. Nothing too hasty." (I thought I heard cosmic laughter right then.) "But until we get what we want, we can live at the farm."

Which brings us, not for the last time, to what in our family and among our relatives and friends always is known as The Farm, although in the real sense when we bought the land in 1967 (my centennial project), it had not been a farm for a long time.

I had walked across The Farm first in the early 1950s when Rassy and I and the boys were quite new in Omemee, and after the shotgun barrage over on the millpond to mark the opening of duck-hunting season, were finding that for weeks hunting, mostly ducks but also upland game birds, was almost the sole topic of conversation. The doctor hunted. Our next door neighbour hunted. Everybody male, old and young, hunted. Rassy was the one of us who understood. Her Virginia-born father had shot his first wild turkey when he was only eight, and after moving to Canada hunted geese and ducks in Manitoba and Saskatchewan, and had, all through her childhood. At the time (this was a few years before the Orenda gift shotgun), I had never owned a gun.

I bought an old twelve-gauge double-barrelled hammer gun for $25 from our neighbour across the street, Russell Ball. I found hunting companions. We'd sometimes go out before dawn, down the river for ducks. Some days after a few hours at the typewriter I would take the gun and drive south along what was known at the time as the Old Railroad. This name dated from when trains ran between the villages of Omemee and Bethany. The last train had been in 1926, after which the tracks were lifted and the narrow spine-like right of way became a road—still there if you ever drive that way, but now wide and paved. When I first drove it, in some places alongside where the trains had run, tree branches touched overhead and made the road a tunnel of green.

I would drive on the Old Railroad a few miles south of Omemee, park, let our dog Skippy out and take to the woods carrying my old shotgun. On those sunny fall afternoons I saw or heard many more partridges than I ever shot, or shot at, was startled sometimes by the explosive takeoff of woodcock, saw in the damp earth the signs of deer, rabbits, foxes.

As the afternoon wore on I might walk into the higher woods and cedar ridges where partridges fed among the hawthorns and wild apple trees. I found great meadow mushrooms, which I took home. I came across apple trees of an abandoned farm orchard and I ate Russets and Snows and filled the big pockets of my hunting coat. I might come home with no partridges but plenty else, plus memories of pileated woodpeckers zooming silently among the trees, big black and grey squirrels chattering from high up.

Once in a while I did manage to react fast enough and successfully shoot what were known locally as partridges but really were ruffed grouse, with which Rassy, brought up on her father's occasional bag of prairie chickens out west, would make a fine stew with dumplings. During those fine fall days Skippy would be ranging far and wide, usually within sight. When the shadows lengthened in late afternoon I would whistle for him. At the car he would stand at the rear waiting for me to open the trunk. Then with a leap he would be in and settled down. One time I forgot to let him out when I got home and woke in bed with a guilty start about midnight. I hurried to the garage, a former barn, in my pyjamas praying fervently that Skippy's silence did not mean disaster. When I opened the trunk he stood up and stretched, as dogs do when they've been asleep, then trotted ahead of me into the house and curled up in his kitchen corner.

I didn't always walk alone on those afternoons. My friend Jay Hayes, born on a farm a few miles away but by then (and since) living in the village, knew the country. Gradually I got to know it, too. We sometimes hunted through a hilly area just south of the First Line of Emily Township that had a grand stand of sugar maples known then and until long after his death as Vince Jones's woods. Vince's sugar shack stood in the middle with its big iron pots. In spring the sap was gathered from the pails attached to the maples and boiled down in those big pots. The resulting maple syrup sold in those days for less than $10 a gallon. Old Vince was still alive then. The woods are still in the Jones family, as beautiful as ever.

A mile south of there, just beyond the road that marks the Fourteenth Line of Cavan Township, Jay once led me over what had been a farm for many years, a hundred acres of steep fields and woods on which, years earlier, the last family to farm the place, the Tweedys, raised ten children. By the time I first saw it with Jay, the house was empty and falling down, the Tweedys scattered and gone. We used to walk along one particular gully of wild apples and hawthorns, where partridges often fed and usually were still alive when we had passed on.

In the next few years when Jay and I still hunted the area, the farm buildings of the Tweedys' time sank gradually into the sumachs and hawthorns and poison ivy until only vague ruins remained: the wreckage-filled hole, once a cellar, of the abandoned and falling down frame house, weed-grown timbers of what had been the east wall of the Tweedys' barn near what might once have been a hen house. Walking more or less easterly with our shotguns ready, Jay and I chatted our way along a grassy gully, seeing under the trees the fallen fruit marked by beak marks (partridges) or tooth marks (squirrels).

The first time I saw the place, it was ideal as a cattle ranch, because of abundant feed and constant water from a sidehill spring. For more than a century the spring had provided water for farm families and their animals and for the tiny stone-foundationed one-room school built on the south side of the Fourteenth Line, on what became The Farm.

In the Tweedys' time the spring's function had been somewhat formalized by someone who had dug a big hole in the path of the brook and in the hole had established an old iron bathtub. This acted as a water trough for deer and cattle, and stayed open and overflowing even in the coldest days and nights of winter, when on mornings I would go there and see the tracks of animals large and small who had been drinking at the bathtub.

I cannot set out accurately enough my feelings of peace and wonder in those days, snow to my thighs, yet the spring still running. The parts of my childhood that I had spent on farms in the west seemed to have stored up, unbidden, my wish to have some of that for myself eventually.

In the five years that I lived in Omemee with my wife and two sons, we had some difficult times. Neil contracted polio in the epidemic of 1950 and barely survived, a time I was to write about thirty years later in *Neil and Me*. For two winters we drove to Florida so that Neil, much weakened, could live in shorts and not much else; he couldn't handle the weight of winter clothes. Meanwhile, I was facing steadily dwindling income in fiction, so began to sell outdoors articles to *Sports Illustrated*. One assignment took me to Manitoba and Saskatchewan to write about duck hunting, another to James Bay on the fringe of the Arctic to write about hunting geese. My marriage with Rassy was in some trouble. Other women in my life were part of it. I can see now that I was casting around as some people do, trying to discover a way out.

In 1955 we rented out our Omemee house and moved into rented quarters in Winnipeg, and then in Toronto, before selling the Omemee house and buying another in Pickering. I wrote whatever would pay our way.

My extramarital involvements became more serious until in 1959, when I met Astrid, our marriage ended in the early stages of divorce. I lived in an apartment in downtown Toronto for a while, corresponding almost daily with Astrid, who visited Toronto occasionally before moving there, taking a job, and becoming my second wife in 1961. When I went to or through Winnipeg on sports assignments I always saw Neil, who was attending my old school, Kelvin. By 1966 or 1967 salaried and freelance work had ended my financial drought. I kept thinking of the good times in Omemee and going there occasionally on weekends, planning to return permanently if I could figure out how to do it. It was in the late autumn of 1967 when one Saturday I happened across that old hundred acres again, The Farm, and wondered if it could be bought, and could we build a house and live there.

Jay quickly found out who owned it—Bruce Sargent, a part-time farmer and Peterborough businessman who ran cattle on what he called the Ranch, what we were to call The Farm. I tracked Bruce down.

"Just thought I'd ask," I said. "I've been looking for some property to buy and wonder if your place on the Fourteenth Line is for sale?"

Bruce, a burly man, pleasant, partner in a real estate and insurance firm, said he hadn't thought of selling but would think it over. I got back to him a day or two later and he said yes, but there was one corner of it that he and his wife wanted to keep: a few acres where they liked to take their grandchildren for picnics and bird-watching and flower-watching and general nature study. But he would sell the rest of it for $6,500. We shook hands on that. He phoned back a few days later to say there had been a hitch: he couldn't separate the southeast corner acreage without a survey, which would be costly.

I asked what price he would put on the entire hundred. He said $8,000. It was a deal and the sale went through.

That winter I went up there every Sunday. Many of my Omemee friends, Jay Hayes among them, had snowmobiles, and I bought one. A crowd of us, Jay and his wife, Betty, their sons Robert and young Bill, and daughter, Brenda, maybe a dozen others from the district, would gather near where the old Tweedy farmhouse had been. Astrid and our two daughters, Deirdre and Astrid, sometimes came along. Across the lane from the old cellar we would build a big fire and heat a great pot of chili go to with the good Omemee-baked bread and a few beers, using paper plates that could be thrown into the fire.

Those were good Sundays. Each time I drove home to Toronto at night I had a mighty feeling of having earned my tiredness. At home in Toronto, Astrid and I would pore over plans to build a house. Left to my own devices, I probably would have done what all my country friends advised—build a house as close as possible to the road. Shortening the inevitable snowdrifts between road and house would be the country way. Astrid had different, wiser, ideas.

We engaged an architect. He wanted to see where the house would be built. We went to The Farm one Sunday after a storm of ice and freezing rain. We couldn't drive more than a few yards off the road, where we parked and walked uphill, slipping and sliding. Astrid stopped on the side of a high hill almost exactly in the centre of the property. A long valley to the southeast gave a vista of many miles of snow, forests and frozen swamp.

"This is where the house should go," she said.

I would have agreed to wherever she pointed. I just wanted a house where we could get out of the city, winter and summer. Over the years, never mind the times when our lane was drifted tight and impassable, never mind our eventual split, I never ceased agreeing with her choice of where the house should be built. One thing that happened soon after might illustrate something about our chosen site. The young architect, up with us to have a look, lost his footing on the ice-covered hillside and slid fifty feet down the hill on his back before we could get him stopped. Even so, he liked the view, and soon produced a design that we greatly liked, centring on a thirty-by-twenty-foot main room with a flagstoned floor.

East facing big windows would look across the deck and along the valley. Along the west, or uphill side, his roof line was designed with long narrow high windows to reduce the effect of summer heat. The deck would lead to steps down to what was envisaged as a parking area. I hadn't thought of a swimming pool then.

There was only one hitch. I had figured that we could afford $25,000. I had quoted that figure to the architect and asked him to bring the house in at that figure, no more. We put his drawings out to several contractors. The lowest bid was $35,000. Builders were busy and would not promise to get the house up and liveable by autumn. Not only the cost but the time element didn't suit me. I wanted us to be using the house for sure by winter. As a temporary solution, so we could enjoy the summer there, I bought a small travel trailer. Deirdre had been working nights and Saturdays, saving to buy her heart's desire, a horse. In my euphoric insistence that it would all work, I okayed the horse.

I continued jumping the gun a little. Excellent prefab chalets were available on the market at that time, one of the most expensive being $12,000, fully erected, with ten percent down and the balance financed through the builder. We decided to pay the architect (I think the fee was $1,800) and buy a Colonial Sunnibuilt chalet that we were promised would be up and liveable by September—which it was if you don't define "liveable" too precisely.

The chalet, with its twenty-four-foot-square living room, wide split-stone fireplace reaching fourteen feet to the ceiling, the stone having been chosen and split off our own stone piles, would be the centre of my life for the next twenty-two years. From the first I knew that sometime I'd live there permanently (or as permanently as I get). Astrid's view of that possibility came out one night at a party of close friends, such parties always close-knit affairs, everyone else with homes or backgrounds in the Omemee or Peterborough areas. Some of us had been bringing in hay that day and someone was kidding Astrid about living at The Farm full time when she said firmly, somewhat provoked, that she had married a Toronto newspaperman, not an Omemee farmer.

So there was friction, although not yet serious. Deirdre at the time had graduated from Guelph University and was about to be married. Young Astrid had her own horse, a quarter-horse gelding named Diamond we'd given her one birthday. She belonged to a pony club that functioned each Saturday morning at Saddlewood Equestrian Centre, a few miles away. When we were at The Farm in the summers she would ride over on a woodsy trail. In winter I would drive her from the city. To be on time to groom her mount and gossip and kid with her equally horse-mad friends, she had to be there by nine.

She and I would be on the highway early from Toronto. She would spend the day at Saddlewood learning to be an English-style rider, bringing home ribbons when she did well in competition, hanging out in the pony club tackroom. At the end of my own relaxing day of doing nothing much, I'd pick her up and we would drive back to Toronto in time for the hockey game at Maple Leaf Gardens. I remember her one day saying quietly to me that I was good to her. "Not many kids have fathers who'll get up early every Saturday and drive eighty miles just so their kids can have fun."

20

Coming Apart:
1969-1976

❦

T HE FARM, HOWEVER, was to play at least a role, if only as a stage-set-
ting, in the eventual breakup of that marriage and family. I can now
recognize that one way of explaining myself to myself is to conclude that
after I moved away from the country, in the middle 1950s, I was always trying to get back there. One time my daughter Astrid told me that once she
and Neil had been discussing the ups and downs of life with me, specifically
the two marriages, both broken by me, that had affected them and their
mothers. Neil asked, "What did our father do to those women, anyway?"

I don't know the answer exactly, but there were clues. I remember one
breakfast in our Moore Park house, which Astrid loved—not only the
house but the district and all it signified and in a way promised, for our
future. I read in the *Globe and Mail* that the Peterborough *Examiner* was
looking for a new editor. Without a word to Astrid, who was across the
table having her own breakfast, I got up and phoned Robertson Davies, a
friend of my Omemee years who, when he was editor of the *Examiner*, had
been putting out one of the most quoted newspapers in the country. All
that Astrid heard was that I was telling Rob that I would like to be considered for the Peterborough editorship. She was shocked. We had never
even talked about moving. She burst into tears. She was settled, she liked
our life in Toronto, and totally without discussion I shattered her hard-
won peace of mind. This was not out of sync with a lot of other things I
had done, including falling in love with her, but she had thought all that
was in the past, and now I was talking about moving to the Peterborough-
Omemee area again.

As it turned out, Rob Davies advised me confidentially that the paper was about to be sold to Thomson Newspapers and that the salary I would require was close to double what the *Examiner* under new ownership would be likely to pay.

My abrupt departure from the *Globe* over the Imlach book in 1969 was also a self-made decision in which consideration of the effect on our family played no part. I even managed to be arbitrary enough that I was out of the *Globe*, and therefore without pay, and out of our Ottawa house, two months before my job at the *Telegram* was to begin. When we drove out of Ottawa that summer we knew that we couldn't get our Moore Park house back and had no place to live except The Farm, which would not be practical when I was going to a new city-based job.

As a stopgap, we rented a townhouse near Highway 401. This vastly reduced the amount of time it took to drive to The Farm, but that was its only asset. Most of our furniture and belongings had to stay in storage because very little fitted into the townhouse. We were both unhappy. What we needed was a house back in the Moore Park area, and a year or so later we found what we wanted—a large house at 17 Rosedale Heights Drive only a few blocks from the old place and a few minutes from Maple Leaf Gardens and other parts of downtown. With some borrowing and mortgaging, we managed it.

It was the best house Astrid and I had ever owned, four bedrooms, four bathrooms, nice grounds, a deck just off our breakfast room. But it became less affordable after the *Tely* folded in 1971, taking about a quarter of my income along with it.

To counteract that trend, I took a job at City-TV as host of the five-nights-a-week *City Show*, produced by Ron Haggart, the guests and topics mainly involved with current events and reflecting his shrewd understanding of local politics. At the same time I was writing my daily column for the *Globe* and several times a week filming a Toronto news report for CHCH-TV in Hamilton.

I would go to the *Globe* and write my column, hurry across town to film my bit for Hamilton's nightly news program, get home in time for a nap (if I had time) and an early dinner, then get to City-TV by six-thirty to work on backgrounds to the several stories lined up for me each night.

It was a crazy schedule that maybe would have worked if, at the same time, Astrid had been in good health. She had been suffering bone loss in her jaw, and had been told that this would endanger many of her teeth unless she underwent a series of bone marrow transplants. First require-ment was a hip operation to obtain a supply of her own bone marrow to use. That operation, badly done, meant that for years her hip was weak and she had to walk with a cane. After each jaw operation she would be in seri-ous pain until it was time for her next transplant. That winter when I got home from each *City Show* stint I would often find her in bed weeping.

At the end of my first winter on the *City Show*, I was exhausted, so I resigned—reluctantly, as I had been treated well by everyone at City-TV. But the happy marriage we had enjoyed for more than ten years was in severe trouble, and for once not because of other women in my life. (Where would I have found the time?) But by then the damage had been done.

~

Eventually I began spending more and more days and nights at The Farm, back in the comfortable routine of writing books, sometimes in 1972 and 1973 moving to The Farm by myself for days or weeks as I worked better there. Astrid, with the operations behind her (but still walking with a cane), would drive up on weekends or in the week. Sometimes we did recapture some of what had brought us together in the first place. But it was a steadily worsening relationship, and in the next two or three years I made decisions that didn't help at all, even when I had the best of intentions.

In the summer of 1974, the World Hockey Association was putting together an all-star team from that league to play an eight-game series with the Soviet national team, four in Canada and four in Moscow. The aim was to recapture the national fascination with the first such series in 1972, when Canada had been represented by a great all-star team from the NHL. At the time, I had been purposely out of sport, writing everything but.

After the *Telegram* folded, some at the *Globe* were sure that I would go there as sports editor, displacing my friend Jim Vipond. But I never con-sidered that kind of a hatchet job and decided to stay away from writing sports, although I still had my season tickets at Maple Leaf Gardens; Astrid and I attended all Leaf games. So I watched the 1972 series on television except for the Toronto game. Roaming from our seats before that game I had a rather pleasant exchange with the Soviet coach, Vsevolod Bobrov, whom I knew. In Moscow when I was there in 1968 as writer of CBC-TV's documentary about Soviet hockey, called *Shaibu!*, Bobrov had had several of us in the mixed Canadian and Soviet crew to dinner at his homey apartment, where his wife cooked her justly famed chicken paprika. Because writers in the Soviet Union always are honoured above producers, directors and everyone else in a film crew, I shared the head of the table with Bobrov. That night between vodka toasts he questioned me keenly about what I thought would be the result of a summit meeting between his team and the best players in the National Hockey League. When Bobrov and I met four years later that famous series had begun in Montreal, with the Soviets humbling the NHL 7–3.

Before the Toronto game Bobrov and I happened to meet again, with hugs, at ice level. Bobrov, happy after his Montreal success, said through his interpreter, "You remember in Moscow at our home when I asked you how we would do against the stars of the NHL?"

I said I did remember.

"You told me," he went on, "that we would do all right."

I nodded.

He slapped me mightily on the shoulder. "You were right!"

But during that series I was still working under the belief, or delusion, that I was through with writing sports on a regular basis, and stayed away from other games. For the 1974 series I felt differently. I had found that I couldn't leave hockey behind me, try (halfheartedly) as I had in 1972. On the 1974 team, coached by former Leaf Billy Harris, were many of my friends in the game: Frank Mahovlich, Bobby Hull, Gordie Howe, Gerry Cheevers and others. I wanted to be there for the whole eight games and the *Globe* agreed. When I knew I was going, Astrid was still not entirely herself after her bone marrow transplants, but I thought, unwisely, that the trip would be good for her. So I urged her to come with me.

It was a disaster, beginning on the long flight of the team from Vancouver to Moscow, when Astrid could not move about the aircraft freely because of her weakened hip. With the bar open all the way on the long flight, I spent a lot of time roaming the aisles with people I knew in hockey, including a close woman friend, while Astrid tried to rest. In Moscow, her condition worsened to the point that she required hospital treatment. I went with her, but that day and others, for one reason or another, or maybe a combination of several reasons, I shamefully did not look after my wife as well as a good husband should have.

I have trouble assessing accurately what was going on with me during the time in Moscow, but I'll try. Astrid was so ill that she had to spend much of her time in her hotel room bed. Attempting, without much success, to write about the non-hockey side of the trip, and to have drinks here and there with Canadian men and women as well as Soviets I'd met in 1968, I was not a good husband. I should not have asked Astrid to come with me on that trip. In the end it had a permanent effect on what was already a shaky marriage.

On our return I made another move that was to cause further damage. In 1975 former Liberal cabinet minister Judy LaMarsh had been named to head an Ontario royal commission on violence in the communications industry. For years as a journalist I had often written in a way that some thought glorified violence (the Lonergan case, for one). Thinking that being part of that royal commission would teach me a great deal that bore on my profession, I wrote a note asking Judy if there was room for me on her research team. Instead, she phoned immediately to ask me if I would be a member of her commission and probably draft the final report. Feeling greatly honoured, I accepted. Dic Doyle was not happy, but agreed on the basis that when the commission was conducting hearings I would take a sabbatical (no work, no pay) from my *Globe* job and therefore would not be tempted to make my column an extension of the commission's work. I agreed. If he had objected I would have done it anyway and taken my chances in the job market afterward.

For nearly two years we held hearings far and wide throughout Ontario. Judy and I became close friends and colleagues, but nothing more. Yet each time I arrived home late from a hearing in a distant part of the province, I would face a barrage of suspicion. I had thought for many years that our marriage was too good to end in bitter recriminations. But as anyone who has been through that mill well knows, in a marital dispute a happy past rarely has a deciding vote.

Not long before the end, we sold our fine house, paid off the mortgage, and with Astrid contributing the proceeds of a legacy that had come her way, bought a new townhouse for which we could pay cash. In retrospect, it was like clearing the decks for whatever might come.

A year or so later, at The Farm we had a terrible argument, its fury partly due to the drinks we'd had, which led to Astrid packing and leaving. Astrid challenged me, and I had admitted to one of my extramarital affairs.

I did all I could to persuade her to stay so we could thrash it out in the morning, but she packed and left. I drove my car downhill to the gate with hers, still trying to get her to change her mind. Less than a minute later, a half-mile or so down the road, I heard a hollow crash. As I drove towards it I prayed, "Please, God, don't let her be hurt." Full of deep guilt and fear, I found her. She had missed the first corner and plunged into some trees. I took her to hospital in Peterborough to have her cuts and bruises attended to. There she told everyone who spoke to her, doctors, nurses, a policeman who was investigating the accident, that I was her husband and that I had a girlfriend.

We stayed together for a short while longer, but on that night our marriage of fourteen years, most of them good, effectively ended.

She kept our newly bought and paid-for Toronto townhouse, and I paid alimony. I kept The Farm. That suited both of us. For some years thereafter we saw one another occasionally for lunch or dinner. In time she married again, meaning that she gave up her alimony, a move that in my opinion not many in her position would make.

From that time on, The Farm became the centre of my life.

2 1

Living at The Farm: 1976-1980

~~~

WHEN I MOVED TO The Farm permanently, late in 1976, it wasn't exactly as a hermit. My daughter Deirdre, twenty-five, was working in Peterborough, her first marriage having ended in divorce. Sitting on the deck early one evening in mid-autumn, looking along the long vista of colour to the east, she outlined her problems. At work there was a supervisor she didn't get along with, and at home her boyfriend, a cheerful young guy whom I'd met, had left her. That, it turned out, was a rather tangled web. She wanted a child and went about it quite directly—simply got pregnant and then told him. He was quite direct, too. He came to The Farm and told me he was sorry, but he, "just wasn't figuring on having a child." I liked him coming to explain. She wanted nothing to do with an abortion, but, as she told me that evening on the deck, didn't know how she could manage the apartment they had shared without someone to share the rent.

"Well, you could come and live here," I said.

So she did, bringing with her a large Doberman that ate my favourite hunting cap. It must have been a tough winter for Deirdre mostly alone on that frigid hilltop. Sometimes I would drive back from Toronto to find her and the Doberman sitting together on our chesterfield watching television.

My grandson David was born the following April. She brought him home to The Farm for a while until she could take a job and rearrange her life, which was soon.

Also, my daughter Astrid, then fourteen and living with her mother, was in difficulty both at home and at school, skipping classes and spending the time in the school library at North Toronto Collegiate. As I drove her to The Farm one day in early winter, we talked it over. More than just the split in our family was contributing to her cop-out at school.

Part of it, she told me, was handling the fact that her brother Neil's growing fame had pretty well changed her public persona at school from "Astrid Young" to "Neil Young's sister." She loved and admired Neil, a sibling relationship that kept on growing with the years long before they began performing together, but part of her inner strength has always been her sure idea of who she is herself. "When they see me coming, Dad, they don't say, 'Hi, how ya doin', Astrid?' but 'Hi, Astrid, how's Neil?'"

She handled it, but it bothered her. At midterm I arranged for her to move to a boarding school at Belleville, where she was grounded once in a while for minor infractions but eventually found herself enjoying life. She had played flute and then oboe at North Toronto, and in subsequent years at other schools was good in anything to do with music or writing, and passable in everything else. Eventually she found that with some summer courses, she could graduate from Grade Thirteen before her seventeenth birthday, get out of school, and get a job. Which she did, as a mailroom clerk with Bell Canada. When I was in the city we would meet occasionally for lunch.

Which brings me, circuitously, to the person who became most important in my life, Margaret Hogan.

From 1976 on, Margaret and I saw one another a lot, both in Toronto and at The Farm. When we both worked at the Toronto *Telegram* and I was married to Astrid, Margaret and I didn't meet. We did meet later at the *Globe and Mail*, when she was an editor in the features department and I was impressed with her looks and style. At the time I was doing my stuff on royal tours and whatever else came along, but was getting tired of it.

Once in a while Margaret and a few others at the *Globe* would have a lunch and a beer or two together in a pub on Spadina, the New Paramount. The relationship grew naturally. I liked her because she knew a lot of things I didn't know and often had a refreshing slant on what I was doing. She came from Regina, worked on the *Leader-Post* there, married young, and bore Erin, the first of her three daughters. Caitlin and Mary Margaret (Maggie), were born in Toronto after Margaret's husband, Brian, an Australian, took a reporting job there.

It turned out that I knew Margaret's father, Johnny Burns, from covering football games in Regina where he sat at the officials' bench and was penalty timekeeper. Regina, as everyone in Canada knows, historically has the most faithful football fans on earth. So we had that in common from the start, not that she was a fan—far from it: she had overdosed on football at an early age. When she and Brian Hogan married, the wedding had to be at 8 a.m. on a Saturday morning because there was a Regina football game in the afternoon, a serious clash of attractions for many of the wedding guests.

When I first met Margaret and her three daughters, Brian had been living in Florida for several years. When the *Telegram* folded and her job there evaporated, she did some freelance writing, then went to the *Globe*.

From my own experience, most people involved in a divorce feel at least some sadness when it actually happens. All those hopes of long ago are hard to bury entirely. Little reminders keep pushing their way to the surface. One night Margaret and I had a few beers and then dinner and talked about marriage and how ours separately had affected us and our families. Our close relationship started there and continued, not always romantically, in fits and starts through the next four years or so. During that time we more or less lived together, a few days apart, a few days at her place in Toronto, a few days at The Farm.

Eventually we bought a house on Albany Avenue, in Toronto, making the down payment with $12,000 we were paid for a compilation of the best speeches from a famous old Toronto organization called the Empire Club. *The Best Talk in Town* did not become a best seller but is still a staple in many libraries, returning each of us some annual income under Canada's Public Lending Rights plan. (Years later in Ireland we gave a copy to our local library in Howth. The librarian one day told me that *Best Talk* was out more often than most of my books, presumably because it gave a picture of Canada other than the familiar.)

The house on Albany Avenue was yet another of our attempts to join our lives together. It was intended as a joint home for Margaret and her daughters and me and my daughter Astrid, who was then in Harbord Collegiate. But since I was living mostly at The Farm, I wasn't much help at Albany, although from the beginning Margaret's daughters and mine got along well.

Margaret and I were lovers and, in our saner moments, friends, but at the time we both saw marriage as a trap we didn't want to fall into again. We finally talked it out on a highway, driving from The Farm to Toronto, and decided to marry in the United Church at Omemee, virtually in secrecy. Two close mutual friends stood up with us, Jay Hayes, a widower after his wife's sudden death in the early 1970s, and his friend Shirley Lowes, a widow with a son and two daughters.

If we had it to do over again, heaven forbid, I would have liked to have our families and closest friends there to rejoice with us. Because it should have been rejoiced. Now, I cannot think of any way in which our marriage could be improved, except that as it goes on we still have some pretty good battles that, if we were wiser, we could head off. But we are not wiser, and the hearts-and-flowers side of our marriage, though a mixture of low comedy and high drama from time to time, suits me. And when it doesn't suit Margaret she lets me know loud and clear. What could be fairer?

At The Farm, after our wedding, one of the matters that bothered Margaret, was her sense of what memories are made of.

"It's Astrid's house!" she sometimes would say, angrily or despairingly.

"It's *our* house, for God's sake," I would reply. "It is a whole empty house, with walls for pictures and for the bookcases I can build and you can fill, and. . ."

It might have been the threat that I would build bookshelves that swung the deal. She had seen my carpentry. At any rate, pictures and photographs went up. I thought of it as our own art gallery. I could sit anywhere and look at what was on the walls and in my mind see reruns of meaningful times. I think that Margaret felt the same. Besides our favourite photos and paintings, her father painted Saskatchewan scenes so evocatively that when I wandered around the house I was walking along that prairie fence, standing at the edge of that pond or slough. Or we're walking our old lane at The Farm together, or the path over the top of the esker, or finding the first wild leeks of spring, or the first bloodroot or trillium or dogtooth violet, or May apples, or the nice blueish plant that for a time we painstakingly identified as Oswego tea. It turned out not to be Oswego tea, but neither of us even now can remember the proper name. There was always a time in late spring when she and I came in to report the year's first confirmed sighting of "Erstwhile Oswego Tea."

22

From the Farm to Ireland: 1980-1992

I T IS ONLY NOW, looking back over our first married years, that I remember in whole cloth the lively life that tended to keep us both looking forward instead of back. Before our wedding we had visited her parents in Regina and my mother and sister in Flin Flon, so that when we did marry, for both those blood connections our marriage was a confirmation, not a surprise.

Within weeks of our marriage, we were among those who defied the boycott of the Moscow Olympics in 1980, a trip we had made reservations for two or three years earlier, along with two of our Omemee friends, Dave Rea (a tall and witty retired customs man who had been a prisoner-of-war after his bomber was shot down during World War Two), and Edna Deyell, the local bank accountant. With others who didn't agree with the Canada-U.S.-Britain Olympic boycott that year (a reaction to the Soviet Union's invasion of Afghanistan), we flew to Helsinki, Leningrad, Kiev and Moscow, the Olympic experience made even better because all the boycott cancellations had left lots of good tickets for Olympic events we wanted to see.

We were building up our memories in other ways as what one might term economy-class jet-setters. From time to time we flew to London on charters for a week of excellent theatre. In 1983, we rented a handy-to-downtown London flat for three months while I researched the British side of the part-biographical and part-autobiographical book *Neil and Me*, about Neil's boyhood and youth and the part I played, or did not play, in his career until that time.

My books in the 1980s included Conn Smythe's memoirs, *If You*

Can't Beat 'Em in the Alley; a second Punch Imlach book, *Heaven and Hell in the NHL;* the novel *That Old Gang of Mine* ; *Hello, Canada,* a biography of Foster Hewitt; a biography of Gordon Sinclair, *A Life and Then Some,* and others.

From time to time, without grants but when I had a little extra money, I wrote things I particularly wanted to—a racetrack screenplay called "Lori" (optioned but never filmed), and the first of my crime novels set in the Arctic, *Murder in a Cold Climate,* around the adventures of my fictional cop, RCMP inspector and full-blooded Inuit Matteesie Kitologitak.

We were both busy, but some days the sameness of our life in the wooded hills of Cavan Township seemed to stretch too far ahead. *Comfortable* was the operative word, more so than *rut.* At the same time, I felt very critical about what was happening in Canada. We had one of the best countries in the world and Canadians never stopped bitching about our government, the clashes with Quebec, and almost everything else. I simply wanted to move to another country and leave all our home-grown complaining behind.

In 1989, after a year or two of talking about it, we decided that if we didn't make a move soon we simply wouldn't be moving. Country living, especially in winter, had its dangers. The routine that I had been following for years—a day's work, a few drinks, dinner, some television, began to take on a sameness. Also, some of my friends thought the time would come when my age would make it more and more difficult for me to fight blizzards and icy roads or washed-out driveways for five or six months of every year.

I didn't worry about that, although when I would be wading through thigh-high drifts to get up the hill to the house I thought of the sudden heart attacks suffered by others of my age and younger. I felt fine. When I shovelled snow I took it easy. When I was trying to kick the garage door free of ice, or chip ice out with a mallet or an axe, so that the automatic opener could function, or carrying wood through the drifts to the fireplace it was just part of the price of living where we did.

Worse than that, or so we occasionally agreed, was that time was slipping away, never to return, and maybe it was time for our lives to change once again.

Once in the early 1980s when Margaret and I were talking about the rather deadly routine we'd fallen into I suggested, "Maybe we should sell this place and go somewhere else." At that time, however, Margaret had not been living at The Farm for long. What struck me as deadening sameness to her was peace. She was upset. "I've moved and moved and moved and now when I'm where I want to be, I don't want to move again."

But as years went on and our routines didn't change much, the subject came up again. How about living somewhere else during winter, coming back in spring or early summer for the wild leeks, morels, trilliums, daisies, wild strawberries, the pool, the flash of a scarlet tanager and the high calm of golden eagles cruising above. Actually, we loved the winters, too, to get up in the morning and look out on the hoar-frosted trees, the wind-sculptured drifts, the long expanse of snow and trees stretching for miles to the east, and I'd look out on the beautiful world and think or even say aloud or even yell to the sky, "God, you've done it again!" Yet by the late 1980s we edged closer and closer to doing *something* to change our lives, which basically would mean going to another country.

~

During that period Margaret's father died, and my mother, getting near the end of her eighties, was in progressively poor health.

I could have written much more in this book about my mother. There are certainly some memorable stories. "Are you enjoying yourself, Mrs. Young?" asked a guest at the reception after Astrid and I were married.

"Oh, yes," Mother replied politely, every inch the lady. "I always enjoy myself at Scott's weddings."

Then there was a time one summer near Flin Flon when my sister, Dorothy Liss, and her husband, Stan, were busy getting ready for forty people to arrive for cocktails at their cabin at Big Athapapesqua Lake. There was a tap on the back door, and Dorothy found their oldest son, Bob, who was living in The Pas, standing there with a slender dark-haired young woman holding a baby.

"This is your new granddaughter, Mother," Bob said, and remembers yet the look on Dorothy's face. None of the family had known he even had a serious girlfriend. Dorothy worried for two days about how to tell Mother but finally, at the lakeside cabin, broke the news.

"Oh, my God!" said Mother. "I guess I better start knitting."

Once when Mother had a bad attack of some kind and was thought to be near death, I was on a book tour in Saskatoon. After a hurry-up call from Dorothy I found that the only flight had to be through Winnipeg and then north via The Pas. Because of weather the flight had to end there, about eighty miles short of Flin Flon. As soon as Dorothy, checking hourly, was told the North's familiar socked-in-by-weather news, she drove to The Pas airport to pick me up. We got to Flin Flon about 2 a.m. Dorothy kept right on going past her home towards the hospital.

"We should go and see Mother," she explained.

I asked, "At this hour? Wouldn't we be better to wait until morning?"

Dorothy shook her head. "She knows you're coming and will be expecting us. After we see her she'll be happy and able to sleep."

So we went to hospital and found Mother wearing an oxygen mask and seemingly asleep or unconscious. When we spoke, her eyes opened and lit up.

"Hello. . . Scott," she said in the slow breath-by-breath speech that goes with emphysema. (She didn't start smoking until she was thirty, but that was fifty-nine years earlier.) I hugged her frail body that used to be so big and vigorous and sexy and game for anything when I was a kid. The night nurse directed us to push her in a wheelchair to a nearby patients' lounge where we could visit without disturbing others.

"Is there anything you want, Mother?" Dorothy asked, once we were settled.

"I'd. . . like. . . a. . . cigarette," Mother said, almost in a whisper.

"I don't have any, Mother," Dorothy said. Then, after a pause and a shrug, "I'll ask the nurse."

This might seem like extreme folly, in the circumstances, but people who have lived that long and are apparently near death do have privileges.

Dorothy came back with one cigarette. Mother's shaky, almost translucent hand held it while Dorothy lit it. Mother took one tiny puff, one thirty-second of an inch of a puff, the tiniest possible bit of a puff, and then began to cough great racking coughs. Her face turned blue. She couldn't stop coughing. I thought she was going to die, choke to death, there and then. But gradually, after a terrible minute or two, she got the coughing under control and spoke again, one slow word at a time: "I'm . . . going . . . to . . . have . . . to . . . stop . . . smoking."

The next day she was a lot better and she survived to go back to the little apartment where for many years she had lived alone, Dorothy and

Stan only a phone call away. In the next bad attack, some months later, she walked out to the ambulance and at the hospital walked by herself to thew x-ray room. A few hours later she went into a coma and died.

After my mother died, Margaret and I again talked of moving. But where to? Toronto? But that would really be going back, while what we wanted was to go on. How about Montreal? Montreal would be okay, we more or less agreed. How about Quebec? Quebec might be better. We didn't want to move to the United States. Okay, then, what about Italy? But my own interest there was mainly to be a visitor, go and visit again Rome and Ancona and the island of Vis and remember wartime, torpedo boats, the village of Komiza, sweet grapes stretching up the hillside, a man tending the vines calling out for us to stop and running to hand us great bunches of beautiful fruit; friendly to anyone from the torpedo boats. I want to go there and see if the women from the harbour-front houses still come out of their doors in the morning and throw a wooden pail tied to a rope into the sea, pull it back overflowing, slosh the water over the cobbled street and sweep the stones clean for yet another day.

We talked of living in England, France, Portugal, Spain, and never of Ireland. Ireland came into our lives by the side door. Margaret's eldest daughter, Erin, met Niall Finnegan, a tall, affable, sports-loving Dubliner who was working as a quantity surveyor in Toronto. They sometimes came to The Farm to visit. When they decided to marry, we offered to host it at The Farm: the deck, the pool, the sheer summer beauty of the place, lots of parking, a tent, a bar set up in the garage . . . all that had been to the good when Caitlin and John Leung married. (Great wedding, but the marriage didn't last.)

But Niall and Erin had their own ideas on where their wedding should take place. Many of Niall's relatives would be coming from Ireland for the wedding and Toronto would be much handier for such a gathering. They thanked us for the offer.

We didn't press it. Instead of having a lot to do as hosts, we would be part of a grand gathering of Irish family, hotel rooms for all, reception and dance, the parties that would go on all night, and the next day getting groggily into our car and returning to our peace and quiet.

The wedding week all worked beautifully. One day Ned Finnegan,

Niall's father, chartered a bus, with a driver and coolers full of things to drink, and took all the visiting Finnegans and families to Niagara Falls. On another day he arranged a lunch in a Toronto club, complete with fervent, funny toasts from Finnegans, Youngs, Hogans, all coming fluently from the heart. Margaret, when we were driving home, said, "I feel as if I'd been at the confluence of two great rivers of gift of the gab."

For our part I arranged a family dinner for a couple of days before the wedding. There were twelve or fifteen of us, all very merry at a long table in the dining room of the Royal Canadian Military Institute in downtown Toronto, a century-old club with a good bar and dining room and walls covered with photos of British royalty. Besides ourselves—and Caitlin and John, Maggie and her friend Adam Newman—the whole Finnegan clan was there, father Ned, mother Kathleen, Niall's three brothers, and sisters-in-law. It was a grand party, and somehow the pervasive imperial Englishness of the place, mixed for the night with the merry, laughing, handsome Irish-made it an occasion never to be forgotten—by me, anyway. Some of those from Ireland stayed for over a week or so because Neil was doing a concert at the Canadian National Exhibition; his people arranged seats and backstage passes.

One of the results of all these good times was that the following spring we were invited to visit Ireland, to stay with the elder Finnegans, Ned and Kathleen, and came to know Ned's pubs—the big and busy Bottle Tower in Churchtown and Larry Murphy's, near the city centre.

They set about arranging dinners, gatherings, driving us to see the countryside and towns while visiting Finnegan relatives at their farms or pubs, some far from Dublin and some near. Of the four Finnegan sons in the close-knit family, Niall was in Canada, the other three worked in the family's pubs—Kieran, Edwin and Shane. Kieran's wife, Ann, and their children, and Shane's wife, Miriam, all became our friends. Edwin was a bachelor then, although much pursued and not long for that state, and behind the scenes was a force in the country's ruling Fianna Fail party.

After filling our first few days with hospitality, plays, famous pubs, Irish music and generally showing us a great time, Ned Finnegan handed the keys of his big car to Edwin to take us on a week-long tour: first south to their seaside place at Courtown, then on to Bantry, Dingle, up the coast to Lahinch and through Galway to Clifden in Connemara before I left the tour and caught a train to Dublin so that Ned and I could go to the races at the Curragh.

I've always loved thoroughbred racing but never before had experienced the Curragh's remarkable country atmosphere. Bettors of experience cruised the line of bookies to check the sometimes varying odds. I used the Tote. Late in the afternoon I heard Ned and others agreeing to meet for a drink. "See you at the Vatican," they'd call. I thought that might be a pub. When we got there, about eight of us including the famous jockey Christy Roche and equally well known trainers and owners, I noticed that the pub's name was not the Vatican at all. Turned out that the woman who owned the place and was behind the bar frowned on bad language and would refuse to serve anyone who used it.

Back in Canada a few months later Neil and his family visited us at The Farm. Out walking in the woods one day I told Neil we thought we were getting bushed, had to make a move now or we probably never would, so we were selling The Farm and moving to Ireland. I was seventy-two, and as we walked along suddenly it struck me how some offspring might react when an aged parent, probably suspected of losing his or her marbles, instead of fading softly into the woodwork under the weight of the years, doesn't.

"Well, Dad," he said, looking at me with a grin, "sometimes you've just got to take a chance."

◆

Late in December we accepted an offer for The Farm, and Margaret flew to Dublin to rent a house. When she returned and the time came when it soon would be final, house and pool spick and span, furnishings mostly in storage for shipping, Margaret, who was much more upset about leaving than she showed, flew to visit her mother in Regina. Alone in the quickly emptying place where I knew that for a long time my heart would be, I finished up what I had to do.

The house Margaret had rented for us was in South Dublin's Stillorgan district (which with that name would have been a natural as a retirement community). It was okay but rather soulless after where we had been, so after a few months we began checking the ads for something we would like better, maybe forever. Both of us wanted to be close to the sea. The house we both fell for was a short walk from the harbour in the North Dublin village of Howth, a fishing community on the Irish Sea. It was on

Dublin's rapid transit and bus lines, a good feature because we had no car.

Even to think of Howth now makes me nostalgic for just-landed scallops and oysters and prawns and cod and mussels and everything else that we could buy in the harbour's fishing pier a few yards from where the busy trawlers daily unloaded their catch. After making a choice, or two or three, we carried the bags home up the steep hill past the Lighthouse pub, post office, wine (plus liquor and beer) dealer, library, newsagent and the big church, greeting friends along the way. The only restraint we ever felt in Ireland was in taking care to let the Irish themselves do any talking that seemed necessary about Britain or politics or religion or condoms or abortions or divorce. Some may be amazed, but I did not miss those topics at all.

Sometimes I think we must have been crazy to leave there, but soon staying was beginning to have new problems. When my drastically up-and-down writing income in Canadian dollars was translated into Irish currency, the punt, the going got very tough—even though the Irish Revenue Commissioners had decided, after reading twenty-five or thirty of my books, that my work had "cultural significance" and that therefore—and like other working artists, writers and actors—I was exempt from income tax.

Beside the money side, our ties to Canada would not go away. The longer we lived away from Canada, the better it looked in comparison to the other countries that we had come to see had their own problems. And Canada was home. On one trip back I bought a nice, simple lakeside cottage on Jack Lake north of Peterborough, to keep a toehold in Canada. But that token respite was short-lived. We returned to Canada in October 1992, not in good shape financially, with a bank loan of about $39,000, a six-year-old car, our Howth house on the market with no takers, our cottage on Jack Lake on the market with no takers. We rented a house in Peterborough. I often went to visit friends in Omemee, but it was many months before I could bring myself even to drive the roads that led to The Farm.

23

Home Again, in
All Respects

≈

O F COURSE, IF WE HADN'T sold it three years earlier, hadn't left it for-
lornly empty as I saw it last (and Margaret had not, unable to bear
it), we would have been going back directly to the place where we had
been so happy, where much of the cementing of our marriage had taken
place, the home where the heart was.

Then came what really qualifies as a miracle. Neil phoned me from
California. He had known The Farm from early days, had walked the
woods with me. His son, my oldest grandson, Zeke, had been there, the
time I captured a big snapping turtle for Zeke to see and it got loose in our
swimming pool giving a certain excitement to swimming underwater until
it finally escaped. Before we left for Ireland, Neil had brought his whole
family, wife Pegi, Amber, Ben, Zeke and their family friend Donna Grant
to visit for a few days. In California on his much larger ranch a few years
earlier we had talked of what we both felt about these properties, his with
its mighty redwoods and all it has meant to him since he bought the core
property in 1968, soon after I bought The Farm. He knew what The
Farm meant to us.

This day in the summer of 1993 when he phoned I saw it as one of
his regular calls to see how we were, until he said, "You know, Dad, we've
been talking it over, I mean our family, Pegi and Astrid and all of us, wondering if there's any way we can put together some kind of a family trust
and get The Farm back."

I didn't faint. I thought about it for a few seconds and then said,
"Well, I could find out."

I phoned the realtor who had handled our sale of The Farm, Mary Ellen McCamus of the McCamus sugar-bush family whose grand maples we could see across the valley from our deck, and asked her what she thought the chances were.

She reported that the man who had bought The Farm from us still owned it, loved it, but hadn't been able to spend as much time there as he intended when he bought it. He'd said, "But I won't sell it to anybody who doesn't love it as much as I do."

Mary Ellen told him I was one of the group involved, and that it would be a family affair, the property to be held by us and our family and for generations to come to be respected as of old. He asked for what he had paid in 1989. The sale went ahead and we took possession again a few months later, early in August, with Neil holding the interest-free mortgage. By the luck of the draw, or maybe Neil had figured out the timing in advance, he had a concert scheduled for Toronto's Canadian National Exhibition grandstand about two weeks later. With his tour bus parked nearby, the whole family gathered at The Farm and talked about things we would do, such as buying a piano.

The uncanny aspect of this reoccupation of The Farm was how little had been done to change the place we had left. Margaret would walk into a room carrying pictures we had shipped back from Ireland, half remembering what pictures had been hung where before. She found that some we had left behind had never been taken down. In one bedroom Astrid had tacked onto the door a brass nameplate that she had removed from her precious German-made English saddle when she had sold her horse and used the money to buy an electric guitar. The nameplate was still there. In some rooms Margaret would take a look and think, "This needs something over there," and she would find that the nails she'd used years before were still in place.

Around the time of the first snow, I began buying feed for the birds and filling the feeder on the deck. Presto, the air was full of evening grosbeaks and hairy woodpeckers and downy woodpeckers and chickadees and sapsuckers, and one lone cardinal, poor chap. The blue jays apparently were unable to handle the fiendish anti-squirrel design of the bird feeder, a hostile act for both bird and animal, which by the second winter there I had rectified.

We had another gathering of the clan when the grand new Scott Young Public School, an honour the community had bestowed on me, was officially opened in Omemee, and I, sitting right up in the educational power structure of Victoria County, Emily Township and Omemee Village, was proud to see my whole family and so many of the people that mean most to me, Hogans and Youngs and our Omemee friends, sitting out front. The next day Astrid and Neil went to Peterborough and bought a piano—delivered the next day—carried up the hill by three men in pouring rain because the delivery truck couldn't make it.

On that visit Astrid, engaged to be married to writer and musician Peter Jerumanis of Glendale, California, the following January, said to me, "Would it be all right with you if Peter and I came to The Farm for our honeymoon?"

A honeymoon on a frigid hillside south of Omemee in the dead of winter? Astrid had lived there and knew all about January weather. What could I say? Of course! We would leave them alone and stay elsewhere. There was lots of wood for the big fireplace, snowshoes, a toboggan, everything a newly married couple from California could possibly yearn for, right? In a few months when Neil sang his Oscar-nominated song *Philadelphia* at the Academy Awards presentations in California, his two backup singers were his wife, Pegi, and his sister, Astrid.

❧

One day in March of 1994, Margaret and I walked, sometimes in crusty snow, while our black-and-white border collie, Fergal, put up grouse and rabbits and sniffed at the tracks of foxes and wolves. We talked about the springtime then on the way, and went back into the house and lit a big fire and talked about what we would do when spring really arrived and all that we loved about the place would be spread out before us again.

Life goes on.

INDEX